Library of
Davidson College

CONCEPT FORMATION IN THE HUMANITIES
AND THE SOCIAL SCIENCES

SYNTHESE LIBRARY

STUDIES IN EPISTEMOLOGY,

LOGIC, METHODOLOGY, AND PHILOSOPHY OF SCIENCE

Managing Editor:
JAAKKO HINTIKKA, *Florida State University*

Editors:
DONALD DAVIDSON, *University of Chicago*
GABRIEL NUCHELMANS, *University of Leyden*
WESLEY C. SALMON, *University of Arizona*

VOLUME 144

TADEUSZ PAWLOWSKI
Institute of Philosophy, University of Lodz

CONCEPT FORMATION IN THE HUMANITIES AND THE SOCIAL SCIENCES

D. REIDEL PUBLISHING COMPANY

DORDRECHT : HOLLAND / BOSTON : U.S.A.
LONDON : ENGLAND

Library of Congress Cataloging in Publication Data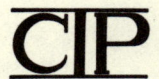

Pawlowski, Tadeusz.
  Concept formation in the humanities and the social sciences.

  (Synthese library ; v. 144)
  Bibliography: p.
  Includes indexes.
  1. Humanities—Methodology.   2. Social sciences—Methodology.
3. Concepts—Methodology.   4. Semiotics—Methodology.   I. Title.
AZ105.P37   001.3   80-14901
ISBN 90-277-1096-1

Published by D. Reidel Publishing Company
P.O. Box 17, 3300 AA Dordrecht, Holland

Sold and distributed in the U.S.A. and Canada
by Kluwer Boston Inc., Lincoln Building
160 Old Derby Street, Hingham, MA 02043, U.S.A.

In all other countries, sold and distributed
by Kluwer Academic Publishers Group
P.O. Box 322, 3300 AH Dordrecht, Holland

D. Reidel Publishing Company is a member of the Kluwer Group

All Rights Reserved
Copyright © 1980 by D. Reidel Publishing Company, Dordrecht, Holland
No part of the material protected by this copyright notice may be reproduced or
utilized in any form or by any means, electronic or mechanical,
including photocopying, recording or by any information storage and
retrieval system, without written permission from the copyright owner

Printed in The Netherlands

TABLE OF CONTENTS

PREFACE   vii

ACKNOWLEDGEMENTS   ix

PART ONE: METHODS OF CONCEPT FORMATION

I. Metrical Concepts and Measurement in the Humanities   3
II. Concepts with Family Meanings in the Humanities   23
III. Persuasive Function of Language   55

PART TWO: APPLICATIONS

A. Aesthetics and Art Theory

IV. Informational Aesthetics   77
V. The Concept of Kitsch   91
VI. The Concept of Happening   112
VII. Interpretation of Art Works   144
VIII. Beauty and its Socio-Psychological Determinants   162

B. Social Sciences

IX. The Concept of Indicator in the Social Sciences   181
X. Semiotic Theory of Culture   197
XI. Theory of Questions and its Applications in the Social Sciences 204

BIBLIOGRAPHY   221

SUBJECT INDEX   225

AUTHOR INDEX   228

PREFACE

Uniqueness of style versus plurality of styles: in terms of these aesthetic categories one of the most important differences between the recent past and the present can be described. This difference manifests itself in all spheres of life — in fashion, in everyday life, in the arts, in science. What is of interest for my purposes in this book are its manifestations in the processes of concept formation as they occur in the humanities, broadly conceived. Here the following methodological approaches seem to dominate the scene. 1. A tendency to apply semiotic concepts in various fields of research. 2. Attempts to introduce metrical concepts and measurement, even into disciplines traditionally considered as unamenable to mathematical treatment, like aesthetics and theory of art. 3. Efforts to find ways of formulating empirically testable, operational criteria for the application of concepts, especially concepts which refer to objects directly not observable, like dispositions, attitudes, character or personality traits. Care is also taken to take advantage of the conceptual apparatus of methodology to express problems in the humanities with the highest possible degree of clarity and precision. 4. Analysis of the persuasive function of language and its possible uses in science and in everyday life.

The above tendencies are present in this book. It is divided into two parts: I. Methods of Concept Formation, and II. Applications. In the first part some general methods of concept formation are presented and their merits discussed. In the second part these methods are applied to analyse some fundamental concepts in aesthetics and the social sciences.

ACKNOWLEDGEMENTS

Three chapters in this book have previously been published; they appear now in a revised form. I want to thank the publishers for their kind permission to include them in the present volume. The chapters: 'Concepts with Family Meanings in the Humanities' and 'Persuasive Function of Language' have appeared in the German version in my book *Begriffsbildung und Definition*,* Verlag de Gruyter, Berlin, 1980. 'The Concept of Indicator in the Social Sciences' appeared previously in *Poznań Studies in the Philosophy of Science and the Humanities*, vol. 2, no. 2, 1976, B. R. Grüner Publishing Co., Amsterdam.

I am also grateful to Mrs. Laura Huxley and to Chatto and Windus, Ltd., for permission to quote from *Eyless in Gaza* by Aldous Huxley, and to Basil Blackwell Publishers Ltd. for their permission to include the quotation from L. Wittgenstein's *Philosophical Investigations*.

T. P.

*Die beiden Kapitel 'Persuasive Definitionen' und 'Begriffe mit Bedeutungsfamilien' sind zuerst erschienen in 'Sammlung Göschen' (Nr. 2213/1980) Walter de Gruyter & Co., Berlin–New York. Sämtliche Rachte liegen beim Verlag de Gruyter & Co., Berlin–New York.

PART ONE

METHODS OF CONCEPT FORMATION

CHAPTER I

METRICAL CONCEPTS AND MEASUREMENT IN THE HUMANITIES

The introduction and use of measurement contributed decisively to the formation of modern science and gave it that social importance which it possesses today. Until quite recently, measurement was applied only in exact and engineering sciences. The spectacular results made possible in those sciences by their mathematization encouraged many to apply mathematics also in disciplines traditionally regarded as unamenable to mathematical treatment. The introduction of measurement to psychology and sociology changed the languages of those sciences. A new discipline has arisen in which the conceptual apparatus of mathematical information theory is used to describe and analyse art works and the phenomena of art reception: hence its name, informational aesthetics.[1]

The introduction of metrical concepts into the language of science has increased its empirical sensitivity: such language is able to discriminate an increasing range of empirical data, whereas for the pre-mathematical language, without such powerful discriminative abilities, those differences remained unnoticeable. Concepts of the classificatory type provide for the differentiation of only two states: those which fall, and those which do not fall, under a given concept. The situation is different with comparative and metrical concepts; they make it possible to differentiate very many states, and thus provide for a much more subtle and precise description of the world. Besides, it is only through metrical concepts that we can formulate new kinds of statements — quantitative statements. The relationships which can be described with the aid of classificatory concepts cover only those of succession and coexistence of phenomena. More interesting, and of greater practical importance, are relationships of the quantitative type, in which it is shown in what way changes in one quantity depend on changes in some other quantities.

The use of measurement outside the domain of exact sciences does not always accord with the principles set up by the general theory of measurement. Sometimes it is used hastily, without proper justification; in other cases its use seems to be justified, but the results are trivial. Sometimes mathematization degenerates into a sort of mania, of which P. Sorokin has already warned, calling it sarcastically 'quantophrenia'. Attempts to use measurement outside the traditional domain of exact sciences set off a lively controversy on the nature of measurement and the limits of its applicability. The measuring procedures used in psychology, sociology or in the humanities were by some considered as contradictive. It was maintained that the magnitudes, whose measurement was aimed at in those disciplines, are not additive, and that only additive magnitudes are susceptible to measurement; that any general quantitative statement outside the domain of the exact sciences is a meaningless expression.[2] These critical reservations, shared by many scientists, can also be found in the practice of everyday life, where the concept of measurement is usually associated with operations similar to those of weighing or measuring length. It is an essential feature of such operations to use a unit of measurement and to join together a number of such units to equal the measured object. Such an image of measurement is accompanied by a disbelief in the possibility of its application outside the domain of the exact sciences. Those objections and doubts are opposed by specialists in various disciplines, outside the domain of the exact sciences, who apply measurement in their research work. They are joined by methodologists and theoreticians of measurement who reflect on the general foundations of measurement and its various kinds. These maintain that to recognize as measurable only additive magnitudes, for which there exists a joining operation isomorphic to arithmetical addition, means to restrict arbitrarily the extension of the concept 'measurement', for the following two reasons. First, the joining operation isomorphic to addition does not have to consist in a physical process of joining. It can be an operation entirely different from putting objects on the same balance-scale, or from placing them one after another along a straight line, as is the case with measuring weight or length. Second, scales defined with reference to an additive operation, even if this operation does not consist in a physical joining, make up only a particular type of scale. There exist other types of scales which are not based on any operation isomorphic to addition. To this the critics retort that such a conception of measurement is an unfounded broadening of the concept 'measurement' to cover operations which do not fall under this concept in its received meaning; and that the aim of all this is to bestow the splendour of mathematical precision upon disciplines whose character and methods give no grounds for such a bestowal.

Are those objections justified? Must we really have a joining operation isomorphic to addition in order to be able to use measurement in the domain of social and humanistic disciplines? The general theory of measurement allows us to answer this question in the negative. Generally speaking, measurement consists in establishing a homomorphic relation between the objects measured and a domain of real numbers. Real numbers, however, possess many properties, and between those numbers there hold various relations. Depending on the amount and the character of the numerical properties taken as the basis of the homomorphism relation, we obtain various types of scales. Only some of those scales are based on a unit of measurement and on the operation of addition. It follows that we can apply measurement outside the domain of exact sciences even if we do not dispose of scales based on a unit of measurement and on the operation of addition.

To be measurable, then, is a property which admits of gradations; we can put scales in an order, beginning with the 'weakest' and ending with the 'strongest'. The conviction that measurement can be used meaningfully outside the domain of the exact sciences is now beginning to gain common acceptance. However, the question of what use can be made of quantitative data in formulating general statements is still a source of confusion and misunderstandings. These misunderstandings center around two matters: 1. the variety of scales, and 2. the connection between the types of scales used and the admissible structure of statements in which relations between the measured magnitudes are expressed. In what follows I shall discuss the general foundations of measurement which concern all domains of science or practice, wherever measurement is applied. I shall also call attention to special problems which arise in connection with attempts to use measurement in various branches of humanities.

The problem of constructing a scale for measuring a certain magnitude consists of two component problems: 1. the representation problem, and 2. the uniqueness problem.

THE REPRESENTATION PROBLEM

Suppose we are to construct a scale for measuring objects in a set S. To solve the representation problem we have to define formal properties of certain relations holding between those objects, and to prove that these relations are homomorphic to certain relations holding between numbers assigned to the objects measured. Let us assume that S consists of a small group of persons, and we want to construct a scale for measuring their intelligence. It will be a weak type of scale — the so called ordinal scale — in which we assign numbers to persons measured in such a way as to give homomorphic representation only to relations of equal and greater intelligence holding between those persons. We have, then, to define two relations: x is as intelligent as y (symbolically $x \, Q \, y$), and x is more intelligent than y ($x \, P \, y$). These relations can, for instance, be defined with reference to some intelligence tests. By specifying the set of persons S and the two relations Q and P, defined on this set, we establish the ordered triple $E = \langle S, Q, P \rangle$ — the so called empirical relational system; S makes up the universum of the system. Next, we assign numbers to persons in S in such a way that the relations: $=$ and $>$, holding between the assigned numbers mirror the relations: Q and P, holding between the persons, to whom the numbers were assigned. Suppose S consists of 8 persons ordered by the relations Q and P. Suppose, further, that the persons were assigned numbers in the following way:

a	b	c	d	e	f	g	h
1	3	4	6	8	9	10	11

Thereby we have specified the ordered triple $M = \langle I, =, > \rangle$ — the so called mathematical relational system; I consists of the above eight integers.

With the aid of the concepts just introduced the representation problem can be described as follows. To construct a scale for measuring objects in the universum of an empirical system E, we have to show that this system is homomorphic to a suitably chosen mathematical system M.[3] The advantages which can be gained by the application of measurement are of great scientific and, therefore, also of social importance. Metrical concepts provide tools for a subtle and precise description of phenomena and for the formulation of quantitative relations between them. They also made it possible to use mathematics as a powerful instrument of deduction.

THE UNIQUENESS PROBLEM

In solving the representation problem we did not complete the construction of a scale for measuring a magnitude. For, it is not enough to know what numbers have been assigned to particular degrees of the magnitude; in addition we must know to what extent this assignment is invariant, or, in other words, what is the type of scale established by this assignment.

Suppose some three objects have been measured on an ordinal scale and the following numbers have been assigned to them: 2, 4, and 6. From this we can infer that the first object precedes the second and the second precedes the third. But we cannot infer that the difference between the first and the second is equal to the difference between the second and the third, even though the differences between the corresponding numbers are equal. Such conclusion about the equality of differences between the objects would be a meaningless statement, because in the ordinal scale only the relations of equality and precedence holding between the objects measured are given homomorphic representation.

We can draw conclusions concerning the relations between differences between objects if instead of an ordinal we use an interval scale. By assigning numbers to objects measured on an interval scale we give homomorphic representation not only to the relations of equality and precedence, but also to the relations holding between differences between objects measured. If by using an interval scale we obtain the following data: 2, 3, 4, 5, 6, 7, 8, we can infer from this that successive objects possess the property measured in a greater degree, or that the differences between successive objects are equal.

On the other hand, the conclusion that the third object is twice as great as the first, or that the fifth object is three times greater than the first, is not admissible, even though $2 \cdot 2 = 4$ and $2 \cdot 3 = 6$. Such conclusions would be meaningless statements, because in the interval scale there is no unique object indicated by the number 0. This number can arbitrarily be assigned to many different objects as, for instance, is the case with different scales of temperature, except the absolute scale. But the existence of such an unique object indicated by the number 0 is necessary if we want to speak about the ratios of magnitudes.

To draw meaningful conclusions concerning the ratios of magnitudes, we must have a stronger type of scale — the ratio scale.

I have stated above that the type of scale established by a given numerical assignment depends on the degree of uniqueness of this assignment. I shall illustrate this point with reference to the given example of the use of the ordinal scale for measuring intelligence. To construct an ordinal scale we have to define a function f whose domain is the set S and whose range is a subset of real numbers, and such that:

(1) x coincides with y if and only if $f(x) = f(y)$
(2) x precedes y if and only if $f(x) < f(y)$

Suppose the following numbers have been assigned to the objects in S.

(3)

a	b	c	d	e	f	g	h	i	j	k	l
1	2	3	4	5	6	7	8	9	10	11	12

It is easily seen that assignment (3) is not the only one that meets the conditions (1) and (2). It can be replaced by many other assignments, for instance by:

(4)

a	b	c	d	e	f	g	h	i	j	k	l
5	9	25	99	111	121	122	135	150	155	156	200

Generally, any assignment which is related to assignment (3) by a monotonic function g meets the conditions (1) and (2) and, therefore, gives homomorphic representation to the relations of equality and precedence holding among the members of S. The function g being a monotonic transformation of (3) leaves the scale form invariant.

The type of scale can, therefore, be characterized by the set of numerical transformations that leave the scale form invariant. For the ordinal scale it is the set of monotonic transformations. The interval scale, on the other hand, is determined by the set of linear transformations. One numerical assignment can here be replaced by another one related to the first by linear function $y = ax + b$, where $a > 0$. In the case of the ratio scale it is the set of similarity transformations that leaves the scale form invariant. Any two numerical assignments are here related by function $y = ax$, where $a > 0$.

The foregoing remarks substantiate the conclusion that measurability is a property which admits of gradation. The weakest is the nominal scale. In assigning numbers to objects we only take care that every object receives a different number. Automobile license numbers or the numbers of football players are examples of this sort of measurement. The strongest is the absolute scale where only the identity transformations are admissible. In the ordinal scale — the scale often used in the socio-psychological disciplines and in the humanities, the assignment of numbers to objects is arbitrary except for order.

Of course, the advantages of measurement are greater or lesser, depending on the type of scale used. Generally speaking, the stronger the type of scales used to measure some quantities, the greater the variety of relations between these quantities that can be discovered and described.

The process of measurement as described above is known in the literature as the fundamental measurement, as opposed to derived measurement. I shall content myself with showing the main difference between the two types of measurement. In defining a fundamental scale for measuring a magnitude, we do not presuppose any scales for measuring other magnitudes. This is not so in the case of derived measurement, where one scale is always defined with reference to some other scales. An example is the derived scale of density, defined with reference to the scales of mass and volume.

MEANINGFULNESS OF QUANTITATIVE STATEMENTS

Suppose we embark on a research project to find out what relations hold among certain magnitudes. Suppose further that we have already constructed suitable scales to measure these quantities. The question now arises what kinds of relations can we observe among the quantities?

Before we answer this question, we must first differentiate between the language of sociological generalizations and the language of data that can be used to corroborate or to falsify those generalizations. All our further remarks are concerned with the first kind of language only.

Now it would seem that one cannot *a priori* put any restrictions on the kinds of relations; that any statement expressing quantitative relations is permissible. Naturally, which statements will prove true depends on empirical data. However, such a conviction is not correct. Certain statements have to be eliminated in advance, because any attempt to test them empirically is useless. Not because they are false, but because they are meaningless, and as such do not admit of empirical testing. On what, then, does the meaningfulness of quantitative statements depend? Generally speaking it depends on two factors: the types of scales and the structure of statements.

It is not the case, therefore, that we can state any kind of relations among quantitative data independently of the type of scale used to obtain the data. This follows from what we have said above concerning the transformation properties of different types of scales. Thus, for instance, if certain quantities have been measured on an ordinal scale, we cannot state relations among them which assume the measurement of distances. The question then arises how we can know whether the relations we intend to state are admissible. Here the transformation properties supply us with a criterion. According to the criterion, a sentence stating relations among quantities measured on a given type of scale is an empirically meaningful sentence if its truth value remains invariant under transformations admissible relative to this scale. In other words, a sentence S_1 is a meaningful sentence if admissible transformations carry S_1 into an equivalent sentence S_2.[4]

Let us use this criterion to analyse a concrete example of a quantitative sentence.

(5) If $\dfrac{C(x) \cdot T(x)}{A(x)} < \dfrac{C(y) \cdot T(y)}{A(y)}$ then $S(x) < S(y)$.

In this sentence a relation is stated between the degree of social status, S, of two persons x and y, their age, A, the length of time they have lived in a certain community, C, and the degree of an attitude measured by a test T. Let us assume that the scale determined by test T is of the ordinal type, and let the data in question obtained for some two persons x and y be as follows:

(6)
$S(x) = 25 \quad C(x) = 3 \quad T(x) = 40 \quad A(x) = 30$
$S(y) = 15 \quad C(y) = 2 \quad T(y) = 80 \quad A(y) = 30$

Substituting these data in (5) we obtain the following false statement:

(7)　　If $\dfrac{3 \cdot 40}{30} < \dfrac{2 \cdot 80}{30}$ then $25 < 15$

Because test T determines an ordinal scale, we can replace numerical assignments 40 and 80 by other ones related to the first by a monotonic function f. Let function f carry these numbers into 5 and 6:

(8)　　$f(40) = 5$　　$f(80) = 6$

Substituting these new numbers in (7) we obtain the following true statement:[5]

(9)　　If $\dfrac{3 \cdot 5}{30} < \dfrac{2 \cdot 6}{30}$ then $25 < 15$

As we saw, the truth value of (5) was not invariant under admissible transformations, therefore (5) is not a meaningful statement. One could say that one is not authorized to accept (or refute) the statement (5), because it states a quantitative relation which would be possible to discover only if the quantities (except quantity S) were measured on ratio scales at least whereas one of the scales (the scale T) is only of the ordinal type.

The scales used at present in social research are mainly of the ordinal type. This is a rather weak type of scale and, consequently, the variety of possible relations that can be stated between measured quantities is not very rich. Unfortunately, social scientists absorbed in their researches do not always remember this or are unconscious of it. In particular it is well to remember the close connection between the type of scale used to obtain some metrical data and the kinds of statistical measures applicable in description of the data. Similarly certain comparative relations, although they appear quite correct are nonetheless inadmissible. For instance, the following sentence:

(10)　　If $T_1(x) < T_2(y)$ then $S(x) < S(y)$

stating this kind of relation between the degree of social status S, and two variables T_1 and T_2 measured on different ordinal scales is meaningless. This can easily be shown, for if we make in (10) the following substitutions:

　　　　$S(x) = 40$　　$S(y) = 30$

(11)

　　　　$T_1(x) = 20$　　$T_2(y) = 50$

we get a false statement:

(12)　If　$20 < 50$　then　$40 < 30$.

Now let two monotonic functions defined on numerical assignments (11) be such that:

(13)　$f(20) = 50, \quad g(50) = 1$.

If we substitute the results of these transformations in (12), we get the following true statement:[6]

(14)　If　$50 < 1$　then　$40 < 30$.

Statement (10) is thus shown to be meaningless. On the other hand a statement like:

(15)　If　$T_1(x) < T_1(y)$　then　$T_2(x) < T_2(y)$

is correct. To prove this let us assume, that functions f and g are monotonically increasing. From this assumption it follows that:

(16)　$f[T_1(x)] < f[T_1(y)]$　if and only if　$T_1(x) < T_1(y)$,

(17)　$g[T_2(x)] < g[T_2(y)]$　if and only if　$T_2(x) < T_2(y)$.

Thus, a monotonically increasing transformation carried (15) into:

(18)　If　$f[T_1(x)] < f[T_1(y)]$　then　$g[T_2(x)] < g[T_2(y)]$.

From (16) and (17) it can be seen that the left and right sides of statements (15) and (18) are correspondingly equivalent, therefore statements (15) and (18) are also equivalent. The proof is analogous when we assume that functions f and g are monotonic decreasing.

We have mentioned before that social scientists often do not take sufficient care to make sure the structure of their quantitative statements is adequate to the types of scales used. Sometimes they neglect the difficulties that arise in this connection; in other cases they simply do not realize them. Whatever the reason, it always lowers the value of their work.

Let us illustrate this with concrete examples. In a well known monograph on the authoritarian personality the authors construct several scales for the measurements of some personality aspects.[7] Among other things they determined a scale of political conservatism, PC, and a scale of ethnocentrism, E. The authors do not state clearly what in their opinion are the types of these scales, nor do they give any reasons to this effect. If one can judge however, from various remarks scattered throughout the text they consider both scales to be of the ordinal type. In any case, we have not found anything in the book that would authorize the assumption of a stronger type. However, one of the authors discussing the results obtained by application of these scales makes the following statement: "Thus, while the rank order of conservatism is similar to that of ethnocentrism, the general level of conservatism is considerably higher. People are, so to speak, more conservative than ethnocentric, at least as measured by these scales". This comparison of the general level of conservatism boils down to the statement:

(19) $E(x) < PC(x)$

according to which every person tested was less ethnocentric than conservative, or that this was the result in the majority of cases tested. It is easy to show that truth value of (19) is not invariant under monotonic transformations. Let us substitute in (19) some of the values from the scales of conservatism and ethnocentrism, say $E(x) = 30$, $PC(x) = 45$. Than we obtain the true statement:

(20) $30 < 45$.

Assuming now that a monotone transformation f carries 30 into 50, and making the necessary substitution, we obtain a false statement:

(21) $50 < 45$.

Statement (19) is, then, inadmissible if the scales are of the ordinal type. On the other hand, a statement like:

(22)   If $E(x) < E(y)$ then $PC(x) < PC(y)$

is correct. Of course, whether it is true or false depends on empirical data. The correctness of (22) can easily be proved by an argument analogous to that which we used to prove the meaningfulness of (15).

The next example is taken from a paper by H. Turk: 'Social Cohesion through Variant Values: Evidence from Medical Role Relations'. In this paper the author presents the results of research carried out in a medical outpatient clinic of a university hospital. As the author says, the results corroborate the hypothesis according to which some variation in the values to which the different members of a social group are oriented can contribute to the cohesion of that group. The main statements of the article have the character of quantitative sentences in which relations are stated between certain sociological variables, as for instance bureaucratic orientation towards patients, cohesion between members of a working team, or expected importance of an actor's role. The author constructs metric indices for these variables based on some questionnaires. Unfortunately, he nowhere touches upon the question of what types of scales he has constructed. On this, however, depends the meaningfulness of the statements which he puts forward. Thus, for instance, all his main quantitative statements have the following form: The higher (the lower) the degree of a certain magnitude P, the higher (the lower) the degree of certain other magnitude Q.

Here is one of these statements:

(23) The higher the student physician's score and the lower that of the student nurse on the initial index of bureaucratic orientation towards patients, the higher should be the index of subsequent interaction between team mates.

This statement can be written down symbolically in the following form:

(24) If $B(p_1) > B(p_2)$ and $B(n_1) < B(n_2)$ then
$I(p_1, n_1) > I(p_2, n_2)$,

where: $B(p_i)$, $B(n_i)$ denote degrees of bureaucratic orientation towards patients on the part of a physician or of a nurse; and $I(p_i, n_i)$ denotes the degree of team interaction.

To make (24) a meaningful sentence, it is enough to assume that the scales of bureaucratic orientation and of team interaction are both of the ordinal type. For the truth value of statement (24) is invariant under monotonic transformation of its numerical assignments. This can easily be shown by an argument analogous to the one we used to prove the meaningfulness of statement (15).

Let us now consider a statement similar in form to (24), but expressing relations between *means* of bureaucratic orientation and interaction:

(25) If $M^B_{p_1} > M^B_{p_2}$ and $M^B_{n_1} < M^B_{n_2}$ then $M^I_{p_1 n_1} > M^I_{p_2 n_2}$,

where: $M^B_{p_i}$, $M^B_{n_i}$ denote the means of bureaucratic orientation in a group of physicians or a group of nurses; and $M^I_{p_i, n_i}$ denotes the mean of interaction in a group of dyads.

It can easily be shown that to make (25) a meaningful sentence it is not now enough to assume that scales of bureaucratic orientation and interaction are of the ordinal type. A stronger type is necessary, at least an interval one.

For linear transformation carries statement (25) into an equivalent statement of the form:

(26) If $aM^B_{p_1} + b > AM^B_{p_2} + b$ and $aM^B_{n_1} + b < aM^B_{n_2} + b$

then $vM^I_{p_1,n_1} + c > vM^I_{p_2,n_2} + c$.

The equivalence of statements (25) and (26) follows from the equivalence of their corresponding parts, namely:

$aM^B_{p_1} + b > aM^B_{p_2} + b$ is equivalent to $M^B_{p_1} > M^B_{p_2}$.

$aM^B_{n_1} + b < aM^B_{n_2} + b$ is equivalent to $M^B_{n_1} < M^B_{n_2}$,

$vM^I_{p_1,n_1} + c > vM^I_{p_2,n_2} + c$ is equivalent to

$M^I_{p_1,n_1} > M^I_{p_2,n_2}$

Statement (25) would, however, turn into a meaningless sentence if we assumed ordinal scales. For then its truth value would not be invariant under admissible transformations. Thus the correctness of each particular statement involving statistical measures can be ascertained with the aid of the general criterion of meaningfulness.

It is known that outside the domain of exact sciences it is possible, although not easy, to determine scales sufficiently strong to permit the formulation of interesting relations among sociological variables. A good example can be found in *Decision Making: An Experimental Approach*, by D. Davidson, P. Suppes and S. Siegel. In this book a theory is developed step by step with logical rigour and clarity not often found in the realm of social research. On the basis of this theory it is possible to construct an interval scale for the measurement of utility and an absolute scale of subjective probability. Unfortunately, the applicability of the procedure there developed is rather limited. Nevertheless it can serve as a model for similar endeavours in related fields.

MEANINGFULNESS OF QUANTITATIVE STATEMENTS AND THE GENERAL CONCEPTION OF MEANINGFULNESS

The criteria of empirical meaningfulness of sentences have undergone numerous changes, taking a more and more liberal character. The last known version of the criterion formulated by Carnap[8] gives a very wide extension to the concept of empirical meaningfulness. It is so wide that it covers expressions which should rather be excluded, and recognized as meaningless. I mean here certain sentences stating quantitative relations between magnitudes. Further on I shall argue that these sentences are nonsensical expressions, and I shall demonstrate that these sentences nevertheless fall under the concept of meaningfulness formulated by Carnap. I shall also discuss an attempt to formulate empirical criteria of meaningfulness for quantitative sentences, Namely the definition of meaningfulness given by P. Suppes in 'Measurement, Empirical Meaningfulness and Three-Valued Logic'.[9] Although his definition cannot be considered as an equivalent condition of meaningfulness and although it does not cover all forms of quantitative sentences, it can nevertheless furnish a basis for a general condition of meaningfulness which, added to Carnap's definition, will eliminate the doubtful quantitative sentences from the set of meaningful sentences determined by this definition.

Let us consider the following examples of quantitative sentences:

(27)   The distance between Nürnberg and Braunschweig is 480.

(28)   The distance between Nürnberg and Braunschweig is half the distance between Stuttgart and München.

(29)   The ratio of a day's temperature to pressure is never bigger than the ratio of humidity to temperature:

$$\frac{t}{p} \leqslant \frac{w}{t}$$

It is obvious that (27) does not state anything definite, its content will become clear only if we specify the unit of length with which the distance has been measured. On the other hand, (28) is fully comprehensible, and even true, without any additional information about the unit used; or more exactly, the sense and the truth value of (28) will remain unchanged independently of the unit used to measure the distance.

And what is the case with (29)? We must say that this sentence, like (27), will not have any definite sense unless it is indicated what units have been used to measure the magnitudes involved in the stated relationship. Let us suppose that the relationship (29) has been stated on the basis of numerous observations, in the course of which temperature was always measured by using the Celsius scale. If we were now to describe the results of the same observations in terms of the Fahrenheit scale, then on the grounds of the known definitional relationship between the two scales (29) would assume the form:

(30) $(\frac{9}{5}t + 32)/p \leqslant w/(\frac{9}{5}t + 32)$

Sentences (29) and (30) are not equivalent, which is shown by the following substitution:

(31) $\quad \dfrac{30}{75} \leqslant \dfrac{22}{30}, \quad \dfrac{86}{75} \leqslant \dfrac{22}{86}.$

If we then were to use the Fahrenheit scale to measure the temperature, the relationship between temperature, pressure and humidity would assume a totally different form from the relationship described in (29).

The situation, then, is as follows: (29) does not state any definite empirical relation until it is specified what units have been used for measurement; on the other hand, if we supply such information it becomes clear that we are not dealing with a single empirical relationship among pressure, temperature and humidity, but with numerous relations, the form of which depends on the units used. As determination of units is a matter of free choice, we can say that (29), if completed with information about the units used, states something more than simply the results of observation. All these reasons suggest excluding expressions of the type (29) from the set of meaningful sentences.

The sentence (27) is in a different situation, as it does not state any general relation, but an individual fact. In its present form it is, of course, deprived of any sense. But completing this sentence with information about the unit used does not lead to the above-mentioned undesirable consequence; nothing then speaks against the inclusion of the sentence (27) thus completed in the set of meaningful sentences. All further remarks about the meaningfulness of quantitative sentences apply only to sentences stating general relations between magnitudes. Of course, when giving the definition of a meaningful sentence it should be exactly determined what is understood by a "quantitative sentence stating a general relationship". Such a general and, at the same time, exact definition has not yet been formulated; further on we shall present a particular form of it, constructed on the basis of a concrete scientific theory the axioms of which are expressed in a syntactically determined language.

I shall now prove that the definition of meaningful sentence formulated by Carnap covers also sentences which do not fulfil the earlier presented condition of invariance, that is, sentences which according to the discussed conception should be considered as meaningless expressions. Following Carnap, the expression A is a meaningful sentence in the language L_T if and only if A meets the formation rules of L_T, and if, moreover, every descriptive constant in A is a meaningful term. The definition of meaningful term, in turn, consists of two parts; we shall here adduce only the first one. The term

MEASUREMENT IN THE HUMANITIES 17

M is meaningful relative to the class K, with respect to L_T, L_0, T, C if and only if the terms K belong to V_T, and M belongs to V_T, but not to K; there are sentences $S(M)$ and $S(K)$ in L_T and sentence $S(0)$ in L_0 such that the following conditions are fulfilled:[10]

(a) $S(M)$ contains M as the only descriptive term.

(b) The descriptive terms in $S(K)$ belong to K.

(c) The conjunction $S(M) \cdot S(K) \cdot T \cdot C$ is consistent.

(d) $S(0)$ is logically implied by the conjunction $S(M) \cdot S(K) \cdot T \cdot C$.

(e) $S(0)$ is not logically implied by the conjunction $S(K) \cdot T \cdot C$.

In constructing the proof we shall use the language and the axioms of the theory of decision making, formulated in *Decision Making: An Experimental Approach*. The language L_T of this theory consists of the constant Z, denoting a small set of observable objects, of the constants P and $\approx E$, denoting relations between these objects, of the functional term ϕ denoting a function defined on the set Z, and assuming values from the set of real numbers; these are the specific constants of the theory. Moreover, the language of the theory contains the names of real numbers and the signs $+, \cdot, <$. L_0 contains the same constant Z, the constants W and JE denoting observable relations between objects in Z, and individual constants and variables. Coordinating definitions C have the following form:

$xPy \equiv xWy$ (the choosing subject prefers object y to x.)

$x, y \approx E u, v \equiv x, yJE u, v$ (the alternative of getting the objects x and y when the event E happens is valued equally highly by the subject as the alternative of getting the objects u and v when the event E does not happen).

The class of terms K is here empty, there is therefore also no sentence $S(K)$. The sentences $S(M)$ and $S(0)$ have the form $\exists(x) \ \exists(y) \ [\phi(x) < \phi(y)]$, $a_1 W a_2$, where a_1 and a_2 are names of objects in the set Z, and ϕ is the term M. Theory T, which we shall use here, makes it possible to explain and to predict the behaviour of a person who is to make a choice from a set of objects. The axioms of the theory are given in the Appendix to this Chapter. It is possible to prove, on the grounds of these axioms, the existence of function ϕ, which assigns to objects numbers representing the subjective value of these objects for the person choosing. The function ϕ meets the following condition:

(32) $\quad \prod_x \prod_y [\phi(x) < \phi(y) \equiv xPy]$.

It can also be demonstrated that ϕ determines an interval value scale, as it is unique up to linear transformation; i.e. if ϕ_1 is such a function, then so is $\phi_2 = a\phi_1 + b$, where $a > 0$, and b is any real number.

To prove that the conjunction $S(M) \cdot T \cdot C$ is consistent we find an interpretation under which the conjunction is true. This interpretation is determined by the following equivalences:

(33) $\quad Z = \{1, 2\}, \qquad xPy \equiv x < y, \qquad xy \approx Eu, v \equiv$
$\equiv x + y = u + v, \; xWy \equiv x < y, \qquad x, yJEu, v \equiv x + y = u + v.$

As we can see, under this interpretation the axioms of the theory, the sentence $S(M)$, and the coordinating definitions are all true. It is also easy to prove that the sentence $S(0)$, here $- a_1 Wa_2$, follows from the conjunction $S(M) \cdot T \cdot C$. In order to do so, we omit quantifiers in the equivalence (32), substituting for the variables x and y the constants a_1, a_2, and we obtain:

(34) $\quad \phi(a_1) < \phi(a_2) \equiv a_1 Pa_2$.

We carry out a similar operation on $S(M)$ and on the coordinating definition $xPy \equiv xWy$:

(35) $\quad \phi(a_1) < \phi(a_2)$,

(36) $\quad a_1 Pa_2 \equiv a_1 Wa_2$.

From the sentences (34), (35) and (36) we obtain $S(0)$.

In order to demonstrate that $S(0)$ is not implied by the conjunction $T \cdot C$, we choose an interpretation identical with the previous one except for the set Z which consists now of a unique element $\{1\}$. Under this interpretation the conjunction $T \cdot C$ is true, while $S(0)$ is false, as it then reduces to the sentence $1 < 1$.

We have demonstrated that the functional term ϕ is meaningful on the basis of Carnap's definition; therefore every well-formed sentence containing the term ϕ (and possibly other meaningful terms) should also be meaningful. For instance, the sentence:

(37) $\quad \exists(x) \; \exists(y) \; \exists(z) \; [\phi(x) + \phi(y) < \phi(z)]$

meets these conditions and is a meaningful sentence under Carnap's definition. But it can be demonstrated that the truth value of this sentence is not invariant under transformations admissible relative to the interval scale. Such transformations carry (37) into:

(38) $\exists(x)\ \exists(y)\ \exists(z)\ [a\phi(x)+b+a\phi(y)+b < a\phi(z)+b]$.

and (38) is not equivalent to (37).

That these two sentences are not equivalent is shown by the interpretation in which the universe is a three-element set $\{1, 2, 3\}$, and the constants a and b as well as the function ϕ are defined by the equations $a = b = 2$; $\phi(x) = x$. Under this interpretation (37) is true, while (38) is false.

We have demonstrated that the definition of meaningful sentence formulated by Carnap covers also quantitative sentences which for reasons presented at the beginning of this chapter should be excluded from that extension. Such exclusion can be obtained by adding to Carnap's definition a supplementary condition, postulating for quantitative sentences the invariance of their truth value under transformations admissible relative to the scales used. As we have said before, a general and fully precise definition of that condition of invariance has not yet been formulated. In a work we have already quoted, P. Suppes discusses a particular form of it which we shall present here. The definition is relativized to the formalized language L_m. This is the language of the theory formulated by A. Tarski in *A Decision Method for Elementary Algebra and Geometry*, enriched by individual variables, individual constants $O_1, \ldots, O_{10}$, denoting ten physical objects, and by the term m, where $m(a)$ is a real number denoting the mass of the object a. The individual constants and the constant m are then the only descriptive terms of L_m. The definitions of a term, of an atomic formula and of a sentence are given for the language L_m. The function m is supposed to determine the ratio scale of mass. The definition of meaningful sentence, formulated on the basis of this language, consists of the following two parts:

A.   An atomic sentence S of L_m is empirically meaningful if and only if the closure of the formula

$$\alpha > 0 \to [S \equiv S(\alpha)]$$

is arithmetically true for every α, while $S(\alpha)$ results from S by replacing every occurrence of m in S by the product αm.

B.   A sentence S of L_m is empirically meaningful if and only if every atomic sentence in S is empirically meaningful.

Suppes consideres two more definitions of empirical meaningfulness, which are modifications of the above-presented definition, formulated in the language of model theory. We do not intend to quote them here, we shall mention only two aspects pointed out by the author in relation to these definitions. If these definitions are assumed, then to the usual values of truth and falsehood we have to add a third one — meaninglessness. The example of the following two sentences indicates the need of introducing such a three valued logic:

$$\exists(x)\,[m(x)=1] \;\vee\; \sim \exists(x)\,[m(x)=1],$$
$$\exists(x)\,[m(x)=1] \;\vee\; \exists(y)\,[m(y)=2].$$

The first disjunction is — according to one of the author's definitions — a meaningful and true sentence, although both of its components are meaningless sentences. In the second disjunction both the components and the whole are meaningless sentences. As we can see, the disjunction does not have here its usual properties of truth-functional connective. The situation is the same in the case of other connectives.

Another important point to which the author pays attention is that, on the ground of his definitions, the set of meaningful sentences does not make up a deductive system, which means that logical consequences of such a set may not be meaningful sentences. For example, a logical consequence of a sentence meaningful on the grounds of the previously quoted definition of meaningfulness:

$$\prod_x [x>2 \to x>1]$$

is the meaningless sentence

$$m(O_1)>2 \to m(O_1)>1.$$

To take care of such cases it is necessary to introduce, in addition to the concept of logical consequence, that of meaningful logical consequence, which is defined by the author. The use of the concept of meaningful logical consequence requires, in turn, the change of formal logical rules. The author proposes such a change for the system of natural deduction. It would consist in the additional restriction that every line of the proof be a meaningful sentence.

Finally, let us go back for a moment to the previously given definition of meaningfulness. The author formulates both its parts in the form of equivalences. It can be seen, however, that the fulfilment by a sentence of the conditions set by the definition does not yet suffice to assure the empirical meaningfulness of the sentence. For those conditions do not take into consideration the relation of the sentence to empirical data. Suppes' definitions can therefore be considered only as formulations stating a necessary condition of meaningfulness with respect to quantitative sentences. Only by adding this condition to Carnap's definition (or else to some other alternative definition) can we obtain a complete definition of the empirical meaningfulness of sentences.

APPENDIX

The ordered triple $\langle Z, P, \approx E \rangle$ is an equal-interval preference structure if and only if for every x, y, u, v, z in Z the following axioms are satisfied:

A_1 The set Z is finite, and the relation P is antisymmetric, transitive and connected in Z,

A_2 $x, y \approx Ey, x,$

A_3 $x, y, \approx Eu, v \rightarrow u, v \approx Ex, y,$

A_4 $x, y \approx Eu, v \cdot u, v \approx Ez, w \rightarrow x, y \approx Ez, w,$

A_5 $x, y \approx Eu, v \cdot xPu \rightarrow vPy,$

A_6 $xNy \cdot uNv \rightarrow x, v \approx Eu, y.$

N is the relation which holds between x and y when y is the only immediate successor of x. The definition of this relation has the following form:

xNy if and only if xPy and for every w in Z: if xPw, then $y = w$ or yPw.

NOTES

[1] Informational aesthetics is the subject matter of a separate chapter in this book.
[2] Cf.: Symposium: 'Measurement and its Importance for Philosophy'. *Proceedings of the Aristotelian Society*, Supplement, vol. XVIII, London 1940.
[3] The expression: "A suitably chosen system M" refers to the fact that in such a system the relations between numbers are not any relations whatsoever, e.g. artificially defined ones, but 'natural' relations – relations which find useful applications in various domains of research or practice; cf. P. Suppes, J. Zinnes, Basic Measurement Theory; in: D. Luce, R. Bush, E. Galanter (eds.), *Handbook of Mathematical Psychology*, vol. I, New York 1963.
[4] This criterion is formulated by Suppes and Zinnes, *op. cit.*
[5] Sentence (7) is false, because its antecedent is true and its consequent false. On the other hand, sentence (9) is true, because its antecedent and its consequent are both false.
[6] Compare remarks in footnote (5).

[7] T. W. Adorno et al., *The Authoritarian Personality*, New York 1950
[8] Cf. 'The Methodological Character of Theoretical Concepts', in: *Minnesota Studies in the Philosophy of Science*, I, 1965.
[9] Published in: *Measurement. Definitions and Theories*, New York 1959.
[10] R. Carnap, *op. cit.*, p. 51 and 60.

CHAPTER II

CONCEPTS WITH FAMILY MEANINGS IN THE HUMANITIES

The development of methodological research has stimulated interest in language as a means of communication. Philosophical discussion of the process of concept formation brought to light many aspects of scientific concepts and concepts used in everyday language. Much stress has been put on finding clear, empirical criteria for the application of concepts, in order to ensure maximal decidability of statements in which those concepts appear. The conception of empirical indicators for such directly inaccessible entities as attitudes, character or personality traits has been developed. R. Carnap called our attention to a large class of only partially definable concepts. Such concepts often refer to various physical or psychological dispositions and are, consequently, called dispositional concepts.

Ludwig Wittgenstein indicated a different type of difficulty concerning attempts to define certain words — words with family meanings. This difficulty stems from certain structural features of such words; their extension does not consist of a set of objects characterized by a number of properties common to all elements of the extension and only to them; rather, it consists of a number of subsets which bear only partial similarity to each other. Due to these similarities they make up a family of subsets; to this family of subsets there corresponds a family meaning. In the course of its evolution the extension of a concept with a family meaning can be enriched with new subsets; but it can also be split into a number of independent extensions each of which is then supplied with a name of its own. The process of evolution is influenced by an interplay of factors of praxiological and psycho-social nature.

'Game' is an example of a concept with family meaning given by Wittgenstein himself. More examples can easily be mentioned: art, avantgard, novel, tragedy, sculpture, sign, sentence, question, subjectivism, anarchy, mental illness, mental health, ideal, animal, plant, etc. Such concepts appear in everyday language as well as in science; in the humanities and the social sciences as well as in biology, psychology, chemistry, etc; even sciences of the logico-mathematical type are not free from them. It seems interesting, therefore, to take such concepts for an object of methodological analysis.

I shall try to find answers to the following questions, as related to the social sciences and the humanities.

1. What are the logical structure and function of concepts with family meanings?

2. Is it possible to define such concepts?

3. What factors determine specific features of such concepts?

4. Do such concepts appear equally in all disciplines or are they prevalent in the humanities?

5. Are family concepts scientifically useful?

6. Does the structure of such concepts change in the course of their evolution, and if so, how?

I shall use Wittgenstein as a starting point in my discussion of family concepts. However, I do not aim at a detailed reconstruction of his views or proclaimed intentions. In referring to Wittgenstein's formulations I nonetheless aim at a presentation of my own views.[1]

As an introduction let me observe that the following can be seen as characterizing family concepts.

1. There is no set of properties common to all objects denoted by such a concept and only to them – a set which would make up an equivalency criterion for the application of the concept.[2]

2. On the contrary, the extension of the concept consists of several different subsets of objects.

3. Every one of those subsets has some properties in common with some other subsets in the extension.

4. Family concepts are open, i.e. there is no boundary separating objects which fall under a given concept from those which do not.

LOGICAL STRUCTURE OF CONCEPTS
WITH FAMILY MEANINGS

To elucidate the logical structure of the concepts in question let us consider how they originate and develop. Their source lies often in everyday language. At first a given word is used to refer to some objects or situations. Subsequently its use is extended to cover also objects similar in certain respects to the primary ones. In the course of development such extension of the former usage takes place several times. Each time the newly added set of objects has some properties in common with some of the objects subsumed earlier. As a result an extension is formed whose elements have no properties common to all of them and only to them. There are, however, properties common to particular pairs of subsets within the extension. In effect there arises a concept with family meaning. Below several examples of such process of concept formation will be considered.

It is to be stressed that the factors which determine the origin and development of concepts with family meanings are both complicated and divergent. Whether some new objects only partially similar to those already in the extension of a given term will also be included in this extension, or whether a new term will be introduced to refer to them, depends on the particular configuration of those factors, and on which of them proves to be the most important in a given situation.

It was stated earlier that the extension of a family concept consists of objects which do not have properties common to all of them and only to them; this requires elucidation. There are always *some* properties common to all objects named by a given word and only to them, to mention only the property of being named by that word. However, what is meant here, and what Wittgenstein apparently had in mind, are not any such common properties, but properties sufficiently 'interesting' or 'important' relative to a given purpose.

Let us now turn to the question of whether it is possible to define such concepts. Wittgenstein's answer to this question was in the negative. He argued that there are no properties common to all objects denoted by such a concept. However, this argument is not adequate. The lack of common properties does not prove that family concepts are undefinable; it merely rules out the ordinary equivalence definition. Such a definition specifies a set of features common to all denotata of the term being defined and only to them. As we shall see, family concepts can be defined with the aid of partial definitions.[3]

I shall present two attempts at formulating general schemes for definitions of concepts with family meanings. One is based on the relation of similarity which is to bind all objects denoted by such a concept; this relation is explicated and made precise. In the other use is made of partial definitions to explicate the logical structure of concepts with family meanings.

Definition Based on the Relation of Similarity

L. Koj refers to difficulties encountered by researchers in biological systematics during attempts to give adequate definitions of 'plant' and 'animal'.[4] It was assumed that the set of animals contained among others the following classes of organisms: *Flagellatae, Rhizopodae, Amoebosporidiae, Ciliatae, Anthozoae, Spongiae*. A series of attempts was made to define the concept of animal with reference to such properties as (1) motility, (2) possession of at least one sense organ, (3) inability to photosynthesize food, (4) inability to grow during the whole life span, (5) having cells with thin membranes, (6) the presence in the organism of haemoglobin or chitin. However, every attempt resulted in a definition which was either too broad or too narrow, or both, or was inadequate on some other grounds. Thus, motility does not supply an adequate criterion, because there are organisms (e.g. some corallines or sponges) which do not move and nonetheless belong in the kingdom of animals. Neither does the presence of haemoglobin or chitin, because not all animals have these substances, and there are organisms counted as plants which produce them.[5]

Koj sees the source of the difficulty in the specific methodological character of the concept being defined. He sees both 'plant' and 'animal' as concepts with family meanings; consequently every attempt at an ordinary equivalence definition which looks for features (in the Aristotelian sense) common to all animals (or plants) and only to them must end in failure. His definitional scheme makes use of the relation of similarity which binds all objects denoted by a concept with a family meaning. He explicates this relation in the following way. First, he distinguishes a number of properties, say $p_1, p_2, \ldots p_n$, characteristic of some initial typical set of objects T. He then considers another set D_T which is an enlargement of the initial set T; he defines an element of D_T as any object which has more than a half of the properties characteristic of the initial type T.

The definitional schema proposed by Koj removes the previously mentioned difficulties to do with separating objects which fall within a family concept from those which do not. Thus, for instance, sponges and corallines whose inclusion in the set of plants or animals met with difficulties may now be counted as animals, because each of them possesses more than a half of the properties taken as characteristic of typical animals.

Koj considers several ways in which his schema can be generalized. Thus, the number of typical properties needed to include some objects in the extension D_T can be fixed as equal to at least half the number n; this makes it possible to dispose of the cases when the number n of properties possessed by typical objects T is an even number. Even greater generalization is achieved if an undetermined fraction r/p is used. The author introduces additional definitional schemata to cover cases when a whole series of concepts corresponding to subsets of a classification is jointly defined. This procedure allows us to differentiate explicitly between subsets the separation of which would otherwise meet with difficulties similar to those mentioned in connection with efforts to set apart plants from animals. I shall omit presenting those schemata, however, because they do not import any new elements relevant to the problems here discussed.

Let us now proceed to consider the merits of the presented schema.

Earlier in this chapter we distinguished four features which characterize concepts with family meanings. Is Koj's definition adequate relative to these points? The first condition is in principle fulfilled. In principle, because his definition admits a special case when all objects denoted by the term D_T have all the typical properties $p_1, p_2, \ldots p_n$. It follows that on the basis of Koj's definition an ordinary concept is an extreme case of a concept with a family meaning. More precisely: ordinary concepts are included in the set of concepts with family meanings. In this respect his definition seems to deviate from Wittgenstein's intuitions.

How about the second condition? We have to answer that in its most general form the condition is not met. To be sure, it is true that every member of D_T has at least one property in common with typical objects T, and therefore with some elements of D_T. However, this is only a special case of the second condition, for Koj admits in his definition only one set of typical objects whereas, in fact, concepts with family meanings often refer to several such sets. Thus, for example, there are several typical games (this is Wittgenstein's own example) a number of typical trends which together form an avant-garde, several types of prose which fall under 'novel'. Similarity does not simply have to denote the relation between one set of objects chosen as typical ones and the rest of the objects falling under a given concept; in the most general case it refers to criss-cross connections which bind together several typical sets and other objects which to some extent resemble the typical ones.

The third condition requires that concepts with family meanings should be open. However, according to Koj's definition those concepts are not open, but closed. For, on the basis of his definition it is in principle possible to decide with regard to every object[7] whether it should be included in the extension of the concept being defined. An object falls under such a concept if, and only if, it is one of the typical objects or else has more than a half of the properties possessed by all typical objects. Thus Koj's explication fails to render an important feature of concepts with family meanings. That Koj's reconstruction deprives concepts with family meanings of their open character is undoubtedly connected with the logical form of his definition. Although his definition does not specify any property (in the Aristotelian sense) common to all objects denoted by the term defined and only to them, it nevertheless gives an equivalent criterion for the application of this term and thus closes its extension.[8]

Let us turn to Koj's explication of the similarity relation.

The author explicates the relation of similarity between two objects by taking into account the number of properties those objects have in common. Such an understanding of similarity suits well the types of examples he analyses. However, there are plenty of cases, in science as well as in everyday life, where similarity refers to an approximate degree of intensity of a property which some objects have in common. It would enlarge the field of applicability, and thus enhance the usefulness of Koj's definition, if it were modified or supplemented so as to cover also similarity in the sense of approximate intensity. It seems, by the way, that similarity measured by the amount of common properties can be construed as a special case of approximate intensity.

According to the author's definition an object is considered similar to objects chosen as typical ones, and is thus included in the extension of the concept being defined, if it has more than a half of the properties possessed by the typical objects. In the generalized version a more liberally defined unfixed proportion r/p is admitted. Now, determining the extension of a concept is an important operation of fundamental methodological significance. The question then arises: why should the operation be carried out on the assumption that the amount of common properties equals 1/2, or r/p, or, for that matter, any other number? Is it at all proper to make similarity dependent merely on the number of common properties? Is it not necessary to take into account also some other aspects of the properties? To be sure, the author admits that it may be useful to differentiate between the properties, e.g. by ascribing to some of them a greater weight than to others. But still, which properties should receive greater weight, how much greater, and why? These questions determine extensions of concepts with family meanings; it is not easy, however, to find satisfactory answers. Now, these are all questions which can be answered only when the theoretical or systematic significance of the properties are taken into consideration; when one takes into account the role that a given concept, defined with reference to given properties, plays in a larger conceptual framework. The history of science, and in particular our knowledge of the development of scientific concepts, supplies examples relevant to these problems. Thus, in biological classification for instance, a large number of properties possessed commonly by some organisms was for a long time considered to be a criterion of the organisms' common origin. As a result these organisms were included in the same taxonomic unit (extension). However, deeper reflection on the systematic significance of particular organic features has led to the identification of cases where organisms phylogenetically homogeneous had fewer properties in common than they had with some other organisms of a different origin.[9] The mere number of common properties is, therefore, not decisive; their systematic significance must also be considered.

We should consider one more problem connected with taking a number of properties as a criterion of similarity. Let us consider three objects x, y and z; x falls under concept A, y under concept B, and we want to decide under which of those two concepts z should be subsumed. Accordingly, we have to count how many common properties x and z have and compare this number with the number of properties common to y and z. So defined, the task is very difficult if not impossible. The cause of the difficulty lies with the great number of properties possessed by every object. To make the task feasible one has to select a certain list of properties considered as important or relevant in the given circumstances. The comparison of objects x, y, and z is now made exclusively with regard to the properties included in the list. In the foregoing analysis of concepts with family meanings such a list of properties was explicitly or tacitly assumed. Koj's list of typical properties is an example. Obviously, object z may be more similar to object x or to object y depending on the list of properties relative to which the comparison is made. The selection of such a list of properties involves important methodological problems of concept formation. In solving those problems reference will have to be made either to the existing terminological usage or to conditions for the scientific usefulness of concepts defined. We resort to the received terminological usage when an analytical definition of a concept is aimed at, i.e. a definition which strives to reconstruct the existing meaning of the concept being defined. On the other hand, reference to conditions for scientific usefulness takes priority when the definition does not aim at an adequate reconstruction of the existing usage, but is to supply a concept useful for given scientific or practical tasks.[10]

CHAPTER II

Explication Based on Partial Definitions

Koj's reconstruction of concepts with family meanings has met with some difficulties. I think that the explication I shall now present avoids these difficulties. In constructing this explication I make use of partial definitions.[11] In contradistinction to the ordinary equivalence definition, which lays down full criteria for the application of the term being defined, partial definitions determine such criteria only partly. Most often they give only a sufficient or only a necessary condition of application; sometimes this condition has only a probabilistic character, i.e. it tells us with what probability the term defined can be used in a given situation.[12] Let the concept being defined be represented by the letter P; then the formulae

If Ax, then Px

If non-Bx, then non-Px[13]

give respectively a sufficient and a necessary condition for the application of P. Sometimes instead of (or in addition to) the necessary condition, a sufficient condition for the application of the negation of P is given:

If Cx, then non-Px

The partial definitions given above determine the applicability of P with regard to objects which have one of the properties: A, non-B, or C. For objects which do not have any of these properties the applicability of the term P remains undetermined. To define P more fully, we can introduce additional partial definitions. However, it is the characteristic feature of a concept which is only partially definable that no number of partial definitions add up to a full definition. The extension of such a concept remains open. This means that there will always be objects about which it cannot be decided whether they should be included in, or excluded from, the extension of an open concept.

Because of their peculiar features, as sketched above, partial definitions offer an especially useful tool for an adequate explication of concepts with family meanings. In order to show this, let us recall briefly how the usage of such a concept is explained. First, one or more kinds of objects are indicated which certainly belong to the extension of the concept in question. This is followed by an additional commentary to the effect that the extension of the concept is not exhausted by the objects indicated, but comprises also objects which are in some respect similar to those indicated. One should notice the characteristically vague and indefinite formulation of this commentary. The specification of factors upon which the relation of similarity should depend is omitted: neither the quality nor the number of common properties nor the degree of their intensity are expressly named. All that can be inferred boils down to the following statement: in order to be included in the extension of the concept the additional objects must show some resemblance to objects explicitly mentioned as members of this extension.

Of course, this omission of specification is not casual, but has its deeper reasons. They go back to the diversity of factors which determine the origin and development of concepts with family meanings. These factors will later be discussed in detail. At this point it suffices to mention the more important ones. 1. Many properties of objects admit of gradation and there is no sharp boundary separating the state of their presence from the state of their absence. A special decision may sometimes be necessary to recognize a given case as more similar to one rather than to the other of those extreme states. 2. Regard for the scientific usefulness of concepts being defined often determines whether some objects should be counted as sufficiently similar and be included in the extension of a given concept. 3. An intention to take advantage of the emotive associations connected with a given word will influence the decision as to what objects should be named with this word. 4. The principle of economy often influences the formation of concepts; for instance to avoid the necessity of introducing a new term for some objects these objects are subsumed under an already existing term whose denotata are considered to be sufficiently similar to those objects.

The diversity of reasons which influence our decision to acknowledge some objects as similar to others and therefore belonging together in the same extension makes it impossible to give a definite description of the similarity relation. As a consequence the extensions of concepts with family meanings remain open. However, this is how they function in all contexts in which they appear. Any attempt at a precise definition of the similarity relation closes the extensions of such concepts and thus fails to give an adequate explication of them. Obviously, in the course of time concepts with family meanings change and evolve. As a result, their extensions may be closed or divided into several extensions, each of which may then be given a term of its own. Of course, when this happens, they change their character and cease to be concepts with family meanings. In the sequel I shall discuss examples of such changes.

After the foregoing explanations we can proceed to describe the logical structure of concepts with family meanings. A definition of any such concept C should meet the following conditions.

1. It consists of one or more partial definitions each giving criteria for the application of C or of its negation non-C.

2. All definitions listed under (1) taken together do not add up to a full, equivalent definition of C. As a consequence the extension of C remains open, i.e. there is a possibility — sometimes expressly mentioned by the author of the definition — of subsuming under C some other objects not covered by the criteria listed in (1). Inclusion of such new objects assumes — expressly or tacitly — additional criteria for the application of C. The introduction of such criteria always marks a step in the development of C.

3. Each of the criteria mentioned in (1) consists of an aggregate of properties characteristic of certain objects considered as undoubtedly falling under C; let us refer to such objects as typical ones.

4. Each type has some property in common with some other type. The existence of properties common to all types is neither assumed nor excluded. However, if such properties common to all types happen to exist, they are not common to those types only, and, therefore, cannot form sufficient grounds for a full, equivalence definition of C — this follows from assumption (2).

5. A new object or type of objects not covered by criteria listed under (1) can be subsumed under C only if it shows some resemblance to the types already included in C. This is only a necessary, but not yet a sufficient condition for including additional objects in the extension C. A decisive role is played here by the already mentioned praxiological and psycho-social factors which influence the development of concepts with family meanings. A given configuration of those factors, the greatest weight ascribed in a particular situation to one of them rather than to another, will decide whether some new objects are considered sufficiently similar to those already in the extension C that they may be subsumed under C, or whether they are held to be so different that a new name for them is required and justified.

I shall presently consider a few examples of concepts with family meanings to show how the above schema can be applied to form definitions of such concepts. At first *the concept of game* will be analysed; the remarks of Wittgenstein providing us with a starting point. He writes:

> ... Consider for example the proceedings that we call 'games'. I mean board games, card games, ball games, Olympic games, and so on. What is common to them all? — Don't say: there *must* be something common, or they would not be called 'games' — but *look and see* whether there is anything common to all. For if you look at them you will not see

something that is common to *all*, but similarities, relationships, and a whole series of them at that. To repeat: don't think, but look! Look for example at board games, with their multifarious relationships. Now pass to card games; here you find many correspondences with the first group, but many common features drop out, and others appear. When we pass next to ball games, much that is common is retained, but much is lost.

... How should we explain to someone what a game is? I imagine that we should describe *games* to him, and we might add: This *and similar* things are called games. And do we know any more about it ourselves? Is it only other people whom we cannot tell exactly what a game is? — But this is not ignorance. We do not know the boundaries, because none have been drawn.

... And this is just how one might explain to someone what a game is. One gives examples and intends them to be taken in a particular way. I do not, however, mean by this that he is supposed to see in those examples that common thing which I — for some reason — was unable to express; but that he is now to *employ* those examples in a particular way. Here giving examples is not an *indirect* means of explaining — in default of a better. For any general definition can be misunderstood too. The point is that *this* is how we play the game. (I mean the language game with the word 'game'.)[1][4]

In order to render adequately the existing structure of the concept 'game' we have recourse to the above schema and not to the ordinary equivalence definition. We do this because there is no set of properties common to all games and only to games. There are only partial similarities and partial differences. Thus, for instance, not all games are amusing; some games involve competition (e.g. football), and others not (e.g. some card games for a single player); there are games which assume winning or losing (e.g. bridge) and those which do not (e.g. some dance games); in some games luck plays a great role (e.g. dice games), in others this role is minimal or null (e.g. chess); for some games high skill is an essential prerequisite (e.g. chess, tennis) while for others no special skill is needed (e.g. some card games, children ball games); some games call for patience (e.g. chess) but in others patience is of no significance (e.g. children's ball games for a single player).

The first step in constructing a definition of 'game' involves listing all sets (types) of objects which undoubtedly fall under 'game'. Each of the types has a certain set of characteristic properties on the basis of which a partial definition can be formed giving a sufficient (but not an equivalent) condition of application for the term 'game'. Let us assume, for example, that the set of properties A, B, C, D, E characterizes card games. Then a partial definition giving a sufficient condition for 'game' relative to these properties would take the form of the following conditional sentence:

If object x has the properties A, B, C, D, E, then x is a game.

Similar conditional sentences can be formulated using as sufficient criteria sets of properties characteristic of other types of objects undoubtedly counted as games. A set of partial definitions so formed is accompanied by a commentary to the effect that all these definitions taken together do not exhaust the extension 'game' — this extension remains open, for there are objects, present or future, which are not identical with any objects undoubtedly counted as games, but merely similar to some of them, which nonetheless may be subsumed under 'game'. The decision, or usage, to count such additional objects as games would supply us with further partial criteria for the term 'game', and would thus further determine its extension. What new objects will be counted as sufficiently similar to typical games and will thus be included in the extension 'game' depends on the praxiological considerations mentioned before.

My next example is the *concept of art fabric*. The extension of this concept has gone through a long evolution which runs parallel to changes in the methods of artistic production. The set of objects counted as art fabrics in earlier periods was in the course of time repeatedly enriched by new objects which in some respects resembled their forerunners and in some others deviated from them.

Among the features which characterized art fabrics in earlier periods were the following: 1. Two-dimensionality — the fabrics spread in two dimensions only; 2. Continuity — there were no interspaces between constitutive parts of the fabrics; 3. The shape of the fabric was predominantly that of a rectangle, of an oval, or of a circle; 4. The threads were plaited densely with the aid of traditional patterns of plaiting; 5. The threads were mostly made of wool, silk, plant fibres, or leather, sometimes interspersed with a few other materials, e.g. gold or silver.

As artistic weaving changed, various properties characteristic of earlier fabrics dropped and new features appeared in their place.

1. Two-dimensionality is no longer the rule in artistic weaving. First threads of varying thickness were used to achieve a relief effect; at present there are fully three-dimensional woven creations, sometimes referred to as woven sculptures, an outstanding example of which are the Abakans — by the Polish artist M. Abakanowicz. In this way the borderline between the two artistic disciplines, weaving and sculpture, was blurred.

2. Many contemporary fabrics are discontinuous: the surface of the web is interspersed with holes of various sizes and shapes; there are even works consisting of several parts entirely separated in space.

3. Shape too has gone through far-reaching transformations. The tra-

ditional shapes — the rectangle, the oval, and the circle — have been supplemented by the wildest variety of forms for which no language has names.

4. Perhaps the furthest reaching changes have occurred in the most fundamental feature of weaving — in the ways yarns (or other elements) are plaited together. The variety of patterns used today is incomparably greater; and the principle of repetition — of repeating regularly one or several kinds of plaits throughout the whole work — is questioned. In some works all neighbouring meshes are plaited according to different principles, which gives the effect of great structural variety. There are works, counted among fabrics, in which plaiting is scarcely to be found: a bunch of cords and ropes of varying thickness and texture, knotted together here and there, streams down from points of suspension and forms a complicated network of curves and lines; or a picture-like structure in which the artist uses scraps of diverse ready-made fabrics, and sews them together, glues them, or joins them in other such ways; the whole, thus formed, is then painted, enriched with other elements, such as glass, metal, or wood, to form a collage. Here again the borderline is blurred between weaving, painting and collage.

5. The materials used to make the fabrics have also gone through fundamental change. In addition to traditional wool, silk, plant fibres, and leather, all conceivable kinds of natural and artificial materials are used: glass, metals, wood, synthetic fibres, paper, rubber, teeth and bones, etc.

As a result of the changes outlined above, the extension of the concept 'art fabric' consists presently of a family of subsets among which there are partial similarities. There is, however, no set of features, relevant to the history or theory of art, common to all art fabrics, let alone a set common to all art fabrics and only to them. Consequently, the definition of the term 'art fabric' would consist of a number of partial definitions each of which specifies a sufficient condition for being an art fabric. To each of the existing variants of fabric there corresponds at least one such partial definition, e.g. in the form of a simple conditional sentence:

If object x has the properties A, B, C, D, then x is an art fabric.

However, the conjunction of all these definitions does not add up to a full, equivalence definition. New types of works, existing or future, may be included in the extension 'art fabric'; every such decision provides additional criteria for the term 'art fabric' and in this way further determines its extension.

The next concept on which we should reflect is that of *language*, a concept which in the course of its development has gone through considerable changes. Of special significance are the modifications which have occurred within the last few decades. They are connected with the efforts — much in vogue these days — to apply linguistic, or more generally semiotic concepts and methods in research on culture and art. These fields of research are often referred to as semiotic theory of culture and semiotic theory of art.[15]

The former usage, in which 'language' appeared in such contexts as the 'English language', 'colloquial language', has been steadily enriched by new usages: 'artificial language', 'language of science', 'language of physics', 'language of logic', 'metalanguage', 'object language'. To these have been further added: 'language of music', 'language of painting', 'language of film', 'language of cooking habits', 'language of family relationships in a given community' etc. Thus the extension 'language' has been repeatedly enriched by new types of objects which only partially resemble the earlier ones.

The features which characterized the concept of language in earlier periods included the following elements: 1. A set of simple expressions (vocabulary); 2. Rules of forming compound expressions out of simpler ones (syntax); 3. Rules of semantic interpretation, often in the form of language custom, which gives each correctly formed expression its semantic coordinate.

In subsequent development of the concept 'language' types of structures were subsumed in which some of the above properties appeared only in a modified, generalized or liberalized form, or were entirely absent. Thus, those who speak of the language of plastic arts see its vocabulary as consisting of lines, forms, solid bodies, spaces, colours, etc.[16] It is obvious, however, that if those elements can be considered as vocabulary, it is only in a generalized sense. The situation is similar with regard to those elements which make up 'vocabularies' of other art-languages, like those of music, of film, etc.

Most often it is the second element which is lacking, namely syntactic rules, especially the rules of forming sentences. Do the languages of music and painting have such rules? How about the language of cooking habits?[17] It is easier to reach agreement, among those interested, on the existence of syntactical rules of forming simpler types of compound expressions, which appear below the level of sentences. However, the existence in the languages of art of rules for forming sentential expressions arouses serious controversies. For instance, many authors deny the existence of such rules in the languages of plastic arts and of music.

In various structures counted presently among languages, it is often the semantic rules that are absent or are given only in a fragmentary and indirect way. In such cases these rules have to be reconstructed in a complicated, round-about way. This is, for instance, the case with avant-garde paintings. When a picture initiating a new artistic movement is shown for the first time at an exhibition, the observer has to stretch his mind exceedingly to understand the message contained in it. The task is so difficult (and also interesting), because no rules of semantic interpretation are given. The viewer has to reconstruct these rules himself on the basis of his observations of the picture. However, such observations do not suffice. In addition he has to draw on his knowledge of various external factors, such as actual problems of a social, psychological or artistic nature, the history of art, etc. He should also have the ability — very difficult to describe, but nonetheless essential — to sense the spirit of his time. It is well to remember that even if all these factors are taken into consideration and the viewer has made a really serious effort at reconstructing the semantic rules, he may nevertheless fail. Thus, for instance, the rules for interpreting Picasso's paintings, formulated by theoreticians of art and known under the name of Cubism, were never acknowledged as correct by Picasso himself. The situation of a viewer who strives to understand a piece of avant-garde painting is not parallel to that of a person who reads a text written in a language whose rules are known to him. Rather, it is similar to the situation of a researcher who tries to decipher an ancient text in an unknown language.

The extension of the concept 'language' as it is used today is the result of changes described above. At present this extension consists of a number of subsets related by partial similarities. There are no features common to all languages and only to them. The definition of the concept would consist of a number of partial definitions each of which specifies a sufficient condition for a particular subset of languages. Up to this point there is a parallel between the concept of language and the concepts discussed earlier, of game and art fabric. However, there is also a difference. We have seen before that the concept of language is presently a subject of lively controversy. As a result of this controversy some negative criteria for the term 'language' may be agreed upon. For instance, they may take the form of one of the following two sentences:

> If a structure x does not have the property P (P may, for example denote syntactic rules for the formation of sentences), then x is not a language.

> If a structure x has a certain property H, then x is not a language.

38   CHAPTER II

The first partial definition gives a necessary condition for 'language'; the second specifies a sufficient condition for the negation of 'language'.

In the foregoing analyses I have tried to recapture the logical structure of concepts with family meanings. It would not be out of place to call attention to the fact that my effort at an adequate reconstruction does not imply my unreserved acceptance of those concepts as always scientifically useful. On the contrary, their scientific usefulness often seems questionable. I shall return to this problem to consider aspects of it in detail.

THE ORIGIN AND DEVELOPMENT OF CONCEPTS WITH FAMILY MEANINGS

An ordinary concept, definable with the aid of an equivalence definition, has as its extension a definite set of objects, even though this set cannot always be delimited sufficiently sharply. With the growth of knowledge a need may arise to change the existing extension of the concept and to adapt it to the discovered facts or newly-accepted theories. Historical and methodological research has shown that many scientific concepts tend to become more and more general in the course of their evolution.[18] Of course, other changes also occur: the new extension may be narrower than the earlier one, or it may partly overlap it. Whatever changes occur, however, the newly-accepted extension always consists of objects which possess certain features common to all of them and only to them. What we are concerned with is not all and any common features — for any extension has some such features — but only those features which are of interest in a given domain of scientific or practical activity.

The origin and development of concepts with family meanings run along different lines. In the course of evolution new objects are added to the existing extension of such a concept, which bear only partial similarities to the former ones. However, the result of this operation is not a more general concept whose meaning consists of properties common to the old objects and the newly-added ones: for such (interesting) properties do not exist. Rather, a concept arises whose extension consists of a number of subsets connected by only partial similarities. The expression 'bud-like development' suggests itself for the description of such a mode of evolution, because it is analogous to certain known organic processes in plants. Why is this so? What factors contribute to such a mode of evolution?

Concepts with family meanings originate and develop as a result of an interaction of factors among which the following seem to play the most important role.

1. The fact that the features which make up the content of such concepts admit of gradation, with the result that it is impossible to delimit their extension sharply.

2. The tendency to economize the media of communication.

3. The tendency to take advantage, for the purposes of persuasion, of emotional associations connected with existing words.

4. Regard for the scientific or practical utility of concepts.

The configuration of these factors, the degree of their intensity, the priority given to one of them rather than to another, all contribute to the origin of concepts with family meanings. Another configuration of the same factors may, however, bring about the opposite effect, by splitting a concept with a meaning family into several separate concepts. According to the situation, this or that particular factor or tendency takes priority. In everyday life, for instance, regard for persuasive effect often dominates the process of concept formation. In science, on the other hand, regard for scientific usefulness plays a major role.

An additional remark is here appropriate. In formulating the factors and tendencies listed above, I do not mean to imply that they are always consciously taken into account in the process of concept formation. Such conscious consideration may, of course, occur, especially in the formulation of scientific concepts. As a rule, however, the process is more or less unconscious. It is only by way of methodological analysis, carried out with regard to evolutional series of concepts, that the factors listed above can be discovered and formulated.

Let us now proceed to consider in detail the factors differentiated above and their influence on the formation of concepts with family meanings.

1. *Properties Admitting of Degrees and Vagueness of Concepts*

Many properties of objects admit of gradation. Red, sweet, long, paranoic, intelligent, naturalistic are examples of such properties. Of special interest for us here are properties whose intensity changes continuously, so that their passage from presence to absence is a matter of imperceptible degrees. In such cases it is impossible to draw a justified, rather than arbitrary demarcation line between these two extreme states. The existence of continuously-changing features is a source of serious difficulties. They confront us in science and in everyday life when we define or use concepts whose content refers to such properties. It is well known how difficult it often is for a biologist to qualify an organism as belonging to this or that species, because the criteria he has at his disposal consist of such continuously-ranging attributes as shade of plumage, subtle differences in shape or size, and so on. Similar, or even greater difficulties, confront practitioners of such disciplines as psychology, sociology, or the humanities. The source of difficulty lies always in continuously-ranging properties and in the resulting vagueness of terms which refer to such properties. To illustrate the ubiquity of the problem here are some more examples of such properties: kinds and shades of colours; peculiarities of shapes; types of intelligence or personality; kinds of psychiatric illness; literary genres; artistic, ethical, or social movements; etc.

It is an important characteristic of vague terms that there are objects with regard to which it is impossible to decide whether they should be subsumed under a given vague term, or should rather be excluded from its extension. As a consequence there arises a state of uncertainty, of suspension. This state of uncertainty creates the general setting within which family concepts originate and develop. Suppose we have a concept C; its extension consists of objects whose features admit of gradation. Suppose, further, we have come across some new objects which, although not identical with those denoted by C, nevertheless bear essential similarities to them. This similarity is, however, neither strong enough to make us include those new objects in the extension C, nor small enough to speak decidedly against their inclusion. To resolve this state of uncertainty, we have to take into account some additional factors from among those mentioned earlier as influencing the development of family concepts. It can happen that those factors supply such convincing and unequivocal reasons that a clear cut decision is possible. As a result the new objects can either be excluded from the extension C, thus leaving it unchanged; or they can be subsumed under C, thus enlarging its extension. This subsumption, however, changes the former meaning of C, which now consists of properties common to both old and new objects and only to them. The new extension does not consist of two similar subsets: the former and the new one, but of one homogeneous set, delimited on the basis of the new meaning.

However, the reasons supplied by taking additional factors into account are not always so clear or unequivocal. Although they may support the inclusion of new objects in the extension C, this is not done by way of giving C a meaning which consists of properties common to both old and new objects and only to them — for such properties have not been found. Rather, the extension of C consists now of two different, although similar, subsets: those of objects newly included and objects which earlier belonged in the extension of C. The new concept thus formed possesses a family of extensions. Of course, this family may consist of more than two subsets; this happens when extension C, even before the inclusion, contained more than one subset. 'Art fabric', 'language', 'art', 'novel', are examples of such concepts. We have seen that many objects counted as art fabrics lie on the border line between art fabrics and sculpture, between art fabrics and pictures, or between art fabric and collage. Another example, chosen from a multitude of others, is that of the happening whose characteristics place it in an intermediate zone between drama, psychodrama, religious ceremony, assemblage and environment. This is caused by the gradational character of features which make up the criterion of art fabric and of the happening.

Further research may lead to the discovery of new, interesting features, common to all subsets of objects which now make up the extension C. Those features may have a more theoretical character, be further removed from the level of directly observable properties. If such features are in fact discovered, they can be used to form a new meaning of C. Relative to this new meaning the extension C ceases to consist of a family of similar subsets, but is turned, instead, into one homogeneous set of objects. Those who form or use concepts with family meanings often hope, more or less consciously, for the future discovery of such new features, common to all subsets and only to them, and at the same time relevant to given scientific or practical purposes.

Should we conclude that concepts with family meanings are symptomatic of transitional periods in the evolution of our notions and of our knowledge in general? Such a conclusion is indeed upheld in the present paper; certainly with regard to scientific concepts of this kind. The transitional character of such concepts, their 'readiness' for further change, for including new sets of objects in their extensions, are closely connected with their open character and their partial definability. Let us add that the transitional character of concepts with family meanings is traceable more easily when we consider the evolution of scientific concepts. With regard to concepts of everyday language the phenomenon is more difficult to observe.

Let us now proceed to discuss the further factors which influence the formation of concepts with family meanings. They will show us how the state of uncertainty caused by the continuous variability of properties and by the resulting vagueness of terms can be resolved.

2. *The Tendency to Economize the Means of Communication*

This is a particular instance of a more general tendency to economize effort which governs all human action. What is of interest for us here is that aspect of the tendency which calls for minimalization of the number of words needed to express a message. By paraphrasing Occam's well-known principle (Occam's Razor) we could give it the following expression: words should not be multiplied without necessity. It is easily seen that this formulation is relative. It contains an implicit relativization to the purpose for which the words are to be used. Generally speaking, the aim of human scientific activity and of much practical activity in every day life is to order the existing multitude of objects and phenomena into groups in a way which would allow us to discover the regularities governing those objects and phenomena. A functioning of language is to help us to carry out this task and to express the findings with the aid of suitable statements or complexes of such statements. Of course, the existing objects and phenomena can be ordered into groups in many different ways, depending on the particular scientific or practical purpose. Moreover, for some purposes it may be necessary to make fine distinctions between objects by taking into account even very subtle differences between their properties and the degrees of their intensity. In other cases a considerably less refined or even a crude differentiation suffices. Our language must be adopted correspondingly. It can be elaborated into an extremely sensitive tool able to describe very fine differences and relations between facts and circumstances. The construction and use of such a language are, however, difficult and time-consuming; in addition they presuppose highly developed sciences and measuring techniques. In cases when such sophisticated techniques are not necessary or simply do not exist we have to be satisfied with a language whose means of expression are much less refined.

We can find concrete examples of languages at different levels of sophistication by, for instance, comparing a text on some problems of contemporary human genetics published in a popular magazine with a corresponding text addressed to specialists. Similar differences in the level of refinement are disclosed by comparative reflection on languages of various nations. Thus—to take one example from a large number of similar ones—some ethnic languages have no word, or at most one word, to denote frozen atmospheric precipitation, e.g. the equivalent of the word 'snow'. At the same time other ethnic languages dispose of many such words, which can be used to differentiate between various kinds of frozen atmospheric precipitation. This language difference is, of course, connected with the practical importance for a given ethnic group of the ability to discriminate between kinds of frozen precipitation and to express such discrimination. A region with little or no such precipitation is in a different situation from a region where the variety and the quantity of this precipitation are large and where many essential aspects of life depend on it. Language adapts itself to such circumstances and the process of adaptation is influenced by the principle of economization.

How does this principle effect the formation of family concepts? The starting point is the situation described above, of uncertainty caused by the continuous variability of objects, features. Should the new objects, similar to those which already belong to extension of C, be subsumed under C or should they rather be considered as something different and be given a new name? Here the tendency to economize exerts a braking effect. It supports the inclusion of the new objects in the extension C, thus preventing the multiplication of words. However, this principle does not act alone. It cooperates with, and in case of conflict even gives priority to, regard for the scientific or practical usefulness of concepts. If, for scientific purposes, the difference between the new objects and the objects already in the extension C is sufficiently large and important, the principle of economization gives way and the new objects are given a name of their own.

To give a fuller picture of the processes outlined above I shall point to factors which exert an influence opposite to that produced by the tendency to economization. New terms are sometimes introduced without substantial justification in cases where existing terms provide sufficient means of expression. Sometimes this is done in order to strengthen the doubtful distinctness of one's own achievements in art or science; sometimes to separate one's own view from the seemingly identical position of a rival; or to evoke by the use of new words the impression of new achievements.

Let us supplement our remarks on economization by considering a few examples. 'Novel', 'sculpture', 'art', as well as many words quoted earlier, are examples of words with regard to which the tendency to economization has shown its effect. New objects, although different in some essential respects from those counted earlier as novels, sculptures, art works, have, nonetheless, been subsumed under these terms. The other factors, the regard for the usefulness of concepts or for the evaluative load connected with existing words, have either acted in the same direction or failed to provide reasons sufficiently weighty to prevail against the tendency to economization. Thus, the concept 'novel' has gone through a considerable evolution: from the classical 19th-century novel to Proust, Joyce or Butor. Most earlier novels were fictional, contained narrative, character delineation and dialogue, and followed a regular time sequence. Some of these properties, e.g. regular time sequence, are absent in certain 20th-century novels. Their place is taken by other features which did not exist in earlier novels, e.g. the interspersion of actual newspaper reports within the text.[19] The new compositions were subsumed under the same term: 'novel'. As a result of this evolution the extension of 'novel' consists today of a family of subsets which bear partial similarity to each other.

The concept of sculpture has also undergone great changes. One of the basic properties of earlier sculptures — that of being a solid, cohesive body, has been questioned. Contemporary sculpture is often perforated by openings of various size and shape: a light, airy appearance supplants the former cohesive body; light passes through the openings and gives the sculpture rich chiaroscuro effects. The variety of materials now used to produce sculptures, and the use of colour, water, sound or motion effects, all contribute to the plurality of aesthetic effects which distinguish contemporary from earlier sculpture. Today the term 'sculpture' refers to a number of subsets bounded by only partial similarities. Concepts like 'mobile', 'happening', or 'collage', on the other hand, are examples where the tendency to economisation gave way to other factors which shape the process of concept formation, especially to regard for the scientific or practical usefulness of concepts. All these concepts denote objects which bear essential similarities to some other objects. Calder's mobiles have many features in common with some contemporary sculpture. Happening borders with drama, psychodrama, religious ceremony, assemblage and environment. Collage is close to painting. With these, however, the differences proved to be more important than the similarities. In consequence the new art objects have not been included in the already existing extensions, but have been distinguished by new terms. The introduction of new terms was influenced by regard for the usefulness of concepts in the theory and history of art, for the purposes of systematization artistic phenomena. It is, however, possible that other factors also played a role, e.g. the intention to take advantage of the emotive load connected with the existing words or to dissociate oneself from such emotive connotations; striving for prestige, etc.

3. *Regard for Emotive Associations Connected with Existing Words*

Linguistic expressions evoke in us emotional reactions. This property of language can be used to shape people's evaluative and emotional attitudes. We can achieve such persuasive effect by taking advantage of the emotive connotations of existing words. By using suitable procedures we can transfer these associations from one word to another, or from one extension to another extension of the same word. We can also change the intensity or the kind of emotional load attached to a given word, e.g. by replacing aesthetic emotive associations with ethical ones, or by reversing its polarity so that a negative load replaces a positive one or *vice versa*.[20] Each of these changes of connotation may influence people's evaluative and emotional attitudes with regard to objects or phenomena denoted by the expression.

What is of interest for use here is the influence exerted by our regard for the emotive function of language, on the formation of concepts with family meanings. Generally speaking, our concern for the utility of concepts will, in cases of conflict, take priority over both the tendency to economisation and regard for the emotive function of language. This priority is most decided and most clearly visible within the realm of the more developed empirical sciences. In other branches of science, where values and value-laden terms play an important role, e.g. in the humanities, and also in everyday language, this priority is not so clearly established; sometimes it is even reversed, i.e. the regard for the emotive load of concepts gets the better.

Let us assume a certain term T is value-laden, i.e. evokes positive or negative associations of some kind. Let us further assume we have come across objects which bear essential similarities to those denoted by T, but are not identical with them — that is, identical relative to a given list of properties. The question arises whether the new objects should be included as a subset in the extension T to form a family of extensions, or not. In this situation, those for whom it is important to transfer to the new objects the emotional attitude towards objects denoted formerly by T, will be in favour of inclusion. Those who are against such transference will also be against the inclusion. This general description entails four different cases depending on the pole of the emotive load possessed by the term T:

A. T has a positive emotive load and this load should be transferred to cover also the new objects.

B. T has a positive emotive load and this load should not be extended to the new objects.

C. T has a negative emotive load and this load should be transferred to cover also the new objects.

D. T has a negative emotive load and this load should not be extended to the new objects.

Here are some examples.

Discussions about pornography often involve practical considerations concerning the prohibition of pornography. Let us imagine a discussion of whether new objects partly similar to existing ones, e.g. some new films, printed pictures or books, should be included in the extension 'pornography'. The answer comes out differently depending on the prohibitionist tendencies of the participants. Those who want the dissimination of the new objects to be prohibited vote for their inclusion (case C), in contradistinction to those who have a less restrictive attitude (case D).

The concept of art work has gone through a long evolution. Parallel to the development of art the extension of this concept has been enriched many times by objects of a novel kind. The inclusion of such new objects is often preceded by long discussions, sometimes bitterly controversial, about whether the new objects should be acknowledged as art or should rather remain outside the extension of this term.[21]

This question seems to be especially pertinent in the contemporary period, when objects or activities extremely different from those acknowledged as art in earlier times are nonetheless claimed to be art. The term 'art' is not emotionally neutral: it is loaded with strong positive emotions, which would be extended to cover any new objects subsumed under 'art'. Besides, the author of an object acknowledged as an art work is entitled to considerable privileges and advantages, including the right to ask a high price for his product, and the right to exhibit in museums and art galleries. All this contributes to making the controversy on what is art so lively. In such controversy, those who include the new objects in the extension 'work of art' fall under case A; those who are against inclusion, who consider the new objects 'unworthy' to be called works of art, fall under case B.

Of course, 'pornography' and 'art' are chosen from a legion of terms around which arise similar discussions. Other conspicuous examples include: 'aggressor' — consider attempts in the United Nations to decide who is guilty of aggression and what measures should be applied against aggression; 'mental health' — compare public discussions on what constitutes mental illness and how mental patients should be treated; 'language' — in the sense we have discussed above; 'sign' — consider the extended use of this concept in informational aesthetics and in the semiotic theory of culture and the justifiability of such extension;[22] 'operationism' — compare discussions on which definitions are operational, conducted at a time when it was in vogue and 'scientific' to define concepts operationally.

4. *Regard for the Scientific Usefulness of Concepts*

A good definition of a concept has to be formally correct i.e. it cannot have formal errors, such as contradiction or circularity. Formal correctness, however, is only a necessary, but not yet a sufficient condition of a good definition. The history of science abounds in examples of definitions which were formally correct and were nonetheless rejected. The additional conditions which a definition has to meet to be accepted in science are often referred to as conditions for the scientific usefulness of definition; one can speak equivalently of the scientific usefulness of a concept introduced by such a definition.

What do we mean by conditions for the scientific usefulness of concepts? When a term is being defined, we have to decide on the following two points which are of fundamental methodological importance;

What set of objects or phenomena should be coordinated to that term as its extension?

What set of definitional properties should be used to distinguish that set of objects?

For, obviously, many different sets of objects can be coordinated to a given term as its extension. Besides, each of those sets of objects can be distinguished with the aid of many different sets of definitional properties. The decision with regard to these two points is closely connected with the central problem of every science: How to order in groups the objects and phenomena of the world around us, so as to be able to discover the regularities which govern these phenomena? The factors which, consciously or not, scientists take into account in these processes of grouping, have to be verbalized in conditions for the scientific usefulness of concepts.

Obviously, both of the choices mentioned above, concerning definitional properties and extension, must take into account a larger system of statements which make up a given discipline, and the aims pursued by this discipline. In this respect there are certain differences between various disciplines, although some criteria for scientific usefulness are common to many sciences. In what follows I shall briefly discuss the more important of these criteria.[23]

A. *The choice of extension.* As extensions of concepts homogeneous sets of objects should be selected. Homogeneity is here relativized to the tasks and interest of the scientific discipline to which the concept being defined belongs. An extension which is homogeneous relative to one scientific discipline may not be homogeneous relative to another. The objects which make up a homogeneous extension have very many properties in common — properties which are of interest for the relevant discipline. That is why concepts with homogeneous extensions make it possible for a discipline to formulate the maximal amount of statements needed for description and explanation of the phenomena which are its subject matter. Let me illustrate this with a simple example taken from the history of botany. Consider the following botanical generalization:

Every grass is wind-propagable

The usefulness of a concept (in our example the concepts are 'grass' and 'wind propagable') is the greater, the larger is the number of empirically corroborated statements which can be formulated with the aid of this concept. Both 'grass' and 'wind-propagable' meet this condition, because they appear in many botanical statements. In contrast, the concept 'Tetriandria' (plants with four stamens) which appears in the plant-system of Linnaeus has not proved scientifically useful. Plants denoted by this concept have few common properties of interest to botany. From the fact that a plant is tetrandrous there follow scarcely any conclusions in the form of general statements similar to the above generalization concerning grass. 'Tetriandria' refers to a set of objects which is botanically unhomogeneous.

B. *The choice of definitional properties.* The extension of any term can be delimited with the aid of many different sets of properties. Each of those sets of properties can be used to form the content of the term. The question arises which set of properties should be chosen for this purpose. Regard for the scientific usefulness of concepts requires that the properties chosen be essential ones. A property of an object is essential when it determines many other properties of that object. It follows that properties essential for a given set of objects can be used, in conjunction with suitable scientific laws, to explain and predict many other properties of those objects. Thus, for instance, the properties which make up the content of the concept 'conditioned reflex' proved to be eseential ones: they are connected with many aspects of human and animal behaviour. As a consequence, the concept of conditioned reflex helped scientists to discover, explain and predict numerous regularities in normal and pathological reactions of men and animals. Similarly, the properties which make up the content of such concepts as atom, electron, atomic mass, molecule, molecular structure have been shown to be essential properties. Thus, for instance, if we know the atomic mass of an element, we can predict a number of other properties of this element.

I have so far discussed two conditions for the scientific usefulness of concepts: that which refers to the choice of extension, and that which refers to the choice of content, of the concept being defined. These will now be enriched by a third condition. This requires that the scientific theory in which the defined concepts appear, should optimally fulfil its tasks. It should cover and explain all phenomena which make up its subject matter, i.e. no phenomenon should remain unexplained. It should not lead to consequences discordant with empirical data. Its formal and conceptual structure should be as simple as possible. If two or more definitions of a given concept compete with each other, then that definition wins and is accepted in science which is based on a theory, *ceteris paribus*, better in some of the mentioned respects. The existence of such competition and selection can be observed by analysing the evolution of scientific concepts. I have shown it elsewhere by tracing the development of the chemical concept of acids as well as the development of biological classification.[24]

Are concepts with family meanings scientifically useful? The answer to this question may vary, depending on which particular concept is taken into account.

The task of science, and in particular that of nomological sciences, is to discover regularities among phenomena and to formulate general statements which express those regularities. Similar general statements occur also, though to a lesser extent, in non-nomological sciences like political history or history of art. No historical phenomenon can be explained without recourse to general statements of this kind. As a rule, however, historical disciplines do not discover such generalizations themselves, but take them from nomological sciences or from common-sense knowledge. Can concepts with meaning families be used to formulate such general statements?

Let B be a concept with a meaning family, and let us consider a very simple type of general statements of the form 'Every x is y'. Can B be used as a subject in a sentence of this type, e.g. in a statement:

Every B is H?

This statement ascribes the property H to each object which belongs in the extension B. We have assumed that B is a concept with a meaning family; this implies that there are no properties common to all elements of B and only to them.[25] This does not exclude the possibility of formulating true statements of the form 'Every B is H', which establish H as a property common to all elements of B, and not as a property common to all elements of B and only to them. According to the working characteristic of a concept with a family meaning formulated at the beginning of this chapter, the existence of properties common to all objects denoted by such a concept is neither excluded nor assumed. The existence of such common properties remains an empirical problem to be solved separately with regard to every concept of this kind. However, the analysis of many such concepts shows that their extensions lack not only properties common to all elements of extension and only to them, but any common properties. It follows that concepts with family meanings are of only limited use for the purpose of formulating true statements of the form 'Every x is y'. Only the very few concepts of this kind, whose extensions have some common properties, can be used as subjects in sentences of this type.

Let us in turn ask if B can be used as a predicate in such a sentence:

Every F is B.

The above sentence is, of course, true on the assumption that F is one of the subsets which together form the family B. We can formulate as many true statements of the form 'Every F is B' as there are different subsets F contained in the family of subsets B. Generally, this is not enough to make B scientifically useful. Its scientific usefulness would rise if more sets were found of which B could truthfully be predicated, or new sets which are connected by some general relationships with the subsets of B. The usefulness of B could also be strengthened by discovering statistical relationships between B and some other sets of objects. If none of the above mentioned circumstances occur, then the usefulness of B is limited to its use as a subject in a statement of the type 'Every x is y', and also to the systematizing and ordering function which B can eventually fulfil. Thus, even if no general relationship is found between sculpture or art fabrics or novels on the one hand, and some other scientifically interesting variables or properties on the other, those concepts can be useful to the degree to which they help to order and systematize the corresponding artistic phenomena.

As we know from the preceding paragraphs, the extension of a concept with a family meaning consists of a number of subsets. There are no properties common to all objects which form an extension of such a concept and only to them; they are bound by only partial similarities. These objects are nonetheless subsumed under one term to form its extension. This is done, more or less consciously, with the hope that future research will discover such common properties and will justify the concepts thus formed. This process can be observed most clearly in science; it is to be supposed that it also occurs, although less consciously, in everyday language. The hope of discovering properties common to all elements of a family and only to them has rational grounds. Objects only partly similar with regard to their more directly accessible properties may nonethelsss be identical with regard to some hidden properties of a more abstract character. The history of science abounds in discoveries of such hidden uniformities among objects whose external, directly accessible features were diverse. When such hidden uniformities are found, the corresponding concept with a meaning family can be transformed into an ordinary concept whose extension forms one homogeneous set of objects. The discovered uniformities supply properties common to all elements of the set and only to them, and are used to form the meaning of this newly introduced concept.

However, the development of concepts with family meanings does not always terminate so happily. Research sometimes reveals that their extensions form unhomogeneous sets of objects and as such are of no scientific interest. It happens sometimes that such unhomogeneous extensions can be divided into two or more sets which are themselves homogeneous and are then established as extensions of several new terms. Transformations of this kind can also be found in the history of science. I shall consider two examples.

The concept 'sentence' in its grammatical and colloquial sense has as its extension a family of subsets which together form an unhomogeneous set. This set embraces affirmative sentences, questions, requests and imperatives, as well as utterances which are shortened equivalents for the preceding types of expressions. From this unhomogeneous set, by way of logical analysis, a set of expressions has been differentiated which is homogeneous with regard to the interest of logic and theory of science. This set of expressions has been given a new name: 'sentence in the logical sense'. It contains all and only such expressions as can be qualified as true or false.

Another example is 'questions' in the colloquial and grammatical sense of this word. Its extension is a family of subsets which also proved not to be homogeneous. It comprises closed as well as open questions; expressions having the grammatical form of a question and that of an affirmative sentence; didactic questions whose aim is merely to check information possessed by the respondent, and questions put with the intention of gaining information. From this set a subset of expressions has been differentiated and provided with a new name: 'question in the logical sense'. The extension of this new term is homogeneous and useful with regard to the interest of logic and theory of science.

The type of transformation illustrated by these two examples can often be observed. It is clearly visible in cases when concepts of everyday language are transferred to the language of science. 'Game', 'logically follows from' 'substantiation', 'proof', 'probable', 'psychic illness' — are examples. Each of these terms refers in its colloquial meaning to a family of sets. Simultaneously with their transference from everyday language to the language of science they have been given narrower extensions, homogeneous with respect to the aims of the sciences into which they were incorporated.

Do concepts with meaning families appear equally in all sciences or rather are they characteristic of the humanities? The latter seems to be the case. In the humanities, family concepts appear more frequently and play a greater role than in the other branches of science, and the same is true of everyday language. How can this be explained? Is it due to linguistic imprecision and the lack of sharp, empirical criteria for the applicability of concepts in the humanities and in colloquial language? Of course, this factor plays its role. However, the main cause seems to lie deeper, in the fundamental methodological features of the humanities, and is connected with the basic scheme of their development. This scheme, namely, is of the non-cumulative type in contrast to the advanced natural sciences which develop cumulatively.

In a science with the cumulative type of development every later stage is a continuation and partial transformation of earlier stages. The achievements of preceding stages are, of course, checked when doubts arise as to their correctness. But some fundamental stock of truths and methods of research, adapted to the new discoveries, is carried to the next stage.

The existence of scientific theories in the strict sense of the word is another feature which distinguishes advanced natural sciences from the humanities. The latter do not have such theories. This is closely connected with, and to a large extent conditioned by, the non-cumulative type of their development. However, scientific theories are the most important factors which shape the process of concept formation. It is with regard to a scientific theory that conditions for the scientific usefulness of concepts can be described most clearly. The structure of a theory and its tasks determine the two factors on which the scientific usefulness of concepts depends: the selection of extension and the selection of content of a given concept. When there is no theory, the criteria of selection are much less definite.

Let us in this context consider again the basic setting in which concepts with meaning families originate and develop. We come across some objects partly similar to those denoted by a concept C; we have to decide whether or not the new objects should be subsumed under C. The scientific theory to which the concept C belongs provides us with criteria necessary for this decision. When there is no theory, we lack such sufficiently clear criteria. It often happens that the degree of similarity of the new objects to objects already subsumed under C is not so small as to make us decidedly exclude the new objects from the extension C. If in addition some other factors, e.g. regard for the emotive associations connected with C, speak for inclusion, then the concept thus formed will have a family of extensions. This is precisely the situation which often occurs in the humanities, but is rarely found in the more developed natural sciences. This is why concepts with family meanings more often appear in the humanities.

I should like to end these remarks on family concepts by calling attention to the fact that it is not always easy to decide whether a given concept refers to a meaning family or is simply ambiguous. Such decisions would be easier if concepts were always introduced by way of clear definitions. However, in the humanities as well as in everyday language it is often custom which determines the usage.

NOTES

[1] I refer to the following works: L. Wittgenstein, *Philosophical Investigations*, New York 1957; L. Koj, 'On Defining Meaning Families', *Studia Logica*, **XXV**, 1969; G. Hallett, *A Companion to Wittgenstein's 'Philosophical Investigations'*, Ithaca, New York, 1977. I take this occasion to thank Professor G. Hallett for his valuable comments which allowed me to improve the text in many places.

[2] Let the equivalence: $Cx \equiv S$ be an accepted definition of the word C with the aid of expression S. As is known, an equivalence is true if both its component sentences have the same truth value, i.e. both are true or both false. It follows that on the basis of the equivalence definition given above we can predicate term C of any object x which meets the condition described by S. On the other hand, the negation of C – non-C – can be predicated about any object x which does not meet the condition S. An equivalence definition thus gives full criteria for the application of the term it defines.

Wittgenstein speaks variably of the absence of properties common to a given set of objects. Sometimes he means that there are no properties possessed by all those objects; sometimes, however, what he has in mind is the lack of properties common to all those objects and only to them. In both cases the possibility of a definition is ruled out (Wittgenstein had in mind an ordinary, equivalence definition). However, it is well to remember that in order to obtain an equivalence definition of a term denoting a given set of objects it is not enough to find properties common to all those objects; one has to find features common to all those objects and only to them.

[3] Compare in this connection remarks formulated in note (2), and also the chapter on partial definitions in my *Begriffsbildung und Definition*, Verlag de Gruyter, Berlin – New York, 1980.

[4] L. Koj, *op. cit.*

[5] Disjunctions of the features mentioned above cannot be used, because the author conceives 'feature' in the Aristotelian way as a non-constructed feature.

[6] One could here object that Koj also admits several typical sets of objects when he jointly defines a whole series of concepts which correspond to subsets of a division. This is indeed so. However, each of those types is then coordinated to a separate concept so that none of those concepts has more than one type. In this respect Koj's explication fits the natural sciences well, especially biological systematics. It is, however, not adequate with regard to all situations in which concepts with family meanings appear. Particularly in the humanities and in everyday language there are concepts of this kind which refer not to one, but to several types.

[7] Unless it is excluded by the extreme vagueness of terms which refer to the typical properties.

[8] I shall return to this problem later when I discuss the attempt at a reconstruction with the aid of partial definitions.

[9] Cf. A. Remane, *Die Grundlagen des natürlichen Systems der vergleichenden Anatomie und der Phylogenetik*. Leipzig 1965, p. 7.
[10] I return to the problem of scientific usefulness of concepts in the sequel. A more detailed discussion of the problem can be found in *Begriffsbildung und Definition*.
[11] Cf. R. Carnap, 'Testability and Meaning'. *Philosophy of Science*, 1936, 1937.
[12] Various forms of partial definitions are discussed in *Begriffsbildung und Definition*.
[13] Read: If object x does not have the property B, then it also does not have the property P. Similarly also the other formulas. I omit quantifiers; this simplification does not bear on the problems here discussed.
[14] L. Wittgenstein, *Philosophical Investigations*, paragraphs 66, 69, and 71.
[15] I consider these problems in the chapter on the semiotic theory of culture.
[16] Compare for instance G. Gollwitzer, *Die Kunst als Zeichen*, p. 21, München 1963.
[17] I am referring here to the article on cooking habits by C. Levi-Strauss.
[18] I have shown the existence of such tendency with regard to the chemical concept of acids and also with regard to concepts which appear in biological systematics. Cf. T. Pawlowski, *On the Methodology of Natural Sciences* (Polish), Warsaw 1959.
[19] Cf. Morris Weitz, 'The Role of Theory in Esthetics'. *The Journal of Aesthetics and Art Criticism*, XV, 1965.
[20] Compare the chapter on persuasive function of language where various types of persuasion are analysed.
[21] Such controversies often have important philosophical, artistic, or ideological grounds which, however, are not the subject of discussion here.
[22] Compare the chapter on the semiotic theory of culture.
[23] For a fuller discussion see my *Begriffsbildung und Definition*.
[24] Cf. my *On the Methodology of Natural Sciences*.
[25] What is meant here are not any such properties, but scientifically interesting properties.

CHAPTER III

PERSUASIVE FUNCTION OF LANGUAGE

We react to phenomena of the surrounding world not only cognitively, through mental or sensory representations, but affectively as well: our perceptions take on an emotional colouring, our feelings are rich in variety and intensity. It is because of our ability to react emotionally to external stimuli that we can enjoy and appreciate art, meaningful perception of which usually presupposes living through an aesthetic emotion. Similarly, human behaviour evokes in us feelings of approval or censure. As a result of repetition the emotional reactions, originally provoked by certain objects, undergo a process of mediation: they shift over onto linguistic expressions which refer to those objects. Subsequently, to provoke a person to an emotional reaction it is no longer necessary to place the person in the situation which originally conditioned the reaction; often it suffices to use the expression which stands for the situation. It is in this way that linguistic expressions can take on an emotive load. Such loads may impede processes of communication, particularly when it comes to transmitting precise, unambiguous information about definite facts. However, the same property of linguistic expressions is useful for other purposes: it can be used for persuasion, to shape people's emotive attitudes. This is a matter of great social importance. Since attitudes help to determine behaviour, by moulding attitudes we can influence behaviour. The persuasive function of language can, of course, be used for any purposes, not only for those we approve of. It is a tool—a tool for shaping people's attitudes—and, as such, is morally neutral. This makes it the more important for us to know the various forms of the persuasive use of language. It is sometimes good to realize that we are objects of persuasion.

The social importance of verbal persuasion techniques accounts for the fact that the attention of sociologists has been focused on them. When discussing the uses made of emotive associations connected with various terms, S. Ossowski wrote in his *Class Structure in the Social Consciousness:*

... terms are not indifferent, especially in the humanities. This is obviously so, because of the propaganda value of certain words. Everyone realizes how important it is to select terms in propaganda speeches and in political writings. Particular words have their spheres of associations, and some of them have acquired strong charges of positive or negative emotions. ... The use of the term 'religion' in Durkheim's sense provokes protests in Roman Catholics who want that term to be reserved for divine matters; it also provokes protests in Marxists, but for different reasons, namely because of the undesirable associations which that term would retain, although the corresponding concept would cover 'atheistic religions' as well. The concept of 'religious function' would be much more acceptable to Marxists if it were called otherwise. The term 'class' could, by a convention, be replaced by the term 'stratum', but as a signal intended to release conditioned responses the term 'stratum enemy' could not easily replace 'class enemy' p. 148.

Changes in emotive attitudes can be produced by various means: linguistic as well as extra linguistic. I am here concerned solely with the former kind. However, even here an abundance of varieties exists. An exhaustive analysis of the linguistic means of persuasion is not possible in this chapter, since it would require a spacious volume of its own. I shall consider mainly definitions of various kinds. My analysis will also cover a certain kind of sequential utterance, spoken or written, which, while not being definitions, perform similar functions. Such sequences of utterances, which I shall call persuasive argumentations, are intended to change the emotive attitudes of the listeners. A persuasive definition often forms part of a persuasive argumentation. Sometimes it plays the role of a summing up, which concisely and emphatically formulates the essence of the argumentation.

What, generally speaking, is the mechanism of linguistic persuasion? It takes advantage of the existing emotive load carried by linguistic expressions: this load is transferred to other expressions or to other extensions of the same expressions; and its intensity, as also its kind or its polarity is changed. The known controversies on the definition of pornography can serve as an example. In its various formulations a narrower or a broader extension of this concept is stipulated, covering this or that particular kind of objects, depending on the intentions and the purposes of the person or the political group which promotes a particular formulation. Of course, one can assume that a definition of 'pornography' is a matter of convention; it is only important that this convention is precise and operative enough, and that it is strictly observed once it has been accepted. However, one who assumes such a stand puts himself in a disadvantageous position, in two respects. Controversy about the meaning of the word 'pornography' is entangled in controversy about practical measures to prohibit its dissemination; and it is not at all irrelevant what is prohibited. Our imaginary disputant could maintain that if the accepted convention stipulated too broad an extension of 'pornography', in a way discordant with his own convictions, he would vote against the prohibition of certain objects. In so doing, however, he would let the controversy move from a rather indirect plane (controversy on the definition of 'pornography') to a direct plane (controversy on the prohibition), which is tactically disadvantageous. In addition he must reckon with the possibility that the negative emotional load associated with the word 'pornography' can easily be transferred by the action of linguistic mechanisms to objects which he himself values, and which have not until now been deprecated by the larger public.

Similar problems are involved in the known controversies on 'the proper' definitions of such emotionally loaded terms as 'art', 'kitsch', 'mental illness', or 'aggressor'.

I have mentioned above a number of transformations which linguistic expressions can undergo with respect to their emotional load. A typology of such transformations will be presented below, but before discussing this problem in detail let us consider a quotation from Huxley's 'Eyeless in Gaza'. The passage grasps finely the atmosphere of persuasive operations, although their objective does not always provoke moral reservations, as is the case in the passage quoted.

> But if you want to be free, you've got to be a prisoner. It's the condition of freedom— true freedom.
> True freedom! Anthony repeated in the parody of a clerical voice. I always love that kind of argument. The contrary of a thing isn't the contrary; oh, dear me, no! It's the thing itself, but as it truly is. Ask any die-hard what conservatism is; he'll tell you it's true socialism. And the brewer's trade papers: they're full of articles about the beauty of true temperance. Ordinary temperance is just gross refusal to drink; but true temperance, true temperance is something much more refined. True temperance is a bottle of claret with each meal and three double whiskies after dinner. Personally, I'm all for true temperance, because I hate temperance. But I like being free. So I won't have anything to do with true freedom.
> Which doesn't prevent it from being true freedom, the other obstinately insisted.
> What's in a name? Anthony went on. The answer is, practically everything, if the name's a good one. Freedom's a marvellous name. That's why you're so anxious to make use of it. You think that, if you call imprisonment true freedom, people will be attracted to the prison. And the worst of it is you're quite right.[1]

Linguistic expressions tend to evoke emotive responses. Under the influence of various factors emotive associations connected with a given expression can be transferred to another expression, which was emotively neutral before, and can thus increase the set of those expressions which are emotively active. This is only one of the many kinds of changes which linguistic expressions can undergo as far as emotive associations are concerned. Another kind of changes consists in the vanishing of such associations; still another, in the driving out of positive associations by negative ones, or *vice versa*. It can also happen that emotive associations of a certain kind are replaced by associations of a different kind, for instance, moral ones by aesthetic ones. I shall present a typology of such changes and analyse certain methods of causing them.

Emotive attitudes find their expression in linguistic terms and phrases which are emotively active, and to which emotively neutral phrases can be opposed. Among emotively active phrases distinction can be made between pure value terms and descriptive-value terms. These relationships are shown in the following classification:

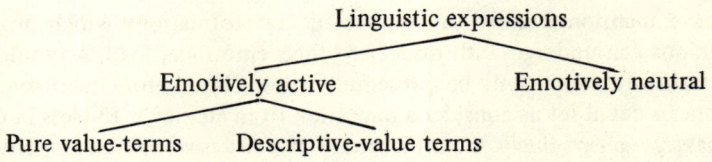

The difficulties encountered in all endeavours to define strictly and to distinguish the kinds of expressions specified in this classification are well known. The source of these difficulties lies in the fact that in colloquial language the meaning of words is, on the whole, not specified sufficiently clearly and unambiguously. It often remains unclear whether the emotive element is a part of the linguistic meaning of a given word, or rather is associated with this word on the strength of empirical coincidences determined by situations in which this word has repeatedly been used. It is known to authors who reflect on colloquial language that its expressions tend to evoke a broad aura of emotive-descriptive associations. Only some of those associations make up the so called linguistic meaning of expressions. The remaining ones are bound with the expressions by way of connections which are impermanent, changeable, often transitory, and have the character of empirical coincidences rather than terminological stipulations. At the same time there is no clear-cut demarcation line which would separate these two kinds of elements. This accounts for the fact that it is often impossible to decide under which of the categories, distinguished in the classification given above, a particular expression should be subsumed. Attention must also be drawn to the necessity of relating expressions to the contexts in which they occur. In colloquial language, in which persuasive utterances are usually formulated, one and the same expression may be emotively active in a certain context, but emotively neutral in another one. Hereafter such a relativization will be assumed, though it will not usually be explicitly stated.

Persuasive definitions have been used for centuries to change emotive attitudes. However, it was only recently that their structure and function were given theoretical consideration. The first formulation of the concept of persuasive definition is Stevenson's.[2] Although I shall make use of Stevenson's formulations, the description of persuasive definitions given here is my own responsibility. Stevenson really restricts his analyses to persuasive definitions which are here characterized as those which aim to change the existing extension of the definiendum. In my discussion I shall cover two additional varieties of persuasive definitions. The first aims to change the emotive charge of the definiendum; in the second the term used hitherto is replaced by another term, charged with emotive associations of the kind preferred by the author of the definition. Moreover, I shall take into consideration not only full definitions in the form of equivalences, but also partial definitions.[3] The latter often lay down only a necessary, or only a sufficient condition for the applicability of the concepts they define.

PERSUASIVE DEFINITIONS
INTENDED TO CHANGE THE EXTENSION OF THE DEFINIENDUM

In this variation, the definiendum is an emotively active term, used in everyday parlance, where its meaning, or at least its extension, has been established. The definition is to specify a new extension for the term, and to transfer emotive associations connected with its former extension to the new one. The definiens is here an expression constructed exclusively of emotively neutral terms or terms loaded with the same charge — positive or negative — as that connected with the definiendum. As will be seen below, this is not so in the case of another variation of persuasive definitions.

Here are some examples of this variation, beginning with two from the work of Gandhi. Gandhi used every opportunity to do something for the realization of the ethical and the social aims which he supported. Amongst other things he often availed himself of the persuasive function of language to shape people's emotive attitudes. In the first example he makes use of the positive emotive associations connected with the word 'music' to strengthen the attitude of mutual benevolence.

During an interview Gandhi was once asked whether he appreciated music and if he would want it to be given to the world. In his reply he said: If we mean by music union, concord, mutual help, it may be said that in no department of life we can dispense with it.

In another example, also attributed to Gandhi, victory is defined as a state in which the defeated does not hate the victor. With the aid of this startling definition of victory Gandhi wanted to diminish the role of hatred in motivating human action. Like no other personality of public life, Gandhi saw clearly the damage caused by hatred in the psychological and the social sphere.

The definition of 'pariah' given below is attributed to Buddha. Pariahs are the class of outcasts, untouchables, people on the lowest level of the social ladder in the Indian society, wretched and under-privileged. Eminent individuals of democratic tendencies and minds of wide scope strived to alleviate the fate of pariahs; they tended to abolish the caste system, or at least to ameliorate the wrongs that resulted from it. Among other things they aimed at changing the negative emotional attitude towards pariahs, manifested by members of particular castes. Persuasive change of the very word 'pariah', and consolidation of that change in the minds of the public, was part of those efforts. In the persuasive definition of 'pariah' given below reference was made to the authority of Buddha, in order to gain public acceptance for it. This definition preserves the existing negative emotive charge connected with the word 'pariah'. However, it changes its received extension, so that now the extension does not cover the former pariahs, the untouchables, but, instead, people who are wicked, who deserve moral censure. The authors of the definition hoped to shift the negative emotive charge associated with the word 'pariah' onto the new extension.

In the new definition, a pariah is a man who is angry and bears hatred; the man who is wicked and hypocritical; he who embraces error, is full of deceit, envious, and can without fear commit any wrong.[4]

It is obvious that the effectiveness of this persuasive operation is rather limited; to achieve a measure of influence the operation should be supplemented by some broader efforts to change the social structure of Indian society, as well as people's attitudes. Serious efforts to change the emotive attitude towards untouchables were also undertaken by Gandhi. However, he applied a different persuasive approach, which falls under the last of the three types of persuasive definitions distinguished here.

The examples given above contain complete definitions, i.e. definitions specifying criteria for the applicability of their definienda in the form of a condition which is necessary and at the same time sufficient. They illustrate particularly flagrant change, for purposes of persuasion, of the usual meanings of words. The next example exhibits a partial definition of an artist:

> Only he is an artist who improves other people morally through works of art.

This definition stipulates a necessary condition for the applicability of the term 'artist'. It also deviates from everyday usage.

PERSUASIVE DEFINITIONS INTENDED TO CHANGE THE EMOTIVE CHARGE OF THE DEFINIENDUM

As with the previous category, here too, the definiendum is taken from everyday language, in which its meaning or at least its extension has been established. It need not, however, be an emotively active term. Moreover, the definiens does not now have to consist only of emotively neutral terms, or terms loaded with the same kind of charge as that connected with the definiendum. On the contrary, the present variation admits of various relations between the emotive charge of the definiendum and that of the definiens. Those relations are shown in the table below, which possibly does not exhaust all the combinations we meet with in everyday parlance. It certainly is not exhaustive with regard to all theoretically possible combinations.

	Definiendum	*Definiens*
1.	emotively neutral	emotively active
2.	emotively active	emotively neutral
3.	has a positive charge	has a negative charge
4.	has a negative charge	has a positive charge
5.	has a charge of one kind	has a charge of a different kind
6.	has a charge	has a strengthened charge
7.	has an incoherent charge	has a coherent charge
8.	has a coherent charge	has an incoherent charge

The task of persuasive definition is here to replace the emotive charge of the definiendum by that of the definiens. This change may, though it need not, be accompanied by a change in the existing extension of the definiendum. The problem that arises is how to make sure that the change in emotive associations takes place in accordance with the intention of the author. If the emotive charge of the definiens drives out that of the definiendum, the change is in agreement with the intention of the author. It is possible, however, that contrary to the author's intention the converse change occurs: the charge of the definiendum drives out that of the definiens. Finally, neither of the two changes may take place, the only effect of the circulation of the new definition being that the addressees become confused, and even develop neuroses. In the latter case we would face a phenomenon similar to that observed in certain experiments on animals. An animal is subjected to two easily differentiable stimuli. The animal's correct responses are rewarded, while the incorrect ones are punished. The stimuli are gradually modified so as to reduce the difference between them. Consequently, the animal's responses become increasingly confused and finally it develops a neurosis. It is not impossible that in some cases persuasive definitions may be deliberately intended to cause such a confusion. Obviously, the effective application of persuasive definitions depends on a number of extra-linguistic factors, such as timbre of voice, gestures and countenance of the speaking person, the information possessed by the listeners, their emotional attitudes, their needs and the degree to which those needs are satisfied, their moods, etc. The effectiveness of the persuasive endeavour depends on the ability to influence those factors.

Here are some illustrations:

Civilization, in the real sense of the word, consists not in the multiplication, but in the deliberate and voluntary restriction of wants. This alone promotes real happiness and contentment, and increases the capacity for service.

This example admits of two interpretations, according to two different senses, or rather classes of senses, attached to the term 'civilization' in colloquial language: the neutral and the emotionally charged one. In the first, a positive charge of the ethical type is given to the previously neutral term. In the second, the emotive charge associated with the concept of civilization in everyday language is replaced by a charge of the ethical type. In both interpretations the change in emotive charge is accompanied by a distinct change in the extension of the definiendum.

Another example:

Let us now try to outline the pen portrait of a contemporary patriot, as stipulated by our young people. ... The perfect patriot is a man who, above all, is courageous, strong, and fit, and endowed with a number of moral virtues among which pride of place goes to honesty; he is ready to sacrifice himself for his country and to defend it against its enemies; he strives to improve existing social conditions and is an honest and selfless worker, endowed with a number of intellectual qualities among which the most important are knowledge and vocational qualifications, profoundly dedicated to the cause of the economic development of his country.[5]

This passage contains a definition of the term 'patriot' with which positive emotive associations are connected in everyday usage. Here, however, it is defined by such a set of properties that those associations are strengthened significantly. At the same time the extension of the term is narrowed.

Consider now an example in which the change consists in replacing an incoherent charge by a coherent one. At one time political writers, among them Lenin, used the term 'patriotism' in a derogatory sense. At that time one of the definitional characteristics of the term 'internationalism' was the lack of a home country, while the term itself had a positive charge. Following subsequent social and political changes the derogatory associations connected with the term 'patriotism' came to be replaced by positive ones, and hence the property of lacking a home country became negative. These changes resulted in an incoherence in the emotive charge of the term 'internationalism' and its derivatives. To eliminate that incoherence it was necessary to redefine it in such a way that all its emotively active definitional characteristics should have a charge of the same polarity. Since the positive charge of the term 'internationalism' was to be retained, it became necessary to remove the property of lacking a home country from the definitional properties of the term. It is worth noting that the above example illustrates the more general trend to eliminate emotive ambiguity and incoherence from movements, ideologies, etc.[6]

In the next example the change in the emotive charge runs in the opposite direction: a coherent charge is replaced by an incoherent one. Schwitters, the eminent German artist of the Dada period, when asked 'What is art?' gave the following witty answer:

> Whatever the artist spits is art.[7]

The jocular form of this answer covers serious matters. The artist strove to broaden the concept 'art' so as to subsume under it objects made of materials hitherto neglected and despised: old tickets, advertisements, or newspapers, pieces of string, wood, or old iron, cast away parts of clothes, or shoes, shreds of rotting fabrics, etc. Every object upon which the artist casts his eye is, according to Schwitters, a potential art work. Schwitters perceived better than anyone else the possibility of aesthetic values in objects hitherto neglected and cast away, which is why the sobriquet 'the archeologist of the present time' was conferred upon him. While making the concept of art broader, Schwitters also wanted to pull art down from the inflated pedestal upon which it was often placed. All these intentions have found their expression in the breezy definition quoted above, thus changing the emotive charge of the term 'art'. The unambiguously positive emotive associations, connected with this term in colloquial language, were enriched by negative ones; as a result the term 'art' receives an incoherent emotive charge.

In the following example a negative charge is imparted to a term that in its usual meaning is emotively indifferent:

Logistics is meaningless, and subjectless logic, dissociated from reality, experience, practice, and objective truth.[8]

Next let us consider the following definition of bureaucracy:

> Bureaucracy is a rationalized, depersonalized, and efficient system of administration.[9]

In his comment the author declares that he had sought a concept of bureaucracy useful for research purposes, free from the pejorative associations, connected with this concept in colloquial language. It seems that with the term 'bureaucracy' in its current meaning negative charges of two kinds are associated: a praxiological one (bureaucracy is tardy, inefficient), and an ethical one (bureaucracy is a system which, among others due to its praxiological defects, works soullesly and unjustly). The definition given above introduces two changes: first, it neutralizes the negative ethical charge, and secondly, it replaces the negative praxiological charge (bureaucracy is an inefficient system) by the positive one (bureaucracy is an efficient system).

PERSUASIVE DEFINITIONS
INTENDED TO REPLACE THE DEFINIENDUM USED HITHERTO BY ANOTHER TERM, CHARGED WITH EMOTIVE ASSOCIATIONS OF THE KIND DESIRED BY THE AUTHOR OF THE DEFINITION.

The starting point is here an emotively laden term T, used in everyday language. The author of the definition strives to change the emotive attitude towards objects denoted by T. To achieve this he replaces T by another term, A, laden with an emotive charge of the kind preferred by him. He then defines A so that the extension of T is included in or equal to that of A. If the persuasive endeavour ends successfully, the emotive charge of A spills over onto the new extension of this term, which—as we remember—includes the extension of T or is equal with it.

Gandhi used the procedure described above to change the negative attitude of Hindu society towards pariahs. I have formerly discussed the attempt at redefining the word 'pariah', attributed to Buddha. Gandhi wanted to supplant the very name 'pariah' as well as other negatively coloured names, e.g. 'untouchables', used to refer to pariahs. "People whom we dare to call pariahs", "so called untouchables", "our brother pariah", "those out of castes", "people from the fifth caste"—these are some of the expressions he used instead to name those whose cause he defended. One can see why he needed a word which would adequately express his compassion, for all the previous expressions evoke negative associations. At last Gandhi found the term 'Harijans'—God's people, charged with an expressly positive load, and began to launch it as the new name for pariahs.

It would be interesting to investigate which of the two methods of changing the negative attitude towards pariahs proved more efficient, and in what social circumstances: the first, attributed to Buddha, or the second, applied by Gandhi? In this context it is well to remember that the influence of linguistic persuasion upon people's attitudes is limited; such attitudes depend on a number of other social and psychological factors.

PERSUASIVE ARGUMENTATION

Persuasive definition is often a part of a broader context, which I shall call persuasive argumentation. By persuasive argumentation I mean a sequence of expressions which satisfies the following conditions. 1. The sequence contains one (or possibly more than one) term taken from everyday language; this will be referred to as the term of argumentation. 2. The sequence is intended to bring about a change in the emotive associations so far connected with that term. 3. The change is to follow the pattern presented in the previously given table.

Particular expressions which together make up a persuasive argumentation are sometimes connected by the relation of premise and conclusion. In other cases those expressions are not logically bound together; nonetheless, the author sometimes strives to create an impression of logical connection to increase the persuasive effect of his argumentation.

There are important differences between persuasive definition and persuasive argumentation. In the former, persuasion always takes on a definite form, namely that of a definition. It is true that in everyday parlance the form of definition is not determined unequivocally, yet the freedom of choice has certain limits, even though they are not strictly determined. In the latter, on the other hand, linguistic expressions of any form whatsoever can be used. Moreover, in both cases the change in emotive charge is based on different principles. In persuasive definition it comes by way of definitional stipulation; in persuasive argumentation it is the whole linguistic and non-linguistic context which effects the change.

The following passage contains an example of persuasive argumentation. It comes from a collection of Nazi documents. In the passage some points of political programme are expounded.

First, we must free our nation from the hopeless confusion caused by internationalism, and must do so by bringing the nation up, consciously and systematically, in the spirt of fanatical nationalism. ... Secondly, we must free our nation from the nonsense of parliamentarianism, by training it to combat the madness of democracy and to accept authority and the principle of leadership as indispensable. Thirdly, we must free our nation from the pitiable belief in the help of others, that is, from belief in reconciliation of nations, world peace, international organizations, and international solidarity, thus destroying those ideas.[10]

The above persuasive argumentation contains a number of terms: "internationalism", "fanatical nationalism", "parliamentarianism", "reconciliation of nations", "world peace", "international solidarity". Each of these terms has some emotive charge.

The aim of the argumentation is to replace each charge by a charge of the opposite pole, i.e. positive by negative and vice versa. The final statement depicts characteristically the persuasive intent of the speech. By 'destroying' the concepts, it purports to eliminate their influence upon people's attitudes and upon resulting social consequences.

SOME METHODOLOGICAL PROBLEMS

All the persuasive operations discussed here may appear in subjective or objective variants. They are understood in the subjective sense when their results have been deliberately intended by their authors. If the results have been achieved independently of whether they were intended or not, the operations will be classified as persuasive in the objective sense. These two meanings are not mutually exclusive: if the author wanted to achieve a persuasive effect, and has indeed achieved it, both the subjective and the objective criteria are satisfied.

All varieties of persuasive definitions deviate from the existing linguistic usage, since they change either the extension or the emotive meaning associated so far with their definienda. Therefore, they are definitions of a non-analytical character. This remark requires certain additional explanations in view of three different ways in which the term 'analytical definition' may be understood. A definition is analytical in the subjective sense if its author strives to render the existing colloquial meaning of the term it defines. An analytical definition in the objective sense is an adequate reconstruction of meaning the definiendum has had so far in everyday language, regardless of whether such was the intention of its author. A definition is analytical both subjectively and objectively if its author set himself the task of grasping the existing meaning of the definiendum and has in fact attained that goal. In the present discussion the concept of analytical definition is used in the third sense. It is obvious that persuasive definition, whether in the subjective or in the objective sense, cannot be analytical in the third sense. But other relations also hold: persuasive definition in the subjective sense cannot be analytical in the subjective sense; likewise, persuasive definition in the objective sense cannot be analytical in the objective sense.

In view of the non-analytical nature of persuasive definition the question arises whether in at least some situations regard for the effectiveness of such definition does not require that its author should divert the addressee's attention from the fact that the extension of the definiendum, as delimited by the definition, differs from its extension accepted so far; or that he should at least abstain from drawing the addressee's attention to that fact. For, should the latter notice the difference, he might reject the definition entirely, or he would not transfer to the new extension the emotive associations he previously connected with the definiendum. On the other hand, the same regard for effectiveness requires that the addressee should link his emotive associations with that extension of the definiendum which has been established by the definition. The problem then arises whether it is at all possible for the addressee to grasp clearly the new extension and yet not notice that it differs from the former one. Now, such a situation is possible. It may occur, for instance, because the persuader's rhetorical manoeuvres prevent the addressee from reflecting on the relation between the former and the new extension of the definiendum, or when the addressee does not realize clearly what the former extension was.

Persuasive definitions are often given a form which can be reduced to the following: The true *A* is *B*, The real *A* is *B*, etc. Here are a few examples:

True happiness consists in a state of perfection.

The really wise man is he who acts magnanimously.

Real beauty means not outward beauty, but a righteous heart.

What is the function of the modifiers: 'true', 'real', etc.? First, it must be noted that they occur mainly in refutations of contrary opinions. Sometimes the criticized opinion is stated explicitely together with the suggested definition, as is the case in the third example. In other cases the opinion can be deduced from the context. Very often, however, neither is the case, and the task of the definition is to evoke an unfavourable attitude toward some opinion which is left unspecified. The tension thus created can subsequently be channeled according to persuader's wishes.

Persuasive definition using the modifier 'true' or a similar one may be intended to make the addressee think that this is the true analytical definition, that people usually understand the definiendum as is stated in the definition. Persuasion conceived in this way would imply a misunderstanding or the intention to mislead the addressee, since persuasive definition always deviates from the usual meaning of the term it defines.

A different interpretation is also possible. The use of the modifier 'true' may be intended to make the addressee believe that a thorough, and not merely superficial, understanding of the definiendum, an understanding that grasps 'the essence of the thing', is what is established by the definition. But in what is that thorough understanding to consist? That issue is not analysed in the contexts in which persuasive definitions occur.

The role of the modifier 'true' may also consist in developing an attitude favourable to the definition containing that modifier, or in making the addressee reject the competitive definition advanced by those of a different persuasion.

An analogous persuasive role is played by the modifiers 'false', 'apparent', etc., added to a definition of a term. Sometimes, placing the term in quotation marks serves the same purpose. In such cases the function of the modifer is to develop an attitude unfavourable to the definition preceded by the modifier.

There is a hypothesis to the effect that people more readily accept definitions which have the external form of real definitions than those in the form of nominal ones. This applies in particular to those nominal definitions in which the definitional copula has the form: 'we call', 'we term', etc; Should this hypothesis be true, out of the two definitions of freedom—

> Freedom is self-imposition of restraints

> Self-impositions of restraints we call freedom

—the former would be more readily accepted.

How could this phenomenon be explained? Certainly, the very form of a definition can play an essential role. The form of nominal definition suggests a certain arbitrariness: a thing termed in one way might also be termed in some other way. Real definition, on the other hand, may savour of a categorical statement of fact. However, a critical person may resist this suggestion. The terms 'real definition' and 'nominal definition' have several different meanings; and only in some cases can we say that real definition is a statement of empirical fact, while nominal definition only reflects terminological conventions. The external form of a definition does not of itself determine its character.

Consider now the problem whether the extension of the concept of persuasive definition has not been delimited too broadly in this chapter. Let it be established, first, which definitions do not fall under the category of persuasive definitions in the subjective sense. These include definitions of those terms which do not belong in everyday language, that is, all new terms, and all technical terms characteristic of various disciplines, etc. Nor are analytic definitions persuasive definitions. Nor do stipulative definitions belong in that category, unless their authors intend to use such definitions to change the emotive attitudes of the addressees. The remaining cases which are covered by the term 'persuasive definition in the subjective sense', satisfy the conditions characteristic of persuasion.

The case of persuasive definitions in the objective sense is somewhat different. The persuasive nature of such definitions is not due to any intention to modify the addressee's emotive attitudes, but to the fact that this sort of change has actually occurred as a result of definition. Since we must always reckon with such a possibility, the problem arises whether the extenstion of 'persuasive definition in the objective sense' is not too broad. Let it be noted, first, which kinds of definitions are not covered by this extension. Neither definitions of terms outside everyday language, nor analytic definitions are subsumed under the extension. On the other hand, the extension covers any stipulative definition whose application has resulted in a change of emotive attitudes. But the extension of the term 'persuasive definition in the objective sense' is not broader than that of the term 'persuasive definition in the subjective sense'. These two extensions overlap. The usefulness of the former consists in that it singles out the class of cases of unconscious persuasion, in which the effect is achieved without any authorial persuasive intention.

It is sometimes objected that the persuasive operations here discussed raise doubts of a moral nature. Is that objection justified? The answer must be in the negative. From the descriptions given above it does not follow that these persuasive operations have by themselves any morally objectionable property.

They are merely instruments of action and, as such, are morally indifferent. The evaluation of goals to which these instruments are applied, and of the ways in which they are used, is another matter. They may arouse both approval and censure. Thus, for instance, moral censure may be justified in cases when persuasive definitions of the type: 'The true A is B' are used. If, when advancing such a definition, an author wants his addressee to believe that this is an adequate analytic definition, and that in everday language the term being defined is understood in the way his definition suggests, he may be blamed for making a statement that is at variance with truth, because—as we have stated previously—no persuasive definition is analytic; they are all stipulative.

Persuasive operations are methods of shaping attitudes. Is the use of such methods admissible in science, and, if so, to what extent? The object of research is usually seen in the classification and description of phenomena, and also in the explanation and prediction of such. Hence it seems that this leaves no room for any persuasive operations. On the other hand, it is certainly true that science is one of the most powerful instruments for shaping attitudes, including emotive ones. But attention must be drawn to the fact that although changes in emotive attitudes do in fact take place under the influence of science, they come about in a different way. Science effects changes in attitudes by providing information about various phenomena and regularities of Nature which are sources of emotive attitudes. Here is an example of such a change in attitudes, brought about by science.

It still happened in 18th century England that mental patients were chained to walls, and the public was permitted to irritate them for a fee of twopence. As the knowledge of mental disorders improved and the belief in Satan's interference in cases of mental disorders was abandoned, such an attitude toward mental patients became impossible.[11]

Persuasive verbal operations bring about changes in attitudes in a different way. They make use of the emotive associations connected with definite terms and transfer them to other terms or to other extensions of the same terms. So would the conclusion be that science leaves no room for the persuasive use of language? The use of language for purposes of persuasion is only a particular instance of using expressions which are emotively charged, or evaluative. Let us, then, put our question in a general way: can value-terms be used in science or should they be barred? Arguments supporting the second stand would, *eo ipso*, bar all persuasion. First, let us recall that it is often difficult to decide whether an expression is descriptive or rather evaluative. Besides, the majority of evaluative expressions are not purely evaluative (e.g. 'good', 'bad'), but descriptive-evaluative (e.g. 'pedantic', 'sadist', 'helpful', 'colouristically refined'). The difficulties met by attempts to rate an expression as purely evaluative, descriptive-evaluative, or purely descriptive result from the fact that the meaning and extension of expressions is not always established with sufficient clarity by linguistic usage. Moreover, it is not always clear whether emotive, evaluative elements are bound up with an expression on the strength of linguistic usage, and, therefore, belong to the expression's linguistic meaning, or rather are associated with the expression by way of changeable, less permanent connections of the type of empirical coincidences. Thus, even if we eliminate evaluative elements from the meaning of a given word we still do not prevent other evaluative elements from associating with the word by way of empirical coincidences.

If, despite those difficulties, we were to accept the postulate eliminating from science all evaluative phrases, we would drastically impoverish the stock of linguistic expressions, the number of evaluative phrases being enormous. Of course, it is possible, at least theoretically, to replace the removed evaluative phrases by expressions of purely descriptive character. However, and this is another serious difficulty, purely descriptive expressions often turn imperceptibly into evaluative ones; similarly, evaluative expressions may gradually lose their ability to evoke emotive associations. In natural languages the processes of such transformations are often imperceptible, and are thus difficult to record, let alone to control. It seems, therefore, that the demand to free science from all evaluative expressions, including value judgements, is impracticable. We shall have to be satisfied with a more modest recommendation that calls upon scientists, when they use value-loaded terms, in their work to do so consciously, and to differentiate as clearly as possible between evaluation and description.

Sometimes an author is recommended, when he writes not in his capacity as a researcher, but as a follower and propagator of a definite value-system, to do so in a separate publication and not to join both these roles in one and the same work. This recommendation does not seem to be justified either. To express one's attitude toward some phenomena in the humanities—e.g. social institutions, customs, works of art, etc.—it is often necessary to give a detailed description and analysis of these phenomena, so that one's subsequent evaluation of them receives proper substantiation and support. In this way a separate publication, intended to be purely evaluative, would, if convincingly written, turn out once again to combine descriptive and axiological elements.[1,2]

It seems, then, that there are no compelling reasons to ban from scholarship evaluative expressions of *all* kinds. What conclusion can be derived from this with regard to persuasive operations? General prohibition does not seem to be justified here either. There is not much room for persuasion in exact sciences, like mathematics or physics. Its use is more justified in the humanities and the social sciences, in some branches of psychology and psychiatry, economics and biology. For instance, researchers in those disciplines often have to re-define a term excessively overgrown with emotional associations in order to neutralize it, and thus to make it more useful for scientific purposes. (Compare in this context the definition of bureaucracy discussed earlier.) Neutralization is, however, a type of persuasive change. Beside neutralization some of the other types of persuasive operations we have differentiated are also used. This is clearly testified by frequent controversies over the 'proper' definition of various concepts. A well known example is the controversy about the definition of mental health. In this case the selection of definitional properties is influenced by the set of values accepted by the author of a given definition, values which constitute his model of mental health.[1][3] Reference, mostly implicit, to a system of values is also visible in what appear to be purely methodological disputes on such problems as: What is the essence of ethical, or aesthetic, value judgements? What features characterize ethical norms? Can ethical norms, especially the supreme ones (sometimes called axioms) be substantiated? Can the relation of logical consequence be said to hold between ethical or legal norms?[1][4] Are norms equivalent to certain value judgments?—in other words, can ethical ideas expressed as norms be equivalently phrased as value judgments? In these controversies various definitions are put forward of the concepts involved, concepts like 'norm', 'value judgment', 'substantiation', 'follows logically from'. All these definitions fall under this or that of the types of persuasion differentiated here. Engagement in values seems to be an unavoidable consequence of the problems discusses.

NOTES

[1] A. Huxley, *Eyeless in Gaza*. Harmondsworth 1955, p. 62.
[2] C. L. Stevenson, *Facts and Values*. New Haven 1963.
[3] Various types of partial definitions and their application in the humanities are discussed in: T. Pawlowski, *Begriffsbildung und Definition*. De Gruyter, Berlin 1979.
[4] Paul Carus, *The Gospel of Buddha*. New Delhi 1961, p. 154.
[5] Cf. H. Muszynski, 'Some Problems of Shaping Patriotic Attitudes in Children and Juveniles'. *Kwartalnik Pedagogiczny*, 1966. Polish.
[6] Cf. J. Lutynski, 'On Valuation and the Manichean Attitude in the Social Sciences'. *Kultura i Społeczenstwo*, No. 4, 1958. Polish.

[7] Cf. K. Coutts-Smith, *Dada*. London 1970.
[8] *A Concise Philosophical Dictionary*. Warsaw 1955. Translated from Russian.
[9] J. Szczepanski, *Sociological Problems of Academic Education*. Warsaw 1963, p. 234. Polish.
[10] *Der Nationalsozialismus*. Dokumente. Frankfurt am Main, 1957, p. 37.
[11] Cf. M. Ossowska, *Moral Thought in the English Enlightenment*. Warsaw 1966, p. 71. Polish.
[12] Cf. I. Lazari-Pawlowska, 'Maria Ossowska as a Moral Scientist'. *Studia Filozoficzne* No. 12, 1975. Polish.
[13] Cf. in this connection, J. Sowa, 'A Critical Analysis of the Conceptions of E. Fromm and K. Horney'. In: *Morals and Society. Papers Dedicated to Maria Ossowska*. Warsaw 1969. Polish. Cf. also: H. Lenk, 'Kann die sprachanalytische Moralphilosophie neutral sein?' In: H. Albert, E. Topitsch (eds.), *Wissenschaftslehre und Gesellschaft*. Darmstadt 1971.
[14] The relation of logical consequence is a concept which has a strictly defined sense only as a relation connecting sentences, i.e. expressions which can meaningfully be qualified as true or false. Neither ethical nor legal norms are usually counted among sentences in this sense of the word. The problem then arises whether it is justified to use the concept of logical consequence with reference to relations between norms or between expressions in heterogenous sets, composed of norms and sentences.

PART TWO

APPLICATIONS

A. Aesthetics and Art Theory

CHAPTER IV

INFORMATIONAL AESTHETICS

The impressive results achieved in exact and engineering sciences, thanks, among other things, to their mathematization, have encouraged many to apply mathematics also in disciplines traditionally regarded as unamenable to mathematical treatment. The introduction of measurement and of mathematical concepts to psychology and sociology considerably changed the languages of those sciences. Even such humanistic disciplines as aesthetics and theory of art rushed in pursuit of exactness. A new discipline has arisen in aesthetics, called informational aesthetics, because in it the conceptual apparatus of mathematical information theory is used to describe and analyse aesthetic phenomena. The purpose of this chapter is to present and analyse the main concepts and assumptions of informational aesthetics, and subject them to critical analysis.

Although informational aesthetics is still a young discipline, the evolution it has undergone, and the relatively rich stock of papers and monographs[1] it has produced over the years, give cause for methodological reflection. A number of interesting problems of fundamental significance suggest themselves for consideration. I shall discuss some of those problems, without pretence at exhaustive coverage. Although the examples I consider belong to aesthetics, the methodological significance of the problems discussed reaches far beyond into many other humane disciplines in which information theory is applied.

The authors who use concepts of mathematics and information theory in their considerations of aesthetic phenomena rely on the achievements of the American mathematician and aesthetician G. D. Birkhoff. The early results formulated by Birkhoff in the thirties[2] were further developed and reformulated with the aid of the conceptual apparatus of information theory.[3]

THE CONCEPT OF SIGN IN INFORMATIONAL AESTHETICS

In informational aesthetics an art work – or, more generally, an aesthetic object – is conceived as a compound whole built[4] of simpler elements, called 'signs' by the followers of the theory. The 'signs' make up a hierarchy, with elementary 'signs' (Wahrnehmungselemente) at the bottom, and 'supersigns' at various higher levels. Aesthetic objects, decomposed in this manner into their constitutive particles, are subsequently described and analysed with the aid of conceptual apparatus of information theory. Of fundamental importance here is the basic Shannonian formula

$$H = -\Sigma p_i \, ld \, p_i$$

with the aid of which one can compute the amount of information contained in any signal i. H reaches its maximal value when the probabilities of all signals i are equal, i.e. none is preferred. This is the maximal state of entropy. Aesthetic value (aesthetic information[5] — as informational aestheticians say) is associated with the existence of preference for particular signals, with some order of appearance other than equal probability for all. In the definition of this order an essential role is played by the concept of redundancy.

Besides redundancy a number of other metrical concepts are used in informational aesthetics to describe various aesthetic magnitudes. I shall discuss those concepts later, after attending first to the concept of sign.

The concept of sign, as used in informational aesthetics, has been given an extremely wide extension. In fact it is so wide as to become nearly a universal concept. Thus, as I have already mentioned, an art work is conceived of as a hierarchy of 'signs' — elementary 'signs' or higher 'supersigns'. However, it is only certain higher-level 'supersigns' which are signs in the usual sense of the word, i.e. objects possessing some semantic function. If, for instance, with the aid of a series of screens a picture is divided into smaller and smaller particles ('signs' of various levels), it is only particles of some higher level, representing an object (e.g. a man), or a recognizable part thereof (e.g. head) which can be called signs in the received sense.

The question arises as to what scientific purpose this enormous broadening of the concept 'sign' serves. How is such a deviation from the normal usage justified? The reasons seem to lie in the same attitude which prompted followers of the semiotic approach to extend the concept of sign so that all cultural phenomena are covered by it (cf. the chapter on Semiotic Theory of Culture). Informational aestheticians assume that advantages can be gained by applying the methods and concepts of information theory — a modern discipline which provides for the quantitative treatment of phenomena. Furthermore, they seem to believe that in order to be able to apply information theory to inquiries about art and aesthetic phenomena, one has to acknowledge as signs all the elements of an art work which are obtained in the process of the kind of screen-analysis outlined above.

Is the above reasoning correct? Does the application of information theory to the analysis of aesthetic phenomena really entail the necessity of broadening the concept of sign? The answer must be in the negative.[6] The Shannonian theory of information does not deal specifically with any semantic phenomena or objects. Its aim is to formulate general laws concerning the transmission of physical signals, such as electric or radio impulses. Those impulses are considered within the theory entirely independently of their possible semantic function.[7] It follows that the Shannonian theory can be applied to any phenomena which meet its axioms, independently of whether these phenomena are signs or not. It follows, further, that the application of Shannonian theory to the analysis of aesthetic phenomena does not justify the broadening of the concept 'sign'. Nor does there exist any other justification.

INFORMATIONAL MEASURES AND THEIR RELATION TO TRADITIONAL AESTHETIC CONCEPTS

In informational aesthetics various measures are formulated to represent aesthetic quantities. Here are some examples. M_A and M_a represent the amount of aesthetic information in macro and micro aspects. A very interesting example of aesthetic measurement is that of maximal effect (Auffälligkeit). It is claimed that if an aspect of an aesthetic object is to exert on the perceiver the maximal effect it has to cover about 37 per cent of the whole object.[9] Concrete examples of maximal effect measures can be found in the papers of the authors mentioned below. For instance, H. Frank writes:

Nehmen wir an, gewissen Farbtönen könnten gewisse Bedeutungen zukommen, etwa weise Gold auf majestätische Pracht hin. Ein Maler möchte ein Bild möglichst intensiv auf diese Bedeutung hinweisen lassen. Er muss dann etwa 40% der Fläche vergolden – vergoldet er mehr, dann nimmt der Effeckt ab. Bei Claude Monets *Felder im Frühling* sind in diesem Sinne sowohl die Bäume wie auch die Felder grob überschlagen maximal betont – während der im Schnittpunkt von Bäumen, Feld und Himmel stehende Mensch stark zurücktritt, wie es wohl die Absicht war.[10]

R. Gunzenhäuser gives an example of maximal effect in poetry and music.

Schon G. D. Birkhoff bemerkt, dass gewisse Laute bei E. A. Poe häufig, jedoch nicht 'überschüssig' auftreten, so das 'e' in den beiden Versen
> Hear the sledges with the bells, silver bells!
> What a world of merriment their melody foretells!

Dieser Laut tritt in 8 von 23 Silben auf, das sind etwa 35% aller Silben. Synkopen fallen bei Musikstücken dann am meisten auf, wenn sie etwa 37% aller Takte beherrschen. Bei Jazz sind sie wesentlich häufiger und gehören sozusagen schon zum 'gewohnten Rhytmus' – im Gegensatz etwa zum 3. Satz des 5. Brandenburgischen Konzerts von J. S. Bach. Dort enthalten von den 310 Takten 124 Takte Synkopen, und das sind beinahe 40%.[11]

Another interesting measure is that for macroaesthetic relevance (makroästhetische Relevanz). According to S. Maser this measure is an exact, informational equivalent for the loose concept of Gestalthöhe used by Chr. v. Ehrenfels:

> Diese Gestalthöhe entspricht der Anzahl der Schritte, die notwendig sind, um eine Gestalt ins Chaos zu verwandeln, wobei unter dem Chaos eine nicht geordnete Menge von Elementen verstanden wird. V. Ehrenfels verdeutlicht seinen Begriff der Gestalthöhe am Beispiel der Rose und des Sandhaufens: um die Gestalt einer Rose bis zum Chaos, bis zur ungeordneten Menge ihrer Elemente, zu zerstören, sind relativ viele Schritte notwendig: Blätter und Stiel zerreissen, mischen und zerstreuen. Eine Rose besitzt daher eine relativ grosse Gestalthöhe.[1,2]

Here the following remark suggests itself. More exact definition of the concept 'Gestalthöhe' would require relativization to a given way of transforming an object into chaos. For, depending on chosen method, the required number of acts also changes, and, consequently, also the number denoting the Gestalthöhe. The concept of chaos would also have to be characterized more precisely, or, if this proves impossible, be relativized to a given state of disorder. For, what particular state of disorder or decomposition is to be regarded as chaos? The above example shows what a difficult enterprise it is to try to define more precise, quantitative criteria for traditional aesthetic concepts. The example also shows that many of those concepts are only seemingly absolute ones; actually they require relativization.

The examples given above, as well as other informational measures, are not, of course, aims for themselves. They are interesting and useful to the extent that they can be used to formulate quantitative statements in which relations are expressed between the corresponding quantities. The question arises as to what quantities those measures represent. What is their relation to traditional aesthetic concepts? I shall consider three interpretations which suggest themselves in this connection.

(a) The informational measures are exact equivalents for some loosely conceived quantities with which we meet in traditional aesthetics and in everyday life. The relation between these two kinds of concepts is here conceived as that of an analytic definition — analytic with regard to the language of traditional aesthetics. As is well known, a definition is analytical with regard to a language L, e.g. everyday parlance, if it strives to render the already existing meaning of the definiendum in the language L. An analytic definition is adequate only if it successfully renders the existing meaning of the term it defines. Otherwise it is inadequate. However, we have to admit that the informational measures are not fit for analytical counterparts of traditional aesthetic quantities. The meanings of both these kinds of terms are different, if only because the informational terms provide for precise, quantitative discrimination where the traditional terms allow only for loose ordering. For that reason neither the maximal effect, nor the macroaesthetic relevance, nor in fact any other informational concept can be construed as an analytic definiens for the corresponding traditional definiendum.

(b) In the second interpretation, the relation between informational measures and the traditional quantities is that of explication. The concept of explication originated with R. Carnap.[13] By this operation, a vague, pre-scientific concept can be transformed into an exact one. The concept obtained as a result of explication — the so called explicatum — should meet a number of conditions, such as scientific usefulness or similarity to the initial concept — the explicandum. It follows that when the explicandum is an everyday term, its explication should grasp some aspects of its colloquial meaning. The process of explication is completed when the defined notion has been incorporated into a consistent theory or at least some loosely conceived system of concepts and statements which explain a definite realm of phenomena. Thanks to this, the accepted definition is not just a product of an arbitrary decision, but has the value of scientific usefulness.

Some, at least, of the results achieved in informational aesthetics can be interpreted as aimed at an explication of various traditional concepts. The informational counterparts for the traditional concepts of Auffälligkeit and of Gestalthöhe are examples. The process of explication will be completed, however, only after an aesthetic theory or an essential part thereof is built in which these concepts are used to express relations among the corresponding quantities.

(c) The third interpretation differs from the foregoing two in that it does not conceive of informational measures as some kind of reconstruction of the existing traditional meanings of aesthetical terms. Instead, it conceives the informational measures as a set of new, independent aesthetic concepts. The problem of whether, and to what extent, these concepts correspond to traditional aesthetic notions is here of secondary importance. What is essential is that the new concepts prove to be scientifically useful. That means they should allow us to formulate statements in which relationships among the new informational-aesthetic quantities are stated. As the number of such aesthetically interesting statements, corroborated by experience, increases, so does the usefulness of concepts involved in those statements.

Of all the three intepretations here differentiated only the second (explication) or the third can be taken as an adequate rendering of the relation between the informational measures and the traditional aesthetic concepts. At least some concepts of informational aesthetics can be construed as explications of the corresponding traditional notions. This, however, is on condition that informational aesthetics in its further development provides for a consistent, empirically corroborated theory to explain aesthetic phenomena.

I take this occasion to call attention to another aspect of aesthetic-informational concepts. Some of them in their present form arouse objections, and call for relativization or additional restrictions. I have already pointed out the necessity of such complementation or relativization in reference to the concept of macroaesthetic relevance which corresponds to the traditional notion of Gestalthöhe. The problem can be illuminated even better with reference to 'maximal effect'. Is it really so that an aspect of an art work, e.g. a given colour in a painting, exerts upon the perceiver the maximal effect if and only if it covers about 37 per cent of the painting's surface? How about some paintings of geometrical abstraction in which a lonely straight line, a small triangle or circle, contrasting colouristically with the rest of the much bigger surface, exerts nonetheless, or perhaps in consequence of its isolation, the maximal effect on the perceiver, engaging fully his capacity to perceive and experience aesthetically? What a powerful thrill of aesthetic emotion is evoked by the pure major chord ending Penderecki's Stabat Mater just because it is the only pure major chord in the whole composition!

The maximal effect is understood, in the discussed conception, as dependent upon a single aspect of an art work — upon the size of that part of the work in which this aspect is manifested. However, the adduced examples show that this effect depends simultaneously on many aspects and on their mutual relationships, which are of a very complicated nature. Thus, for instance, the effect exerted by a picture depends also on relations among coloured spots with respect to their richness, their size and shape, their complementary or contrasting character, etc. The concept of maximal effect requires, therefore, further elaboration and relativization before it can be used as a useful tool of research in the realm of aesthetic phenomena. In its present form the concept can, at best, be used as a name for but one of many different conditions upon which the maximal effect depends.

THE AMOUNT OF INFORMATION CONTAINED IN AN ART WORK

The investigations undertaken by A. Moles, and continued by K. Alsleben, F. Cube, H. Frank and others, aimed at discovering quantitative laws which govern the processes of gaining, storing, transforming and transmitting information. Those researches opened up a perspective for numerous, useful applications. For example, in socio-psychological research on the reception of art — and in particular of art which unfolds in time, like film, television, theater, ballet, music — it is important to find out and define what is the optimal amount of information that an art work should carry in order to be sufficiently rich and interesting, without being overloaded and thus too difficult for perception. The optimum is here estimated in reference to two factors: the amount of information contained in an aesthetic object, and the person who perceives the object. That is, the optimum is relative to a given person's informational capacity, or the amount of relevant information he had before the perception took place. However, on closer consideration the concept 'optimal amount of information' proves not to be well defined, for the following reasons.

First, the analysis of various authors has disclosed that the component concept 'the amount of information contained in an aesthetic object' is not an absolute, but a relative one. It is relativized to the level of superization that is, the level of signs or supersigns taken under analysis. Depending on the level chosen the same aesthetic object may have different amounts of information. S. Maser proposed a solution of this difficulty in which 'the amount of information contained in an aesthetic object' is construed as 'the sum of information contained on all superization levels'.[14] However, this solution does not lead to unique results either, and this because of two additional relativizations which the analysis of the concept reveals: 1. to the set of 'signs' chosen as the elementary ones; 2. to the chosen way of superization, i.e. way 'supersigns' are formed at higher levels. One could try to avoid this relativization by taking into consideration all possible sets of elementary 'signs' and all possible ways of superization. However, as it is difficult to see how these two sets can be uniquely defined, we have to conclude that the concept 'amount of information contained in an aesthetic object' cannot, at least at present, be uniquely defined. Consequently, the optimal amount is also not uniquely definable.

Another solution connects the concept of optimal information with a particular level of 'supersigns' at which a given aesthetic object is perceived.[15] The optimal information is here measured by comparing the amount of information which an aesthetic object contains on a particular level of 'supersigns', with the amount of information the perceiving person is able to assimilate.

However, this solution too encounters a difficulty which makes its usefulness questionable. Namely, to be able to predict whether a given aesthetic object has the optimal information relative to a given person we must be able to tell at which level of 'supersigns' this object will be perceived by this person.

INFORMATIONAL AESTHETICS, MEASUREMENT AND MEANINGFULNESS OF QUANTITATIVE STATEMENTS

Metrical concepts in informational aesthetics are not aims in themselves, but have to be useful in formulating quantitative statements in which relationships are expressed between the corresponding quantities. In this connection the question arises whether quantitative statements and concepts of informational aesthetics meet the conditions postulated by the general theory of measurement. Is it at all possible, and is it correct, to apply measurement in informational aesthetics? The problem of measurement, of its applicability in the humanities, as well as the conditions for meaningfulness of quantitative statements, are discussed at length in the chapter on Measurement and Metrical Concepts in the Humanities.[16] Although informational aesthetics is still a young discipline, the time seems to be ripe for the type of methodological analysis outlined there. Among others the following two questions should be consciously formulated and systematically considered. 1. What are the types of scales used to measure the aesthetic quantities? 2. Under what assumptions do quantitative statements in informational aesthetics meet the conditions of meaningfulness postulated by the general theory of measurement? The satisfactory solution of these problems is of fundamental importance for further development of informational aesthetics.

In reference to the problem of the meaningfulness of quantitative statements in informational aesthetics I should like to point out that the answer may be different depending on which particular aesthetical statement we take into consideration. Let me illustrate this with an example taken from *Numerische Asthetik* by S. Maser.[17] Considering the relation between subjective and objective aesthetic information, the author writes:

Bei der Wahrnehmung ästhetischer Objekte kann nun einmal Kommunikation derart vorliegen, dass die realisierte ästhetische Botschaft bezüglich der einzelnen Aspekte nur teilweise wahrgenommen oder wiedererkannt wird [. . .]. In diesem Falle wäre der subjektive, erkenntnistheoretische Wert W_{Ai} bezüglich eines makroästhetischen Aspektes *i* kleiner als das objective makroästhetische Mass M_{Ai} des entsprechenden Aspektes *i*. Es gilt dann

$$W_{Ai} < M_{Ai} \quad \text{oder} \quad W_{Ai} = \alpha_i \cdot M_{Ai} \quad \text{birk, mit} \quad 0 < \alpha_i < 1.$$

I have two remarks with reference to this statement. First, it is a disjunction whose two parts differ as regards the meaningfulness requirements. To make the right hand part of the disjunction a meaningful sentence, we have to assume different types of scales for the magnitudes W and M than in the case of the left part of the disjunction. Second, in terms of meaningfulness, the left part of the disjunction, the sentence $W_{A\,i} < M_{A\,i}$, is in a situation similar to the sociological generalization concerning the relation between authoritarian and ethnocentric attitudes — a generalization which I discuss in my chapter on measurement.

To make this sentence meaningful, it is not enough to assume that scales for measuring W and M are of the ordinal type; a much stronger type is here necessary.

SOME UNSOLVED METHODOLOGICAL PROBLEMS IN INFORMATIONAL AESTHETICS

As I mentioned at the outset, the questions here discussed do not exhaust all methodological problems which arise in connection with informational aesthetics. In what follows I should like to indicate briefly some of the remaining problems.

The concept of information used in informational aesthetics is that of statistical, Shannonian information. This is opposed by the concept of semantic information (R. Carnap, Bar-Hillel). Although both concepts measure the quantity and not the quality of information (meaning), they are measures of two different quantities. From this there follows a number of problems concerning the application of information theory to the analysis both of art works themselves, and of the processes of their reception.

Works of art bear not only statistical, but also semantical information. The reader will recall that in informational aesthetics an art work, e.g. a picture, is conceived of as a hierarchy of 'signs' with elementary 'signs' at the lowest level followed by 'supersigns' of higher and higher levels.[18] At a certain level in this hierarchy there appear signs which contain semantic, as well as statistical information. This changes considerably the general amount of information carried by an art work; also it burdens to a larger extent the informational capacity of the perceiver. This fact cannot be accounted for by informational aesthetics until the concept of semantic information is incorporated into it, and a theory is formed which interweaves both concepts into a system of cogent relations. It is only on the basis of such a theory that the full amount of information carried by an art work can be computed. There arise in this connection a number of methodological problems of fundamental importance. In particular, the meaningfulness of quantitative statements in which relationships are expressed between the two kinds of information should be carefully examined in the light of the general theory of measurement.

In papers on informational aesthetics, most often only the simplest Shannonian formula is referred to —

$$H = -\Sigma p_i \, ld \, p_i$$

— on the basis of which, the average amount of information carried by any signal i can be computed. This is probably done with the aim of simplifying the argumentation. It is well known that the above formula is applicable only in cases where particular signals i are statistically independent from each other. In real art works this condition is scarcely ever fulfilled. The 'signs' (elements) of which those art works are built are statistically dependent; these relations of dependence occur in two or more dimensions. Taking those relations into account when computing the amount of information carried by an art work would tremendously complicate the computing procedure. The resulting complication would be of such a high order that only computers could possibly cope with it. Is the application of informational aesthetics in such cases feasible? Would the expected results justify such an enormous expenditure of labour?

In mathematical aesthetics, besides the general concept of statistical information the concept of aesthetic information is used. Sometimes aesthetic value is mentioned instead. The relation between the last two concepts is by no means clear. Now and then they seem to be used interchangeably. However, there are no clear-cut declarations to this effect. Also, so far as I know, there is no common consent as to how the concept 'aesthetic information' should be understood. R. Gunzenhäuser defines it with the aid of Birkhoff's formula $M = O/C$, interpreted in terms of information theory and generalized so as to cover all aesthetic objects (Birkhoff referred his formula only to some chosen sets of objects, e.g. flat polygons). In Gunzenhäuser's interpretation M denotes aesthetic information; O—redundancy, and C—statistical (Shannonian) information.[19] I am not sure whether all followers of informational aesthetics would agree with such an interpretation of 'aesthetic information'. However, there seems to exist common consent to the effect that aesthetic information is some kind of function of two variables, redundancy and statistical information, although the form of this function may in particular cases be interpreted differently. Also, depending on which of the several known variants of redundancy is taken into consideration a different kind of aesthetic information is obtained.[20]

Is it at all possible to apply information theory to the description and analysis of aesthetic phenomena? Even if such applications are possible, do they refer to such properties of aesthetic objects as are aesthetically relevant? For, in information theory the fundamental concept is that of the source of information which sends out signals of various frequencies. From these signals messages are formed; the statements of the theory do not refer to particular messages, but to the source as a whole, i.e. to the average amount of information carried by any signal or any message of a given length. How does this correspond to the computation of information contained in particular art works? What constitutes in this case the source of information? Where are those long series of signals sent out by a given source? And from where do the probability characteristics of the source's signals derive? It is true enough, as we saw before, that in informational analysis an art work, e.g. a picture, may be decomposed with the aid of a screen into series of 'signs' of lower and lower levels from which the frequency of particular 'signs' is computed. But are the series thus formed of the same kind as those which are referred to in information theory? After all, a particular art work does not correspond to the source of information, but rather to an individual message. Should we then take into account some other art works, in order to compute the probability characteristics of the signals? What other works? Works of a particular artist? Or rather all works which together make up an artistic movement, a style, or belong to a given milieu? Whichever alternative we choose, our statements will not refer to particular art works, but to the 'source' as a whole; to the average amount of information carried by a signal or a message of a given length — *any* message of that length. Do we not lose sight, then, of the most important aspect of a message which is also a work of art — its uniqueness? Is anything we can say about a particular art work in terms of such a general language sufficiently important and interesting from the aesthetic point of view? In order to arrive at a clear and well grounded opinion on the possible usefulness of information theory in its applications to art and art reception, we have to consider thoroughly such questions.

It is possible that the new, qualitative information theory proposed by M. Mazur[21] will be of help with solving those problems. We find in his book the following passage which is of relevance in this connection:

... the concept 'amount of information' does not comprise all cases when there is a need for quantitative treatment of information. The problem is that in using this concept we assume the existence of a well defined set of occurrences whose probabilities are also well defined. However, often there is a need for a quantitative description of information, although the set of possible occurrences remains indeterminate and their probabilities do not come into play at all. For instance, school curricula in history may comprise a smaller or a greater number of historical facts, and it is obvious to the teacher that the richer the curriculum the more information the students obtain. However, to express this difference in quantitative terms the teacher cannot use the concept 'amount of information' in the sense given to it within the framework of information theory. For, nobody can say how many historical facts there are; and it would not make much sense to speak of the probability of particular historical facts, since each of them has already happened.[22]

The case may be similar with computation of the amount of information contained in an art work.

I have presented above a series of problems whose solution is essential for further development of informational aesthetics. Granted that satisfactory solutions have been attained: what are the main advantages to be gained by the application of information theory to aesthetic phenomena? The most important is the precise language whose metrical concepts make it possible to formulate quantitative relationships. It is sometimes contended that the introduction of the precise, mathematical language of informational aesthetics will automatically solve all traditional aesthetic problems, such as the dispute about the nature of aesthetic value judgements, or the controversies over absolutism – relativism, and subjectivism – objectivism, etc. The answer to this contention must be – No! No traditional problem is automatically solved by informational aesthetics; they all continue to be fully actual. All that can reasonably be expected is that the language of informational aesthetics will make it possible to formulate traditional problems in a clearer and more precise way, and may thus contribute to a better understanding of them. Also, informational aesthetics may, as it develops, provide us with a richer and more precise language for the description and criticism of art and of its reception.[23]

NOTES

[1] Cf. e.g. M. Bense, *Aesthetica*, I, II, III, IV, Stuttgart, 1954, Krefeld, 1956, Baden-Baden, 1958, 1960; H. Frank, *Informationsästhetik. Grundlagenprobleme und erste Anwendung auf die mime pure*, Waiblingen: Verlag Hess, 1959, reprinted in B. S. Meder, W. F. Schmid (eds.), *Kybernetische Pädogogik. Schriften 1958–1972*, 1–5, Stuttgart: Verlag W. Kohlhammer, 1973–1974; R. Gunzenhäuser, *Ästhetisches Mass und ästhetische Information*, Quickborn: Verlag Schnelle, 1962, new edition: *Mass und Information als ästhetische Kategorien*, Baden-Baden: Agis-Verlag, 1975; S. Maser, *Numerische Ästhetik*, Stuttgart: Verlag Karl Kramer, 1970, neue Ausgabe 1971.

[2] 'A Mathematical Theory of Aesthetics and its Applications to Poetry and Music', Rice Institute Pamphlet, July 1932, vol. 19. Reprinted in *Collected Mathematical Papers*, vol. 3, New York: Dover Publications, 1958.

[3] Cf. e.g. A. Moles, *Theorie de l'information et perception esthétique*, Paris, 1958; cf, also bibliography given in footnote 1.

[4] This should not be understood as a real process of construction, though even such extreme interpretations can be found, but rather as a description of a theoretical analysis of an existing art work.

[5] The relation between the two concepts: 'aesthetic value' and 'aesthetic information' is not clear; I shall refer to this matter in the sequel.

[6] This broad understanding of 'sign', introduced by M. Bense, is abortive as a theoretical conception, but it exerted considerable influence upon art, especially upon computer graphics. In many works of this kind graphic effects are achieved by building up a composition using signs of varying shape, size and degree of blackness. It is an interesting example of how science influences art. This influence is traceable also in a volume of collected papers dedicated to M. Bense on the occasion of his 60th birthday. It is characteristic that the authors are mainly artists, not art theoreticians.

[7] This is obvious to anyone who cares to read Shannon's text attentively. Shannon himself states it explicitly in the introductory note: "Frequently the messages have meanings; that is they refer to or are correlated according to some system with certain physical or conceptual entities. These semantic aspects of communication are irrelevant to the engineering problem." Cf. The Mathematical Theory of Communication, Urbana: The University of Illinois Press, 1959, p. 3.

[8] Similar problems arise in regard to the semiotic theory of culture where the concept of sign is also given an exceedingly broad extension. This is allegedly necessary to make it possible to apply in cultural research methods and concepts of semiotics and linguistics. I consider this problem more closely in the chapter on Semiotic Theory of Culture.

[9] Maximal effect so construed seems to be a rather controversial concept. To make the concept useful for scientific purposes it is necessary to introduce in its definition the necessary relativizations. I shall return to this problem in the sequel.

[10] H. Frank, op. cit., vol. V, p. 53.

[11] R. Gunzenhäuser, 'Informationstheorie und Ästhetik', *Die Umschau in Wissenschaft und Technik*, 1963, Heft 20, p. 626.

[12] S. Maser, op. cit., p. 141.

[13] Cf. R. Carnap, *The Logical Problem of Induction*, Chicago, Chicago University Press, 1950. An extensive discussion of explication and its use in the humanities can be found in: T. Pawlowski, *Begriffsbildung und Definition*. Verlag de Gruyter, Berlin 1980.

[14] S. Maser, op. cit., pp. 94 ff.

[15] Cf. H. Frank, 'Über den Informationsgehalt von Bildern', in *Kybernetische Pädagogik*, I, pp. 445 ff.

[16] Cf. also: T. Pawlowski, *Methodologische Probleme in den Geistes- und Sozialwissenschaften*, Vieweg Verlag, Braunschweig 1976.

[17] S. Maser, *Numerische Ästhetik*, Stuttgart, 1971, p. 117.

[18] Cf. remarks formulated above in reference to the concept of sign in informational aesthetics.

[19] Cf. *Informationstheorie und Ästhetik*, op. cit., p. 654.

[20] In regard to various kinds of redundancy cf. e.g. K. Alsleben, *Ästhetische Redundanz*, Quickborn: Verlag Schnelle, 1962.

[21] M. Mazur, *Jakościowa teoria informacji* (Qualitative Theory of Information), Warszawa: Wydawnictwa Naukowo-Techniczne, 1970.

[22] Ibid., p. 17.

CHAPTER IV

[23] In the foregoing analyses bibliographical references were limited to the works discussed. Now I should like to add some additional bibliographical information. Among Polish authors who wrote on problems related to informational aesthetics I should like to mention R. Ingarden, 'Sprawa stosowania metod statystycznych do badania dzieł sztuki (The Problem of the Application of Statistical Methods to the Analysis of Art Works)', in: *Kultura i Społeczeństwo* 1968, No. 4; S. Lem, 'Niebezpieczne związki (The Dangerous Connections), in: *Nowa Kultura* 1962, Nos. 21, 22; M. R. Mayenowa, 'Możliwości i niebezpieczeństwa metod matematycznych w poetyce (The Possibilities and Dangers of Mathematical Methods in Poetics) in: M. R. Mayenowa (ed), *Poetyka i informatyka*, Warszawa 1965; M. Mazur, 'Cybernetyka a sztuka (Cybernetics and Art)' in: *Nowa Kultura* 1962, No. 27; M. Porębski, Sztuka a informacja, Warszawa 1963. In the Soviet Union A.N. Kolmogoroff and his collaborators apply mathematics in researches on poetry; more general problems are discussed among others by J. Filipiev, *Signaly esteticeskoj informacji (The Signals of Aesthetic Information)*, Moscow 1971; L. Piervieziev, *Iskusstvo i kibiernetika (Art and Cybernetics)*, Moscow, 1973.

CHAPTER V

THE CONCEPT OF KITSCH

In the course of its evolution the concept of kitsch has undergone considerable transformations. The number and diversity of situations to which this notion is referred have increased. The attributes put forward as criteria of its applicability have changed, assuming today a more theoretical character with reference to such disciplines as psychology or sociology. Kitsch has been shown to play a role in certain mass social phenomena of our age. The nature of kitsch and its function in individual and social life have become the subject of animated controversies. Some look upon kitsch as a dangerous phenomenon which should be counteracted. Others see the use of kitsch to break old habits as a sign of avant-garde social and artistic ideas. All are, however, unanimous in considering the phenomena and the related concept as worthy of interest.

The rich stock of papers and monographs that have been produced over the years on the subject of kitsch invites methodological reflection. How is the concept of kitsch currently used? Is there one concept of kitsch, or are many different concepts involved in discussions? Is it at all possible to define kitsch? What is the logical structure of this notion? To which discipline does it properly belong: to aesthetics, psychology, sociology, or cultural anthropology? Perhaps to ethics? What is the connection between repetition and kitsch? Are copies and reproductions of paintings to be viewed as kitsch? I shall begin discussing these problems with a few examples illustrating how the concept of kitsch has been applied.

According to Vittorio Gregotti, "... a glass becomes 'new and original' in kitsch terms if its size, for example, is inflated out of all proportion to its function".[1] Gillo Dorfles remarks that "... all 'literary masterpieces', merely as a result of becoming universally famous, have had to undergo the kitsch process. We need only think of Les Misérables, Quo Vadis, The Divine Comedy, Hamlet, much of D'Annunzio's work, and even Proust's Remembrance of Things Past, as well as Kafka's novels",[2] Discussing kitsch in the art of cemeteries Gillo Dorfles writes: "The image of death needs vigour and severity, innocence and putrefaction, blacks and whites; it certainly needs no half tints, sky blues, pinks, angels' wings, frilly chapels or sterilized technology devoid of any real ethical meaning."[3]

CHAPTER V

As the above examples show, the concept of kitsch is understood in a number of ways. Today methodological considerations cannot be restricted to analyzing this or that particular meaning. To be able to cope with the existing diversity one has to construct a comprehensive typology which would order it according to some general principles. This kind of procedure has been adopted in this book. As a result the following typology of kitsch has been introduced:

1. Kitsch as a product of human action as distinguished from kitsch man, kitsch attitudes, kitsch experience, and kitsch behaviour.

2. Intentional and non-intentional kitsch.

3. Kitsch characterized internally and externally.

4. Kitsch as a natural creation and as a human product.

5. Relative and absolute concepts of kitsch.

6. Subjective and objective concepts of kitsch.

7. Classificatory and comparative concepts of kitsch.

8. Historical and universal concepts of kitsch.

Particular instances of kitsch may fall under several types, though sets distinguished within any of the eight classifications are conceived of as mutually exclusive. This condition is, however, met only in case of homogeneous types. Mixed types, e.g., kitsch characterized by a set of attributes some of which are intentional and some non-intentional, are not mutually exclusive.

In the above classification schema the principles of division have been chosen in regard to methodological considerations which are of interest in this paper. For other purposes some different principles may be useful. So, for instance, a classification of kitsch is known where the following types are differentiated in reference to the kind of art or activity in which they appear: museum kitsch, cinematic, theatrical, religious, national or war kitsch, etc.

The concepts of kitsch distinguished in the classification adopted here differ in regard to their logical structure. They also differ in the methods by which one may corroborate the ascription to objects, of kitsch properties denoted by those concepts.

THE VARIETIES OF KITSCH

Kitsch as a Human Product Contrasted with Kitsch Man, Kitsch Attitude Kitsch Experience, and Kitsch Behaviour

One of the conceptions of kitsch sees it as a human product, usually an art work, possessing a set of attributes which characterize it in respect of its form, contents, function, etc. With the advancement of knowledge about kitsch phenomena attention has been drawn to situations for which such a conception would not suffice. For sometimes an undoubtedly kitsch object, e.g., a tawdry tapestry depicting white swans on a blue pond, can be appreciated in a way that shows no signs of kitsch. On the other hand, some art works, e.g., certain lines by Heine, though far from being kitsch, may give rise to kitsch experience.[4] Clear symptoms of kitsch have also been discovered in certain attitudes and behaviour patterns, e.g., those characteristic of contemporary mass tourism.[5] The recognition of such situations has prompted some authors to postulate extending the term 'kitsch' so that not only human products, but also man himself, his attitudes, his behaviour, and his experiences would be covered by it.

Is this operation really an extending of the concept? Rather, it introduces into the language several new concepts of kitsch all represented by the same ambiguous word.[6] This can easily be seen by considering situations which fall under the term 'kitsch' only in one of the several meanings here involved. Suitable illustrations are supplied by the examples given above. Also, it has to be stressed that research operations needed to ascertain the presence of kitsch are different depending on the meaning in which this term is used. If kitsch is conceived as a human product, such operations consist in finding out what are the formal, semantic, functional, etc., properties of the object considered. If kitsch is construed as referring to human attitudes, experiences, or behaviour, proper research procedures consist of sociological and psychological investigations in which use is made of tests, questionnaires, and statistical techniques.

Intentional and Non-Intentional Kitsch

In distinguishing these two types of kitsch we refer to the intention of the author. Descriptions of non-intentional kitsch point only to the properties of the kitsch object itself. An excess of decorative effects, or giving streamlined, aerodynamic shape to static objects, like an ashtray or a desk lamp, can be mentioned as illustrative examples. Non-intentional characteristics often do not suffice to identify kitsch. Some critics maintain that there are objects which, although aesthetic failures, cannot be considered kitsch, because they do not pretend to be something different or something more than they really are; or because they have been produced exclusively for didactic purposes. A definition of kitsch taking into account such considerations would have to include reference to the intention of the producer. This can be done in various ways, the two following being the more important ones. First, certain aspects of a kitsch object can be interpreted as signs used by the author to represent or express something. In this way an author's intention is referred to when his work is accredited with such qualities as insincerity, or incompleteness of expressed feelings. At other times, the intentional characteristic of kitsch consists in the author's supposed desire to evoke in the audience certain experiences. Definitions of intentional kitsch describe it as, for example, a work of art meant to produce dilettantish experience, or else as a work designed for a person who does not understand art, but who wants to buy a touching picture.

What are the proper methods of corroborating statements which assign to art objects the kitsch properties distinguished here? In the case of non-intentional kitsch the corroborating procedure should be based on observation of qualities present in the kitsch object itself. The other variety of kitsch calls, in addition, for an inquiry into the intention of the artist. Authors writing about kitsch often refer to an intentional property, but they do not always substantiate their statements in a clear and methodologically correct manner. Even if they make a conscious effort to ascertain the intention of an artist, they can do so only indirectly by way of drawing conclusions from observation of the kitsch object and from available external information. If for instance, in criticising the work of a formally educated painter who is well versed in art history, one ascribes to his painting an intentional property of naiveté, intended to simulate primitivist 'freshness of heart', such an ascribtion can be substantiated by observation of that painting and by reference to such external information as knowledge of the artist's *curriculum vitae*, and acquaintance with his other paintings as well as with paintings of authentic primitives. It should, however, be stressed that inferences used to reconstruct an artist's intentions do not have an infallible character, so the conclusions to which such inferences lead should be accepted only with caution. This, however, is not always the case. Critics and aestheticians often ascribe intentional kitsch properties to objects in an arbitrary manner without even trying to find out what the intentions of the artist's were, or else without considering all the pertinent data necessary to justify their statements. On the other hand, there are instances of using terms which only appear to imply intention.

This happens when intentional kitsch qualities are assigned to an art work independently of the artist's intentions, but instead by reference to rules of interpretation accepted in a given period or milieu. It has to be remembered that in such cases terms seemingly intentional do not have their usual sense: they do not contain any reference to the particular artist's intentions. For instance, to describe an art work as pretentious does not imply that its author intended his work to appear to be something other or something more than it in fact is.

Kitsch Characterized Internally and Externally

In giving an internal characterization of a kitsch object we have recourse to such properties as its colour, shape, texture, or the kind of material. On the other hand, its external characterization calls for data which refer to some other objects or situations. Some kinds of such data will be here distinguished.

One often comes across references which assume that one property of kitsch consists in its looking secondary, imitative, or stereotyped. In such references a comparison with other objects is tacitly assumed. To have good grounds for ascribing these properties to an object one cannot confine himself to observing the object itself. One also has to obtain suitable data about the objects which are imitated. The situation is similar with the property of obsoleteness which we can only ascribe to an object on the basis of some comparative criteria of progress.

If we declare an art work kitsch, because it is universally appreciated, or is too easy, our judgment has to be based on social and psychological data here involved. Also, when we say that an art object is not being taken seriously by its author — which property is often considered as a kitsch symptom — we have to appeal to psychological data concerned with the author's attitude toward his work.

External characteristics are often used in describing kitsch objects, yet such statements are not always properly substantiated. The reason may be the difficulty in obtaining the necessary data. Sometimes, however, critics are not quite clear about the difference between an internal and an external characteristic, or about the methods of corroboration proper to each.

Kitsch as a Natural Creation and as a Human Product

Are there any grounds for moulding the concept of kitsch so as to cover natural creations? Here the theoreticians are far from unanimity and not without doubts or hesitations. Such doubts do not refer to such situations as laying out new parks, or shaping the landscape, when nature is transformed as a result of human action, and is, therefore, a human product. Rather, they concern primitive nature. It is often said that it is more and more difficult these days to find a spot of really primitive nature. Besides, the very concept of primitive nature is not without vagueness. Certainly, not every human interference would be considered an infringement upon the primitive state of nature. Where, then, should the dividing line be drawn? What kind and extent of human intervention deprives nature of its primitive character? It would be difficult to make any final decision without an arbitrary stipulation.

Let us, however, assume that we are confronted with a really primitive spot of nature. Can it be called kitsch? Those who answer, 'No', will certainly point to the fact that an important property of kitsch derives from the intention attached to an object produced by man. Indeed, this argument excludes the possibility of kitsch in nature. But it does so only with regard to a particular meaning of the term 'kitsch', namely intentional kitsch. Kitsch characterized exclusively by non-intentional attributes could still be ascribed to some natural creations. For it can rightly be maintained that since certain non-intentional properties of human products, such as some juxtapositions of colours, smells, shapes, surfaces, and materials determine the kitsch character of those products, the same properties can supply grounds for qualifying as kitsch some fragments of nature.

There are situations mentioned by some authors as examples of kitsch in nature which, however, properly exemplify kitsch man, kitsch attitude, or kitsch behaviour. Thus, for instance, a Scottish landscape with a Scotsman in the foreground wearing the kilt and playing his bagpipes is not an example of natural creation, but rather a human product: a landscape transformed by placing in it a Scotsman dressed and posed in accordance with the best rules of tourist advertising. Neither should we count as natural kitsch those much-frequented beauty spots, visits to which are turned by mass tourism into 'pseudo events'.[7] It is rather the tourists' attitudes or behaviour which here display the symptoms of kitsch.

Should we recognize as kitsch, instances where nature 'imitates' itself or resembles some works of art? How about famous spots of natural beauty known to the point of boredom from innumerable posters and advertising folders: are they kitsch? These are not easy questions, and they pertain to the problem of relation between kitsch and repetition.[8]

Relative and Absolute Concepts of Kitsch

Theoretical problems of kitsch are closely bound with central problems in aesthetics, such as conceptions of beauty, of aesthetic value judgment, or of what constitutes an art work. Aesthetic controversies between absolutism and relativism have their analogues in the realm of kitsch.

According to the relativist any sentence which merely states that a certain object is (or is not) kitsch is meaningless, or, at best, is an abbreviated substitute for a full expression containing reference to a relativizing factor. It is only with respect to this factor that an object can be qualified as kitsch. On the other hand, a follower of the absolutist position does not require such a relativization, and even considers it improper. In the literature the relativist position is dominant. Sometimes one and the same author pronounces statements characteristic of both viewpoints. This testifies to his inconsistency, or is one more proof for the existence of many different kitsch concepts denoting separate phenomena.

There are various sorts of relativizing factors. Leaving aside any attempt to list them exhaustively I shall confine my discussion to considering the three kinds most frequently met: relativization to a historical moment or period; to a person or a social group; and to a goal, or function, relative to which the kitsch character of a given object is considered.

Propositions with time relativization ascribe various kitsch properties only to objects within a certain period outside of which the same properties would not be counted as kitsch. Here are some examples.

A secondary, imitative character is commonly considered as one of the kitsch symptoms of an art work. However, " . . . in pre-romantic poetry the rule was to create according to existing conventions, to imitate accepted patterns, and to make use of the common fund of topics. This is enough to conclude that not all repetition is kitsch."[9]

Another variety of time relativization can be found in the instances " . . . when art works and expressions full of contents, originality, and creative imagination turn into kitsch afterwards, because of shade cast upon them by later repetitions."[10]

According to some authors, antiquity, or the patina of time is another relativizing factor. Certain objects, at one time qualified as kitsch, have subsequently been rehabilitated and raised to the dignity of venerable art works. In this case, however, the diversity of judgment is more clearly marked, and the opinion is often voiced that objects which are kitsch will remain kitsch forever, their venerable antiquity notwithstanding. The illusory conviction that time has an ennobling influence is here the result of confusing historic value with those attributes whose presence or lack in an object decides its kitsch character.

Time relativization can be of two kinds: formal and substantial. In the former, it is only the date or the historical period which is specified; in the latter, certain aspects of the period are characterized by which properties of a given art object have been conditioned, and on the basis of which those properties can be explained. The use of formal rather than substantial relativization often results from our ignorance of factors which have influenced ways of producing certain objects, or manners of presenting certain motifs in a work of art. Here is an example of substantial relativization taken from the above mentioned book by A. Banach. Discussing changes in ways of presenting the Madonna and Child, and their connection with kitsch, the author writes:

> Fouquet in his picture Madonna with Christ Child and Angels depicted Her breast unveiled, the most beautiful ever painted, a masterpiece of drawing and geometry. Such portrayal was needed to symbolize motherhood. Roger van der Weyden and many others were even more direct in the way they depicted the Madonna nursing the Infant Jesus. Those artists were well aware that any erotic associations would be sacrilegious considering the milieu. . . . Later in the Renaissance beauty of body attracted sensuous interpretation, and it became less proper to depict the Madonna with Her breast unveiled. What is acceptable from one perspective may not be when considered from another.[11]

It is not difficult to adduce instances when the same object qualified by some as unquestionable kitsch produces in others sincere appreciation. Consider, for example, a recording of a maudlin song about a mother's death — composed, moreover, in the rhythm of a waltz — which has, nonetheless, evoked deep emotional responses in some listners. According to some authors, such situations speak for the necessity to relativize the concept of kitsch to a person or a social group.

Consider now the question of goal relativization. To qualify an object as kitsch it is necessary in this case to take into account not only the attributes present in the object itself, but also the purpose for which the object has been designed. So, for instance, ". . . no popularization is kitsch, even though it distorts and coarsens some features of the original to make it more accessible and, consequently, conventional."[12] On the other hand, objects whose shape, size, or material do not correspond to the purpose for which they have been designed, are to be counted as kitsch. We can here point to objects of aerodynamic, streamlined shape made for use in situations which have nothing to do with motion; or Bismarck beer-mugs, Eiffel Tower coffee-mills, etc.[13]

It is not my intention to discuss the validity of arguments advanced by the relativists for the defence of their position.[14] I shall only remark that I see an essential difference between goal relativization and the two other kinds of relativization. It seems that there are good reasons for goal relativization. For it is often only by considering the aim for which an object has been designed that two important kitsch attributes are revealed: disfunctionality and pretentiousness. On the other hand, the arguments adduced to support the first two versions of relativism do not seem to be very convincing, because, among other things, they are not based on a clear differentiation between various types of kitsch. In particular, they seem to mix up varieties distinguished in our first two classifications.

Subjective and Objective Concepts of Kitsch

This distinction has its analogue in the general controversy over the nature of evaluative attitudes toward art works. I shall formulate two main variants of subjectivism in regard to the problem of kitsch.

First, a statement qualifying an object as kitsch may be subjective in the sense that it only seemingly refers to that object, but is, in fact, a psychological utterance which gives expression to the feelings of the person making the judgment. It is worth remarking that with this variety of subjectivism any controversy over the kitsch character of an object becomes meaningless. For the opposing parties are not, in such cases, pronouncing contradictory opinions on one and the same thing — that particular object — but each is speaking about something else, namely, about his own experiences. A second variety of subjectivism proclaims that there does not exist any empirically testable property whose presence in an object decides its kitsch character. Through negation of these two versions of subjectivism one can derive the corresponding variants of objectivism.

I shall not analyse the arguments adduced for subjectivism. It suffices to mention that the existing variability of value judgments appealed to by subjectivists does not really support their case. For it results from the variability of circumstances under which art works are evaluated with respect to their kitsch character.[15]

Classificatory and Comparative Concepts of Kitsch

The structure and function of these two concepts are different. The logical structure of the classificatory concept can be presented with the aid of the following sentential function: $C(x)$, (x has the property C). The classificatory concept divides a given domain of objects into two subclasses: those with the property C, and those without it. To present the logical structure of the comparative concept we need the following two sentential functions: xPy (x

precedes y in regard to a given property) and xEy (x equals y in regard to that property). The comparative concept unlike the classificatory one cannot be used to divide a set of objects into two subsets; instead, it makes it possible to rank those objects in regard to the intensity of a given property.

In the literature of kitsch the classificatory type of concept is most commonly seen. Sometimes, however, the comparative concept seems to be used. Not all elements in a work of art are of kitsch nature. Their number and importance vary depending on which particular art work is considered. This supplies grounds for ranking works of art in regard to their kitsch character. Besides, many definitional kitsch attributes, such as pretentiousness, mawkishness, or sentimentality, admit of degrees. It is not an easy task to lay down empirically testable criteria for a comparative concept of kitsch. However, an attempt at formulating analogous criteria for a classificatory concept will come upon difficulties just as great.

Authors who discuss problems of kitsch do not always bear in mind the difference between the two types of concepts; this may result in logical mistakes. For instance, a writer may claim that one particular object is more kitsch than another. But it does not follow that the first object is kitsch, for such a conclusion involves a concept of kitsch whose logical structure and criteria of applicability are different.

Historical and Universal Concepts of Kitsch

This distinction is implicit in yet another controversy over the concept of kitsch.

According to some authors kitsch is a phenomenon characteristic of our epoch and was absent in earlier historical periods. They indicate the close of the XIXth century as the beginning of this epoch, and tie up the appearance of kitsch with the development of industry and the resulting uniformization of culture. A contrary position claiming that kitsch also existed in other historical periods, e.g., in the art of Ancient Rome or of the Renaissance, is encountered equally often.

Supporters of the first position take their stand on the historical character of the kitsch concept. The distinctive feature of historical concepts is their space-time localization. Consequently, if a phenomenon does not belong to the specified period, it is not kitsch by definition.

With the universal concept of kitsch the reverse is true. Its meaning does not contain any space-time localization, and, consequently, does not preclude the appearance of kitsch phenomena in any historical period. Neither, however, does it imply that such phenomena have in fact existed throughout history. The question of their appearance in a particular epoch remains an empirical problem to be solved by suitable research.

METHODOLOGICAL PROBLEMS CONCERNING THE DEFINITION OF KITSCH

As a result of previous explorations of kitsch phenomena a number of its attributes have been distinguished and described. Attempts have repeatedly been made to define kitsch, but no particular definition has won universal acceptance, even though several kitsch properties are commonly acknowledged by many authors. What is the methodological status of discussions concerning the choice of a definition? Does such discussion involve a controversy over factual matters, or is it merely a verbal contest? What factors should govern our selection of definitional kitsch attributes? Logical theory of definition distinguishes the following three possibilities which we shall discuss in turn.

The Analytic Definition of Kitsch

In constructing such a definition we strive to render the existing colloquial meaning of the term 'kitsch'. Not an easy task, it requires arduous research of the socio-semantical type. The extent and the cost of such research would be enormous if it were to achieve a reasonable measure of representativeness. The main difficulty stems, however, from the fact that the colloquial meaning is extremely vague and ambiguous. The construction of an analytic definition seems often to be the aim in discussions about kitsch phenomena, but, as a rule, the formulations put forward are not supported by suitable investigations, and, at best, can be looked upon as only tentative hypotheses to be tested by later empirical research.

The Stipulative Definition of Kitsch

Here the difficulties mentioned above do not appear. The stipulative character of the definition makes it entirely independent of the colloquial meaning of the term being defined. Of course, this does not imply unlimited arbitrariness in the selection of definitional attributes. If a definition is to be something more than a mere expression of the author's gratuitous decision, it has to be justified by its usefulness in research into the aesthetic, psychological, and sociological aspects of kitsch.

CHAPTER V

Explication of the Concept 'Kitsch'

By this operation, which originated with R. Carnap,[16] a vague, prescientific concept can be transformed into an exact one. First, certain formulations are laid down, sometimes called conditions of adequacy, which have to be fulfilled by the finally accepted definition. The process of explication is completed when the defined notion has been incorporated into a consistent theory explaining some definite realm of phenomena. Thanks to this the accepted definition is not just a product of an arbitrary decision, but has the value of scientific fruitfulness.

The explication lies midway between the analytic and the stipulative definitions. It is like the first in that the conditions of adequacy may embrace certain colloquial aspects of the term defined. The fact that those conditions may also include regard for scientific utility assimilates explication to the stipulative definition. It is, however, much more difficult to meet the requirements inherent in explication. The mere fact that the defined concept may be useful in research and discussion is no longer enough. The concept has to be joined in a consistent network of statements which make up a scientific theory, or at least a significant fragment of one.

Can any of the definitions of kitsch attempted to date be qualified as an explication? So far as I know the answer to this question should be in the negative. The formulations put forward can, at best, be recognized as conditions of adequacy. Above all, it is the theoretical constituent of explication which is lacking.

A reader well versed in the literature might here voice his reservations, appealing to the changes in approach to this problem which have taken place in recent years. Indeed, various authors refer in their considerations to psychological and sociological theories and try to assimilate the concept of kitsch to the systems of those sciences. One of the first attempts was made by Ludwig Giesz in his work on kitsch and tourism. A. Čelebonović, whom I have already quoted, refers in his paper to C. G. Jung's theory of projection:

Together with bad films, popular magazines, etc., kitsch objects serve as a cue to project the misery ... of the inner world into the outer world. In this way latent problems are projected into objects whose value is purely fictitious, because it makes things easier.[17]

Here is one more attempt at an explanation of kitsch phenomena:

... jazz music accords with primitiveness and civilization, and is in the service of kitsch, for it relies on primitive instincts and the soothing past common to all. ... in the company of his peers, all subjected to the same pictures, posters, music, and clamour, an individual does not want to appear different from the others. With the others, he feels tender and warm. Joint experience of kitsch in art, politics, or religion allows him to immerse himself in common past experiences, not only of his own, but also of those with similar experiences who surround him.[18]

The examples cited make it possible to grasp the character of the attempts made so far to include the notion of kitsch in the conceptual framework of a science. These attempts are not systematic enough or exact to be recognized as fully fledged explications. Besides, the systems of statements into which the notion is to be incorporated, themselves do not meet the requirements of scientific precision to an extent which would make them scientific theories in the strict sense of the word. With all the progress made in recent years the present knowledge of kitsch phenomena allows only for a partial fulfilment of the conditions needed to build an explication of the concept involved.

Is it at all Possible to Define Kitsch?

There is no unanimity on this point. Some authors bluntly state that all attempts at a definition must end in failure: "A final definition of kitsch is impossible. If anyone expects that as a result of analysis an exact description of it will be given, he will be disappointed. The essence of kitsch cannot be described, but has to be experienced, like pain, or green".[19]

Are there any objective grounds to support such a view? For one thing, many terms denoting various kitsch attributes, such as pretentiousness, insincerity, or incompleteness of expressed feelings, are of the psychological type. In trying to define them one has to use terms relating to certain experiences or attitudes. Such terms are notoriously vague, and it is not easy to give them a precise, empirical meaning, so that the sentences in which these terms appear be empirically testable. One can see this by tracing the efforts made in recent years by psychologists and sociologists to define their concepts in an exact way.

Besides, some kitsch attributes are directly observable properties or phenomena, like colour, shape, or various kinds of emotions. The configuration or degree of intensity of those properties determine the kitsch character of objects in which they are present. The terms denoting such properties are patently imprecise, and to diminish their impreciseness one has to take recourse to the so called ostensive definition.[20] Such definition is not a purely verbal operation, but consists also of demonstrating a selected series of objects or situations which fall under the term being defined, and those which are excluded from its extension.

Taken generally, the opinion mentioned above, that kitsch cannot be defined but has to be experienced, does not seem to be justified. It is applicable only to those directly observable kitsch attributes which are to be defined by ostensive definitions. The difficulties mentioned before, which every definition of kitsch must encounter, do not justify the assertion that the concept is basically undefinable. It seems that this task can be solved, at least to an extent, through the application of the so called partial definitions.

The Partial Definitions of Kitsch

A full definition has the form of an equivalence. Such definition makes it possible in regard to every object to decide whether or not it belongs to the extension of the definiendum. With partial definitions the situation is different. They specify only partial conditions of applicability, for instance, only a necessary condition, or only a sufficient one.[21]

Existing full definitions of kitsch are not adequate, or else they contain some semantic defects. This is understandable in view of the enormous difficulty of the task. It should be easier, on the other hand, to advance a number of partial definitions, taking advantage of various kitsch properties mentioned in the literature. None of those properties, taken separately, constitutes a sufficient, or a necessary, condition of kitsch. It is only through their combination that one can obtain partial criteria which may prove to be characteristic of various types of kitsch. What is meant here is one particular sense of the term "kitsch" to which those partial criteria would be pertinent. Other meanings would require partial criteria of their own.

It is possible that some of the partially definable subsets of kitsch are bound by similarities which turn them into a family of subsets.[22]

Can we anticipate that as a result of future research partial criteria will in time be replaced by one full definition? Or rather should the concept of kitsch be considered as only partially definable? At the moment it is difficult to give a definite reply to this question, although seemingly the dispositional character of some kitsch attributes speaks for the second alternative.[23]

Definitional and Factual Kitsch Properties

As a result of observation and research so far a number of kitsch attributes have been distinguished. Of course, not all these properties can be ascribed to kitsch objects, on the basis of definition alone. An attempt at a definition should be preceded by a decision as to which properties are to be considered definitional, and which factual, i.e., ascribable to kitsch objects on the basis of established empirical relations. If such a decision is to be something more than a mere expression of the author's personal predilection, it has to take into account the fruitfulness of the resultant definition. It follows that selection of definitional kitsch attributes involves the same considerations I spoke of in connection with the usefulness of explication.

To which Discipline Does the Concept of Kitsch Properly Belong?

Due to the ambiguity of this concept an answer to the above question will be different depending on which of the expressly formulated or tacitly assumed definitions is taken into consideration. In discussions a certain set of kitsch attributes is repeatedly mentioned from which all existing definitions derive. Rather than consider particular definitions I shall reflect upon those attributes. The theory of kitsch — if anything worthy of that name can be said to exist — assumes statements and concepts of many other disciplines, such as logic, sociology, psychology, or aesthetics. Its central concept, therefore, may have to be defined by properties which belong under several of those disciplines as their subject matter. In fact, such is the case with many proposed definitions.

I do not intend to enumerate all the kinds of properties which are or can be used to define kitsch. Rather, I shall concentrate on the three kinds mentioned most often: socio-psychological, aesthetic, and ethical attributes.

Characteristics of the socio-psychological type contain such elements as the specification of the class of audience, and description of their behaviour, experiences, and needs. Here are some examples of socio-psychological features: degenerate art of the elite; a universally famous art work; a work of art calculated to evoke a dilettante experience; an art work which mitigates loneliness and helps the observer to escape from reality.

Characteristics of the aesthetic type refer mainly to the qualitative, the formal, and the semantic properties of an art work. The following are few illustrations: a secondary art work; an art work which repeats acknowledged patterns; an art work overloaded with decorative details; a disfunctional, outdated or 'cheap' art work.

Ethical terms, appearing either as pure value terms or as descriptive value terms, constitute an important element of kitsch characteristics. The role of these terms is clearly visible, especially in such conceptions which look upon kitsch as a phenomenon loaded with socially undesirable consequences. As examples we can cite references to the insincere, false, or pretentious character of an art work; a work of art in which phony emotions are substituted for true ones; an art work which deviates from desirable ethical and aesthetic standards.

Persuasive Character of Some Definitions of Kitsch

A purely descriptive definition of kitsch seems to be possible; e.g. its definiens could be made up only of terms which refer to formal and semantic properties of an art object. However, definitions actually found in the literature contain, as a rule, value terms which are of three types: aesthetic, moral and praxiological. The evaluative character of the kitsch concept, the emotive load with which it is charged in everyday parlance, contributes to the fact that its definition can easily be coloured with persuasive intent.

There are three basic types of persuasive definitions: those intended to change the extension, those intended to change the emotive charge of the definiendum, and those intended to replace the term formerly used by another term with an emotional load desired by the author of the definition.[24] In colloquial language negative emotive associations are connected with the term 'kitsch'. This is so independently of whether its emotive charge is, of the aesthetic, the ethical, or the praxiological type. In the passage quoted below a definition of kitsch is tacitly assumed in which the negative charge is replaced by a positive one. Also, paradoxically enough, kitsch is there considered as a factor of social and artistic progress.

... the charm of kitsch ... consists also in that today the purity and unity of style are to be looked upon as boring and conceited pretenses which reduce to the following: look, here is the whole truth, the whole sensible world. It seems to me that kitsch is the very factor that disturbs the status quo, the established order, for it is certainly not platitudinous. It is academism which is associated with officialdom, concerned with ordering cultural activities and promoting a closed attitude. Kitsch was born in the suburbs and lived in cramped quarters. It is related to popular restlessness, as well as to the restlessness of searching intellectuals ... I call for a rehabilitation of kitsch, as a progressive, though preartistic, medium to clear the path for an authentic art expression representing an independent attitude in a world otherwise full of incomprehensible, solemn authorities, always contradicting each other, yet transient, remote, and arbitrary.[25]

KITSCH AND REPETITION

The relation between kitsch and repetition seems to me an especially interesting object of inquiry. Let us at the beginning set apart two kinds of repetitions which are often confused: repetitions evinced in an art work itself, and repeated perceptions of that work which may result in formation of a specific attitude toward it.

Of course, not all repetitions present in an art work have a kitsch character. Only those repetitions which make the work look secondary, imitative, or stereotyped are qualified as kitsch. These properties whose presence in a work of art can be ascertained objectively do not, generally, form sufficient grounds for such a qualification; they are considered symptoms of unwillingness or incapacity for creative effort, of a tendency toward a facile imitation of existing patterns.

It is another property of repetition to generate kitsch through the kind of modifications to which the repeated motif or element is subjected. Usually, kitsch reaches for the easiest aspects of the original; besides, it makes them distorted, shallow, and trivial. Numerous adaptations of novels for the cinema can be cited as illustrations. Similar examples can be found in the province of painting or music. We can point to the known recordings of orchestral compositions by J. S. Bach adapted for a popular vocal ensemble: the 'geometric' music of Bach, full of manly energy, loses all its sharp contours and is transformed into pretty-sweet pulp. Another illustration is afforded by recordings of Tchaikovski's more popular compositions, such as the Piano Concerto in B minor or the VIth Symphony, in simplified, shortened versions. From these compositions, which are not difficult even in their original form and are played to satiety, there have been selected and woven into one slick whole, only the most melodic and ear catching fragments.

Kitsch and repetition are closely linked also in the way some artists blatantly strive for popular success, with an attendant lack of creative aspiration. To gain a quick and sure appreciation by the public, at least by a certain section of it, it is better not to propose things entirely new, because their reception requires a great deal of effort. On the other hand, works embodying many known elements are more likely to win public appreciation. This fact is well known to publishers. It has even been established, or so they claim, that a book containing more than ten percent of new material has little chance of success.

Are copies and reproductions of paintings to be viewed as kitsch? This is by no means a trivial question. It is mostly and sometimes even exclusively through the medium of reproductions that we get acquainted with existing works; and as the quality of reproductions improves, their role becomes more and more important. First, we shall distinguish two purposes for which reproductions can be used: to supply information about the original, and to evoke aesthetic experience. If an original is not kitsch, neither, I think, is its reproduction or copy, if treated exclusively as a source of information. Anyway, I have not found in the literature any opinion to the contrary. The diversity of attitudes begins when we turn to the aesthetic function of reproductions. What is the source of this diversity? It may be due to changes which occur in reproductions. However, do such changes necessarily have the character of kitsch-generating distortions and therefore turn reproductions into kitsch? Such is only the case, I think, with reproductions of poor quality. A good reproduction, although it may deviate from the original in respect of size, material, texture, and the shades of some colours, does not have distortions sufficient to change it into kitsch, nor of course does a copy so masterly that it can be distinguished from the original only by an experienced specialist.

Another cause for doubt may be the plurality of reproductions as against the uniqueness of an original. Does this provide sufficient grounds for considering reproductions kitsch? What kind of a value is uniqueness? Is it an aesthetic value? Here, it seems, we do not contend with a homogeneous value, but rather with a fusion of several different values. Undoubtedly, one of them is of an aesthetic nature. It is distinctness, otherness. Reproducing and copying a work destroy this value. Let us remember, though, that we cannot recognize the disvalue of plurality by mere observation, however meticulous, of formal and semantic aspects of a chosen reproduction. We need additional, external information to the effect that other reproductions of the same work exist. We may add that the loss of the value of distinctness is experienced less painfully when reproductions are not too numerous and not found too often. The last two considerations speak against qualifying reproductions as kitsch, or at least they take the edge off such a qualification.

The value of uniqueness also has a snobbish element. It gives the owner of the original (or of the only existing reproduction) the feeling that it is only he who has the thing in question. One would hardly say that the absence of this sense of unique proprietorship provides sufficient grounds for considering reproductions kitsch.

It is sometimes believed that reproductions are kitsch because they multiply works of art which by their authors were intended to be unrepeatable. Of course, this conviction does not refer to such departments of art as the multiple, graphic arts, or posters, where multiplication is intended. Is reproduction really at variance with unrepeatability? Unrepeatability, like uniqueness, is not a homogeneous value, and it contains, among others, the two above mentioned constituents. The remarks I previously made in regard to uniqueness apply also to unrepeatability. We conclude that it is not so much reproducing as imitative and pretentious exploitation of existing patterns which is the source of kitsch. Of course, it is possible to use reproductions in a kitsch way, but this constitutes a different problem.

Sometimes an opinion is expressed that all literary works turn into kitsch simply because of their becoming universally famous.[26] Is this opinion justified? What idea does it express, strictly speaking? Universal esteem contains an element of repetition. However, it is not repetition evinced in the art work itself — which after all remains unchanged — but repetition of contacts with that work which may result in forming favourable attitudes toward it. It is, therefore, not the work of art itself, but the attitude of acceptance toward it which may take on kitsch characteristics. Is it true that appreciation of an art work, if it is universal, necessarily bears the marks of a kitsch attitude? The universality of an attitude may stimulate aversion in persons who value highly their own individuality. Such motives do, in fact, supply certain grounds for qualifying universal acceptance as a kitsch attitude. Let us, however, bear in mind that these motives may lead to contradiction. It may happen that a work of art which is universally esteemed, and deservedly so, is also appreciated by a person who, however, tries to change his attitude in order to preserve his distinctness. Thus in seeking to escape from kitsch this person finds himself under its rule.

Universal esteem is not always an expression of real liking. It sometimes results from a tendency to adapt one's own behaviour to accepted patterns or authorities, or else it is a consequence of clever advertising, propaganda, etc. That is why a work's universal fame is sometimes regarded, not without grounds, as a sign of the kitsch character of the work itself, of its cheapness and sentimentality.

*   *   *

For a number of years the concept of kitsch has been a subject of growing interest. Among its definitional characteristics have appeared properties which make it possible not only to describe the phenomenon, but also to undertake attempts to explain it within the framework of some sociological and psychological theories. The role kitsch plays in mass social processes has been investigated. Growing interest in the concept of kitsch has been accompanied by an increase in the number of different meanings attached to this word. The question arises whether it will not be possible in the future to reduce the existing plurality of meanings to one concept with a universal extension. I do not think it plausible. It should rather be expected that controversies will continue and new definitions will be put forward. Of course, I do not mean to say that no reduction of diversity is possible. It is, however, my conviction that the kitsch phenomena make up a non-homogeneous set which requires at least two mutually irreducible types of concepts: one referring to human products, the other to attitudes, behaviour, or experiences.

It is, I think, possible although not easy to lay down a definition of kitsch. The attempts made so far are inadequate; besides, they do not give sufficiently clear criteria for the applicability of the term. I connect greater chances of success with the application of partial definitions. This will call for a detailed inquiry into the formal and semantic attributes of kitsch objects. That is why it is not advisable to attempt directly a definition covering all departments of art. Rather, one should start by grasping symptoms of kitsch characteristic of particular artistic disciplines and then use them to form a series of partial definitions. Attempts at a generalization could be made afterwards.

Irrespective of which scientific discipline one chooses as properly embracing the concept of kitsch, its connotation should contain an aesthetic element. It is the common opinion that this element comprises a negative value term. Is the term 'kitsch' simply a new name for ugliness? The relation between these two terms is not sufficiently clear to me. If the term 'ugliness' is taken to cover not only the deficiencies of artistic craftsmanship and flaws of form, but also semantic defects; and if, in addition, we would agree to consider such properties as insincerity, pretentiousness, or cheapness as combinations of these three kinds of faults; then, I think, the extension ugliness would include the extension kitsch. Art works of good craftsmanship but counted as kitsch because of their being pretentious or insincere, would then also be covered by the term 'ugliness'. It is, however, doubtful whether the above mentioned kitsch properties can be reduced to the combinations of those three kinds of faults. It seems that at least some of these properties have to be characterized with the aid of a negative value term of the ethical type. In that case the extension 'kitsch' would overlap the extension 'ugliness'.

NOTES

[1] Vittorio Gregotti: 'Kitsch and Architecture'. In: Gillo Dorfles (ed.), *Kitsch. An Anthology of Bad Taste*. Studio Vista, London 1969, p. 261. Cf. also: Gillo Dorfles, *Der Kitsch*. Tübingen 1969.
[2] G. Dorfles: 'The Betrothed' and Co., *op. cit.*, p. 91.
[3] G. Dorfles: 'Death'. *Op. cit.*, p. 137.
[4] Cf. A. Banach: *On Kitsch*. Cracow 1968. Numerous examples of literary kitsch are discussed in *Deutscher Kitsch* by Walter Killy. Vandenhoeck and Ruprecht, Göttingen 1966.
[5] Cf. Ludwig Giesz: 'Kitsch Man as Tourist'. In: G. Dorfles *op. cit*. Cf. also: Ludwig Giesz, *Phänomenologie des Kitsches*. Wolfgang Rothe Verlag, Heidelberg 1960.

[6] In the best case 'kitsch' is not simply an ambiguous term, but refers to a family of meanings. Compare in this respect another chapter in this book: Concepts with meaning families.
[7] G. Dorfles considers the above situation an example of kitsch in nature.
[8] I shall return to this problem later.
[9] Cf. A. Banach, *op. cit.*, p. 88.
[10] *Op. cit.*, p. 95.
[11] *Op. cit.*, p. 296–297.
[12] *Op. cit.* p. 88.
[13] Alexa Čelebonović: 'Notes on Traditional Kitsch'. In: G. Dorfles, *op. cit.* p. 280 ff. Cf. also Gert Richter' *Kitsch-Lexikon von a–z*. Gütersloh 1970.
[14] I consider this question in relation to the general problem of aesthetic value judgments in the chapter: Beauty and its socio-psychological determinants.
[15] Compare the chapter: Beauty and its socio-psychological determinants.
[16] The concept of explication originates with R. Carnap; cf. 'On Explication', a chapter in: *Logical Foundations of Probability*. Chicago University Press, Chicago 1950. The use of explication to define concepts in the humanities is discussed in: T. Pawlowski, *Begriffsbildung und Definition*. Berlin 1980.
[17] Alexa Čelebonović, *op. cit.* p. 289.
[18] A. Banach *op. cit.* pp. 177, 186.
[19] *Op. cit.* p. 67.
[20] Cf. J. Kotarbińska: 'On Ostensive Definitions'. *Philosophy of Science* 27, 1960.
[21] Partial Definitions and their application in the humanities are discussed in: T Pawlowski, *Begriffsbildung und Definition*. The conception of partial definitions which originated with R. Carnap has been formulated in connection with the difficulties encountered by attempts to give full definitions of some dispositional concepts. Cf. R. Carnap: 'Testability and Meaning', *Philosophy of Science*, 1936, 1937.
[22] Compare in this respect the chapter on concepts with meaning families.
[23] The concept of kitsch would in this respect be similar to the concept of beauty and to some other concepts in the humanities.
[24] Compare the chapter on persuasive definitions.
[25] M. Czerwiński, 'A voice in discussion about kitsch'. *Polska Sztuka Ludowa*, No. 3–4.
[26] Cf. G. Dorfles, *op. cit.*, p. 91.

CHAPTER VI

THE CONCEPT OF HAPPENING

The happening, like any other avant-garde movement, grew up in opposition to established art. It conceived in a new way the role of the audience in the spectacle. Chance, absent from the art of earlier periods, became admissible as an artistic determinant, and was even allotted a high rank in the hierarchy of aesthetic and social values. In contrast to traditional art, the happening should not have a plot, nor should it represent, symbolize, or express anything. It should not have characters, or roles to be played, as in theatre. It questions traditional limits of time, place, and spatial extension of the spectacle. Happeners preached the abolition of the special status accredited to art and to artists, as well as the abolition of the individuality of authorship: a piece initiated by one person could be continued by any other. These are immense differences and their implementation, although only partial, has changed art deeply. Of course, the happening did not arise all of a sudden, but grew out of tendencies present in earlier art, like Dadaism, Surrealism, or Ready-Made art. Nothing has been initiated or ended with the happening, states Michael Kirby, all elements of happenings and even their characteristic combinations can be found in historically earlier forms of art.[1]

Happeners and other avant-garde artists have often expressed a critical attitude toward existing art and the role it played in society. One such radical manifesto questions all the attributes hitherto considered to be the characteristic and indispensable properties of the art work: its uniqueness and individuality, its special value and social position which elevates the art work (and the artist) above other phenomena. The manifesto, ironically entitled *Nine Directions in Art*, contains the following items[2]

1. Absence of ....Art
2. Destroy all ....Art
3. Everything is .... Art
4. Don't sign .... Art
5. Copy .... Art
6. Do as usual .... Art
7. Change .... Art
8. You are .... Art
9. .... Art

Item nine, left blank, invites the reader to fill it in as he pleases, and thus stresses the main point of the manifesto: that all dividing lines between art and life are artificial and should be abolished, and that all constraints on the artist's creative freedom are unfounded. The manifesto is not without a certain touch of nihilism, a destructive tendency towards art.

What values are carried by the happening? Throughout its declarations and manifestos there run aims of an artistic as well as a social and philosophic nature. The happening preached full freedom of artistic activities: freedom from established rules of creative production, freedom in choosing and shaping materials. Everything could be art, everyone could be an artist — no special talents are required. The happening postulated the full integration of art in real life and the abrogation of lines separating various domains of art. It criticised the existing framework of social life and aimed at destroying conventions and customs which impoverished it; it strived to transform people's attitudes and to liberate them from psychic inhibitions which mutilate their personalities. Sometimes it simply wanted to be entertaining, but it also set out to entrance people or sometimes to introduce them into the mysterious experiences of Zen-Buddism.

Opinions about the happening are far from being unanimous. The happening was born of boredom, it is maintained, and is full of conventional clichés; is unable to afford any real experiences, and the shocks it is supposed to provide are false and faked. Such an impression is certainly given by descriptions and photographs relating to Jean Jacques Lebel's 'The Funeral Ceremony of the Anti-Procès', Venice, 1960. This happening alluded to old pagan rites of human blood sacrifice, and to myths connecting love and death. It was intended to induce the participants to join in the collective unconscious, to live through an archetype-experience. Cocktails are served at one of the palaces in Venice (Palazzo Contarini—Corfù); about 150 persons attend. They have been asked to come in formal dress and to bring white flowers. The ceremony begins. A man enters, his face under a black hood — the executioner. He kills a human figure with a large butcher's knife (it was a sculpture made for this occasion by Jean Tinguely). Lebel reads a violent page by the Marquis de Sade on the theme of death and love. A man behind a small metal curtain masturbates. Then the body is carried out of the palace into the street, and taken to waiting gondolas. The gondolas slowly advance up the Grand Canal. Occasional pedestrians take their hats off, convinced that it is a real funeral. The body is thrown into the water. One of the photographs shows four men carrying the body out of the palace: they are well fed, cultivated figures; their faces are unable fully to conceal the simulation; the impression of the ridiculous is intensified by black rings painted round the eyes.

The happening has its adherents, who fervently plead its merits. They sharply oppose those who consider happeners (or other avant-garde artists) as abnormal or even charlatans. "Sometimes, when a person cannot understand something" — says Michael Kirby, sculptor, painter, happener, and historian of avant-garde art — "he is not able to believe that anyone else could be profoundly interested; avant-garde art is often seen as a trick or a 'put on'. But I can assure you that this is not the case. I know personally almost every contemporary artist whom I discuss here. They are all deeply committed and honest people. None of them is trying to 'kid' anyone."[3]

The most important realizations took place in the late 'fifties and in the 'sixties. The happening flourished mainly in the United States, in Japan, France, Germany, Austria and England; also in Eastern Europe, e.g. in Czechoslovakia and Poland. The processes of unification which have for some time now been integrating various domains of art contributed to the development of the happening. The declarations of creators place the happening somewhere between theatre, ballet, show, circus, rite, psychodrama, and real-life situations, distinguished by a special gesture or intention of the performer. It owes an immense debt to the plastic arts and to music. The assemblage and the environment are among its direct predecessors. The happening is an enlivened environment — this statement expresses adequately one of its essential features. Depending on a particular realization, some or other elements characteristic of various domains of art or life come to the foreground. So, for instance, in some of Kaprow's happenings ('Words', 1962, 'Push and Pull. A Furniture Comedy for Hans Hofmann', 1963) the dominant role is played by the plastic aspect, a way of proceeding characteristic of the assemblage and the environment. An interior filled with objects invites the audience to enter. Objects of everyday life are haphazardly arranged in the space. The associations linked with the objects until now are broken — new associations have been made possible. The objects are often impermanent easily perishable: tatters of paper, wood-shavings, apples. They match our ephemeral moods and experiences. In those happenings nothing special occurs: the audience perform simple acts, spend some time in object-filled space, go round the objects, pass between them or enter them. As a matter of fact, these pieces lie on the line between the happening, the assemblage and the environment.

Elements of circus and of circus acrobatics are essential constituents in Robert Whiteman's 'The American Moon', 1964. In one of the events a big ball of red cloth is swinging on a rope; the layers of cloth slowly fall down; a man is uncovered who starts to perform acrobatics.

In 'Abreaktionsspiel' by Hermann Nitsch, 1963, the aim is to help the participants free themselves from unconscious complexes and inhibitions. They joint a lamb, whip each other and splash themselves with blood. A naked woman is lying on the floor, covered with lumps of meat, splashed with blood; two men treat her 'sadistically'. A similar therapeutic effect is intended in Carolee Schneeman's happenings in which she aims to release the participants' sexual inhibitions; a photograph relating to 'Meat Joy', 1964, shows a swarm of naked or half-naked bodies of men and women wriggling on the floor.[4]

The diversity of programs, declarations and realizations outlined above indicates that the happening is a phenomenon much more complex than it is usually admitted; an additional complication is introduced by divergence between manifestos and realizations. All this must have an influence upon the structure of the concept which refers to these phenomena. Is it possible to define the concept of happening? If so, what should its definition be like to match adequately the existing usage? Would a definition of the usual equivalence type do the task? What other modes of definition could eventually be used? Does the variety of aims and a certain diversity of features prove that the concept of happening is ambiguous? These are some of the questions which I should like to answer in this chapter. To do this, it is necessary to investigate the actual usage of the term 'happening', taking into consideration attempts at a definition as well as other pronouncements, e.g. programs, manifestos, individual statements in which certain concrete realizations are counted as happenings. This will make it necessary to analyse the attributes of those realizations for the sake of making comparisons and discovering similarities and differences.

FEATURES AND AIMS OF THE HAPPENING

Is it possible to distinguish a set of features which uniquely characterizes all happenings? An attempt to single out such a set meets unsurmountable difficulties. To be sure, in many realizations and programs a certain set of social, philosophic, and artistic aims is reflected; however, this set is not common to all happenings and only to them. Particular authors lay the main stress either upon social aims, for instance, upon a radical transformation of individual and social life, or upon philosophic aims, for instance, offering experiences inspired by Zen-Buddism. They differ, moreover, in their selection of artistic aims and means as well as with regard to the hierarchy of importance allotted to particular artistic or non-artistic aims. These circumstances make it impossible to indicate a unique set of features characteristic of all happenings, provided, of course, that the aim is to render adequately the existing usage of the term 'happening', and not to stipulate arbitrarily a new extension. It is more correct to speak about something like several variants of the happening, or, more precisely, about a meaning family coordinated to the word 'happening'; this will be substantiated in detail at a later point. One can, however, distinguish a set of attributes, some of which will appear in particular realizations or artistic programs. I shall present a concise description of this set and then go on to indicate differences which separate particular authors.

Artistic programs refer to general postulates of social or philosophic nature; in a way, they follow from those postulates and at the same time present means which can contribute to their realization. This connection can most clearly be seen with regard to two, apparently most important, aspects of the happening: the aesthetic function of chance and the role of the audience. According to many authors, full freedom of artistic activity is a fundamental aim of the happening. Such freedom is curtailed by rules and conventions left over from earlier art, which should therefore be rejected. This liberating tendency can be supported by admitting chance as an artistic solution. Further presuppositions of the happening, resulting from the postulate of artistic freedom, and to an extent unfolding its contents, can be embodied in the points given below. At least some of these presuppositions are assumed in many programmatic declarations, but by no means in all of them. This is a source of serious difficulties which beset all attempts at a definition of happening.

1. The happening is a certain structure of objects related in space, time, and motion. The word 'object' is here taken in its broad sense as referring not only to things, but also to people, their behaviour, sounds, lights, smells, etc. In a pronouncement characteristic for this aspect of happening, Claes Oldenburg states:

What I do as a happening is part of my general concern, at this time, to use more or less altered 'real' material. This has to do with objects, such as typewriters, ping-pong tables, articles of clothing, ice-cream cones, hamburgers, cakes, etc., etc. — whatever I happen to come into contact with. The 'happening' is one or another method of using objects in motion, and this I take to include people, both in themselves, and as agents of object motion. . . . I present in a 'happening' anywhere from thirty to seventy-five events, or happenings (and many more objects) . . . in simple spacial relationships. . .[5]

The structure which makes up the happening divides into parts — events. The relations between the events are casual; they are not determined by plot, or by the relation of means and ends, which are absent. None of the events is a consequence of, or a prelude to, another. Neither persons nor objects are assumed to have a particular identity, valid for the whole time-span of the happening. It follows that the time-order of events in a happening can be determined arbitrarily, some events can be omitted or new ones added, without detrimental effects on the structure.

Chance performs an aesthetic function in the happening. The more accidentally the elements have been put together, and the more difficult it is for the audience to relate them together, the stronger — some theoreticians say — is the audience's reaction to the happening. Chance is supposed to help the artist free himself from restraints imposed by conventions which have up to now regulated the selection and juxtaposition of elements. Chance should also help assimilate the happening to real life which is likewise governed by chance. The assimilation, and incorporation of art into the stream of life, should end its harmful isolation and promote its influence upon life, thus imparting to it great social importance.

2. In the happening use should be made of real material and not of objects artificially produced for this purpose. At the same time the scope of the material admissible in art is extended to cover objects hitherto rejected, like industrial refuse or worn-out items of everyday life.[6] The established conceptions of what can, and what cannot be art are thus questioned, and the way is opened to new forms and qualities, unattainable with the aid of conventional means. So, for instance, ". . . when a piece of hardware is juxtaposed to some wood-shavings, and this in turn is placed upon a crumpled rag, a series of abrupt shifts occur with the passage of the eye (and of the touch) that simply are not found in the most highly contrast-full paintings. For in the latter, no matter what may be the shapes and colors, the medium of paint offers a sensible unity in which all other differences may take place."[7] As with the time-order of events, the selection of materials and their juxtaposition are also determined by chance and not by plot.

3. The happening should not have any mimetic functions, like presenting, symbolizing or expressing. Instead, it should be 'real' action taking place among 'real' objects, as in ordinary life.

The attributes embraced in points 1—3 can be interpreted, after Hanna Ptaszkowska, as abolition of the hierarchy of information, of time, of space, of objects and situations.[8]

4. The happening does not have roles or characters to be played as in theatre. Every participant is just himself. No actors are needed. More than that, in some happenings — for instance, in those whose aim is to bring the

participants into a mediumistic trance or to free them from their unconscious complexes — the use of actors would not serve any purpose and would even preclude the intended aim. That is why happeners are generally against using actors and preach abolition of the artificial line, as they see it, between actors and spectators.

5. All lines dividing particular domains of art are artificial and should be abolished. That is why in the happening the use of all possible kinds of materials, means and techniques is admitted, independently of the domain of art or life they derive from.

6. The happening questioned the limits of time and place so far accepted in art. To be sure, spectacles often continued to be arranged in closed quarters of galleries or exhibition-halls, for — as Kaprow says — we cannot wait for new architecture, adapted to the new tendencies in art. However, many happeners go out into the open space: some happenings by Wolf Vostell ('Cityrama', 1961, 'In Ulm, um Ulm, und um Ulm herum', 1964) take place in numerous spots scattered throughout a city (Cologne, Ulm); Kaprow's 'Calling' continues for two days, partly in a city and partly in the country; "The place in which a happening occurs may be of any size", says Oldenburg, "it may be a room or a country." One of the reasons which made happeners abandon closed rooms and extend the spatial reach of spectacles was their hope of increasing tension between the events in a happening; this was supposed to be greater when the events took place in several widely spaced locales.[9]

The duration of happenings also transgressed accepted limits: beside short spectacles of one to one and a half hours, we find performances extending over many hours or many days; there are even actions without any time limit or any definite end-effect.[10]

7. Happeners wanted to shock their audiences out of their role of passive consumers. This is not an easy task, and it has two aspects: the conceptual one, which I shall treat later, and one that refers to the role of the audience in the happening. As we shall further see, the problem of audience-engagement is solved in different ways: apart from partial, sometimes spurious participation, there are various forms of more intensive engagement, up to cases when the audience is entirely eliminated and replaced by fullfledged participants.

DIFFERENCES AND DIVERGENCES

Let us presently examine the more important differences of opinion on the essence of the happening which occur between various authors or result from evolutional changes in the views of a given author. These differences may consist in omitting this or that particular feature from among the seven attributes listed above, or else in a different interpretation of the feature's character, function, or degree of intensity. Sometimes the differences take on the form of a conflict: a feature ascribed to one variety of the happening is just the opposite of a feature ascribed to another variety. A detailed discussion of these differences will be used to focus attention upon the problem of the definition of happening, and of the logical structure which the definition should have if it is to render adequately the existing usage.

A. Chance and its Role in the Happening

Complete agreement seems to prevail with regard to the following three points: a. the aesthetic function of chance; b. chance as a factor which obliterates the 'artificial' division between the happening (and even art in general) and life; c. chance as a liberating factor — liberating the artist from constraints imposed by the established rules and canons of artistic creation, as well as liberating the individual from conventions which damp his personal freedom. Beyond that there begin divergencies which can be reduced to different understanding of chance and to the variable extent of its intervention in the structure of the happening.

How can chance fulfil the functions ascribed to it? Before we can answer this question, we have to consider how the term "chance" is understood in discussions on these matters. Closer analysis of programmatic declarations and of particular realizations shows that the term "chance" is used in those contexts in at least six different meanings.

Chance as improvisation; i.e., acting without special previous preparation, reflection, or detailed plan. In this sense many aspects of happenings are left by their authors to the free decision of performers. Governed by their intuition, their physical or mental endurance, and taking into account the reactions of the audience, the performers decide whether, and in what manner certain fragments in a happening are carried out, how long they last, what new elements, unforeseen by the score, shall be introduced, etc. An example is the introduction into the script of 'The Burning Building', by Red Grooms, 1959, of a new item, caused by the audience's reaction. During the first performance the doorman (who was one of the performers) asked the audience for matches. They were really needed for the performance, and it happened that none of the performers had them. The shabby, cramped room in which the performance was taking place, along with an imperfect acquaintance with the term 'happening' – in short the general confusion among the spectators who did not know what was to be expected – all this caused the doorman's question to release a nervous laughter among the audience. After this incident the doorman asked the audience at every performance for matches; in this way he was gathering for himself, as were the other performers for themselves, a repertory of activities which would evoke the audience's reaction. In the same happening the length of particular fragments, their course and character were modified by way of improvisation, depending on the audience's reactions.[11]

Chance as free choice: understood as choice without substantiation, e.g. by reference to rules, principles or conventions. An example is 'The Thousand Symphonies' by Dick Higgins, 1967.[12] The script is made by casual machine-gunning of music paper with the standard ensemble indicated on it. In this way 'music signs' are marked on the paper. The machine-gunned fragments are then gathered together, and the conductor attaches them to intact pieces of paper to make the 'script' of the 'Symphony'. The question of how many fragments should be attached to the part played by a given instrument is freely decided by the conductor. Any shred of paper crossing a performer's part indicates the shape of the musical event performed by him. The lack of any means silence. Fragments may be repeated *ad libitum*, unless the conductor decides otherwise. The possibility of repetition ends when the orchestra moves on to the next fragment; this, again, is decided freely by the conductor. This happening contains a number of elements whose course and character are freely determined by the conductor or the musicians. From the information supplied by H. Sohm it is not clear, however, in what sense the machine-gunning – on which, after all, important aspects of this happening depend – is determined by chance. Is this too a consequence of somebody's free decision? I shall return to this question.[13]

Chance as determination by the unconscious: the acting subject is not aware of the motives of his conduct, he finds it accidental, whereas it is really determined by his unconscious; sometimes he feels his behaviour is controlled by forces beyond his influence. Chance in this sense is involved, for instance, in happenings whose aim is to influence the unconscious: psychotherapeutic performances to release inhibitions or complexes; actions which induce the participants to join in the collective unconscious and to live through an archetype-experience (cf. happenings of Lebel, Nitsch or Schneeman). Of course, a statement which purports to assert the action of chance must in any particular case be corroborated in reference to suitable psychological or psychoanalytical relationships. Needless to say, many things are here unclear or doubtful, and the statements put forward should be met with criticism.

Chance as determination by the unconscious may co-determine improvisation and, therefore, be involved in all happenings in which the selection or the arrangement of elements depends on improvisation. However, it would be wrong to surmise a necessary connection between them; improvisation does not involve determination by the unconscious, the former may occur without the latter.

I have mentioned the two most typical situations involving chance as determination by the unconscious. It is obvious, however, that the unconscious may influence all human behaviour, and may, therefore, play a role in all variants of the happening.

Chance as absence of logical connections: there are no connections which would explain the selection or the arrangement of elements. The manner in which the objects used in a happening are juxtaposed should tear down all the relations connecting those objects in real life situations, without replacing the old logical connections by new ones. It is repeatedly stressed by many authors that such a way of proceeding intensifies the audience's reaction to a happening. The absence of logical connections between objects as well as the stress put on objects not used in art hitherto was to sharpen and enrich the perception.

Chance as unintended or unforeseen occurrences: caused, for instance, by weather or animals, by behaviour of the audience or casual passers-by. Natural phenomena, like rain, wind, snow, thunderstorm may influence in an unforeseen way the course and the character of happenings arranged in the open air. In happenings set in a city scene a similar role is played by casual passers-by or by passing vehicles. Thus, for instance, in Kaprow's 'Calling' one of the episodes is set at a New York subway station; a crowd gathers around, with the resulting possibility of emotional tension or unforeseeable behaviour. A crowd of passers-by or passing vehicles may separate spatial or time fragments of a happening, thus introducing an unforeseen caesura. The selection of objects or activities may also be determined by unforeseen occurrences. Searching for objects to be used in his 'Autobodies', 1963, Oldenburg decided to buy some ice. The sales clerk stumbled while going out of the shop, and the ice-cubes scattered on the roadway. They glistened in the lights of the passing cars and were crushed under the wheels. Oldenburg felt as if he was witnessing the rehearsal of his happening.[14]

It is to be stressed that the factors mentioned above — forces of Nature, elements of city scenery — are not always unforeseen or unintended. So, for instance, in Kaprow's 'Fluids' an immense structure of ice-cubes is being built in the open space of a city. The slow melting of the ice as well as all the other accompanying effects caused by temperature — i.e. by a force of Nature — were, of course, intended and foreseen. Equally intended were the effects of rain in Kaprow's 'Raining', in which objects undergo changes as a result of rain. The last example shows, in addition, that an intended occurrence does not have to be foreseen with all its details: the exact timing of rain, its violence and character remain, at least with the present state of knowledge, unforeseeable.

Chance as a probability mechanism: here for instance a roulette wheel or dice determines the selection or juxtaposition of elements. In designing a happening the creator makes a number of decisions: he selects objects, participants, locations, ways of juxtaposing the selected objects, their movements, the time order of events which make up the happening, etc. It is sometimes the author's concern to make his decisions dependant on 'pure' chance only, and not on his predilections or his unconscious, on established rules of art, or on any other factors except 'pure' chance, conceived as a probability mechanism which secures an equal probability to every alternative, of a set of alternatives from which the selection is made. Taking a set of alternatives as a starting point, we can carry out random selection in many ways, depending on the probability mechanism we adopt (e.g. dice throws, the roulette wheel, etc.). Happeners who use probability mechanisms seem to be concerned in a procedure which secures an equal chance to every alternative, out of those taken into consideration. However, there are probability mechanisms which can be used in a different manner. They can coordinate a different probability to every type of alternative. In this way certain objects, movements, or actions in a happening appear with increased or diminished frequency with resulting effects on the appearance of the happening.[15]

It follows that in the procedure described above two choices will always depend on some factors other than a probability mechanism, for instance, on somebody's free decision; the two choices are: **1**. the stipulation of the set of alternatives to choose from with reference to an adopted chance mechanism, and **2**. the selection of the mechanism itself.[16] These two choices, made without reference to any chance mechanism, determine in advance certain important aspects of a happening. Thus, for instance, by throwing a coin we can ensure that every object, of a given set of objects, has an equal chance to appear in a happening. However, we can choose randomly from different sets of objects: industrial refuse, items in a big food store, or a clothing store, objects in everyday use by the rich or by the poor, etc. Objects derived from each of those sets, when used in a happening, will give the spectacle a different atmosphere, a different expression. Even in happenings designed strictly in accordance with the probability principle certain essential features depend, therefore, on factors of a different nature, often on a free decision of the creator.

Allan Kaprow is one of those who repeatedly used probability mechanisms to determine various aspects of their happenings. So, for instance, dice or the roulette wheel were used to decide how many persons, besides Kaprow, would take part in a happening, the upper bound being freely decided upon by the author with reference to the number of those wishing to participate. Coin-tossing may be used to decide on the inclusion of natural forces: tails—for, heads—against. Full randomness of choice is here also limited by the existing conditions: the prevailing climate, the season, the state of weather, the presence (or lack) of animals or plants, and their kinds, etc.[17] All these limitations of the role of 'pure' probability reduce to a free, or at least non-random choice of the set of alternatives from which the adopted probability mechanism will make a final selection.

Various methods of making chance decisions used in art are often wrongly considered to be random selection. A method of choice only spuriously random can be found, for instance, in the procedure adopted by Jean Arp to design his collages. He used to throw scraps of paper on the floor and then stick them down exactly as they fell. No probability mechanism is here employed; rather, the course of action is governed by chance in the sense of an unforeseen occurrence — unforeseen for the artist, although theoretically the way the scraps of paper fall could be predicted with reference to physical laws and to knowledge of conditions prevailing at the time and place of throwing.

And what of the procedure, described earlier, used to design the script for 'The Thousand Symphonies'? Is the machine-gunning of music paper performed in accordance with a probability mechanism which secures an equal probability to every single occurrence? What is such a single occurrence to consist in? Is hitting any point within a staff such an occurrence? Or hitting any point whatsoever on the music paper? Many other interpretations come easily to mind. Unfortunately, the available information does not supply sufficient grounds for a well-founded answer. It does not seem very likely, though, that they adopted any probability mechanism to secure an equal chance to each single occurrence, independently of how such occurrence is defined. Rather, the occurrences are there determined by chance understood as a free decision of the gunman, and as an occurrence not wholly foreseeable.

These various meanings of the term 'chance' are essentially different; the situation referred to by each of them may exist independently of the situations described by others. So, for instance, the fact that rain soaks objects and people in a happening, thus changing their appearance and creating a specific atmosphere, may be unforeseen; however, it has occurred in accordance with definite natural laws and, therefore, can be logically explained. Similarly, improvisation does not necessarily have to coincide with determination by the unconscious; the latter, in turn, does not exclude logical connections between acts determined by the unconscious. Free choice may exist without an application of a probability mechanism, and vice versa; by the way, the use of a probability mechanism, once it has been selected, precludes free choice, because choice is then determined by the selected mechanism. Of course, the selection of the mechanism itself remains an open question, and can be decided by somebody's free decision.

The extent to which chance intervenes will vary, depending on particular realization. Chance may influence the choice of objects, participants, locations, ways of arranging objects, time sequences of events, etc.

The most radical intervention of chance (conceived as probability mechanism) is to be found in the procedure described by Kaprow.[18] The selection and arrangement of elements is there determined by various probability mechanisms, for instance, roulette, dice, or the random selection of items listed on the business pages of a telephone directory. Even in this procedure, however, — states Kaprow — many things are left to free decision of the performers and, therefore, not to chance in the sense of probability mechanism.

In pieces where the intervention of chance is less radical than described above, it determines only some features of performances, for instance, only the selection of locations, or only of participants.

It is not difficult to adduce examples illustrating divergencies with reference to the intervention of chance — of its reach, character or intensity. The extreme, radical case described above can be opposed by pieces in which the intervention is minimal. Thus, for instance, in Lebel's 'The Funeral Ceremony' chance in the sense of probability mechanism appears scarcely at all, instead, a certain role may be played by chance as determination by the unconscious (in the reactions of the participants), and as unforeseen occurrence (in the reactions of passers-by). Between those two extremes there are many intermediate realizations. With Kaprow himself, whose views have undergone a considerable evolution, we find "probabilistic" happenings beside pieces in which the role of chance was rather limited.

The aesthetic function of chance. Let us consider how chance can fulfil the aesthetic function ascribed to it by happeners and by other avant-garde artists. It seems to me that this question presents itself most clearly with reference to chance conceived as probability mechanism. Besides, the answer comes out differently, depending on the variety of chance taken into consideration.

The aesthetic function of chance as probability mechanism reduces, I think, to the following three points. 1. Intensification of emotional-intellectual reaction to art-products, revitalising perception, and stimulating the audience's imagination to creative effort. 2. Liberating the artist from restraints imposed by the established conventions, rules or habits. 3. Enriching art with new elements, hitherto unknown. The use of probability mechanisms is intended to contribute to these aims in that it should make it possible to break radically with all principles and habits which hitherto shaped the creative process; speaking generally, the creative process means the selection of objects (in the broad sense here assumed), and ordering them according to various hierarchies: of time, space, semantic and functional connections, etc. The use of a probability mechanism breaks all such connections, because it replaces the established regularities (e.g. regularities characteristic of the traditional stage theatre, the dodecaphonic music, or the cubist painting) by something entirely different — by the principle of randomness. However, the principle of randomness is also a principle; it follows that it can bring new aesthetic values only in those domains of art in which probability mechanisms have not hitherto been applied to determine the creative process. In those domains of art, in which such application has already taken place, only modifications of the existing aesthetic values are possible, by way of changing the mechanisms or the extent or the manner of their application.

The aesthetic function of chance as free choice or unintended occurrence also consists in its ability to break with regularities established by the existing conventions. However, the breach is neither so radical, nor so consistent, as was the case with probability mechanism. An artistic effect, however unforeseen, may accord with the received rules of art; as is the case when chance means free decision. Of course, this does not preclude situations when free decisions may bring interesting artistic effects. An example in the realm of music is the use by W. Lutoslawski of an aleatoric technique. This brings the effect of refined irregularity and richness of rhythm, so characteristic of Lutoslawski's works.

The greatest doubts arise in connection with the aesthetic function of chance as determination by the unconscious. An example often quoted is the method of painting (if the word 'method' can at all be used in this context) applied by Jackson Pollock, or action-painting in general. Those doubts do not concern the achieved artistic effects, which are undisputable, but rather the way these effects have been achieved. Pollock himself speaks about this in the following words. "When I am *in* the painting I'm not aware of what I'm doing. It is only after a sort of 'get acquainted' period that I see what I have been about. ... the painting has a life of its own. I try to let it come through."[19] So far, the facts discussed above have not been examined in a systematic way. To what extent are the phenomena determined by the unconscious? Why did the unconscious consistently suggest to Pollock always the same general scheme of painting, named by art-theoreticians abstract expressionism? Did not conscious choice play a role? In the subconscious as well as in dreams, pictures and elements are associated by way of connections different from causal or logical bounds, known in waking experience. However, such is not always the case; besides, these connections are certainly not of the probabilistic type, but result from pertinent psychological interdependencies. Something is already known about these interdependencies, and, as our knowledge grows and is better corroborated, the feeling of casualness and surprise will vanish. Besides, much of this has already been exploited by surrealism.

In statements about the aesthetic function of chance various assumptions are made with regard to the relationship between application of chance and achieved artistic effects or phenomena of art-reception. An example is the quoted assertion that chance revitalizes perception, and intensifies the emotional-intellectual reaction to art-works. What is the methodological status of those assumptions? Are they essentially empirical statements, accessible to empirical testing? Or rather analytical ones, logical consequences of terminological stipulations? Or else consequences of the assumed system of aesthetic values? Are the assumptions justified? Does chance always increase the intensity and vividness of reactions to art-works? Perhaps it does so only in certain cases, whereas in other cases chance evokes dullness and boredom? What should the general characteristic of such cases be like? These problems await thorough examination.

There also arises the fundamental problem, whether chance as such brings aesthetically valuable effects, or whether this is the case only with some of its applications. In the latter case the delineation of the valuable effects of chance-application would call for special aesthetic criteria, independently of, or in addition to chance. Instructive experience has been gathered in this connection by the limited (or controlled) aleatorism in music, and by computer-graphics. In these domains of art only some of the effects brought about by the application of chance are acknowledged as artistically valuable. In cases where the application of chance does not bring any positive artistic effects, its function boils down to the negative effect of abolishing the established conventions and procedures of composition. It is, of course, problematic whether these two functions of chance — the positive and the negative — can be separated with any reasonable measure of precision. Until now, I have not come upon a full and consequent application of chance as a factor determining all elements of the creative process. Chance is only used to complement choices made consciously, intentionally although the extent and the ways of its application widely differ.

The important role of chance in contemporary art is commonly acknowledged, which makes warnings against its misuse the more pertinent. The stand taken by John Cage, one of the pioneers in the use of chance in contemporary art is very telling. He duly recognized the artistic function of chance, and applied it in his numerous realizations. He also inspired many avant-garde artists in this respect. However, when he found that some of them were going too far, and ascribing an exaggerated importance to chance, he came forward against its facile misuse.[20]

B. *The Audience, its Presence and its Role in the Happening*

The problem of the audience is one of the most important aspects of the happening. It is connected with a number of general postulates put forward by happeners — postulates of an artistic as well as social and philosophic nature: 1. To shock members of the audience out of their role as passive consumers, and to stimulate them to active, creative participation in the spectacle. 2. To deny that any special talent is needed to practice art; on the contrary — everyone can be an artist. 3. Through active participation in the happening to release the audience from their inhibitions and restraints. Attitudes toward audience participation range from full acceptance of an audience, in accordance with the rules of traditional stage theatre, to total elimination of an audience — whether by exclusion, or by transformation of the spectators into participants.

It would be a misunderstanding to surmise that happeners wanted to eliminate the audience, in order to exclude non-artists, people professionally not engaged in artistic activities. Such a thought was generally alien to happeners, although even here there are exceptions. Rather, they wanted to prepare people for the role of active participants, and to prevent their participation from reducing to a spurious one. This requires a previous acquaintance with the script, rehearsals and preparatory talks. Allan Kaprow is one of the happeners who in many of his realizations, especially the early ones, consequently adopted the procedure described above.

The audience [states Kaprow] should be eliminated entirely. A group of inactive people in the space of a happening is just dead space. A happening with a seated audience is not a happening, but stage theatre. On the other hand, to assemble people unprepared for an event and say that they are participating if apples are thrown at them or they are herded about, means essentially to give up the whole idea of participation. It conflicts the aim of the happening, and even evokes negative reactions of people. After some time, in any case, such 'audience response' turns into pure cliché that should not be tolerated by anyone serious about the problem. I think that it is a mark of mutual respect that all persons involved in a happening be willing and committed participants who have a clear idea what they are to do. This is simply accomplished by writing out the score for all and discussing it thoroughly with them beforehand.[22]

According to Kaprow, such way of proceeding does not differ from the preparations for a parade, a football match, a wedding, or a religious service. It is sometimes stressed that participation in a happening calls on the audience to meet the same conditions which the artist is resolved to fulfil — it calls for liberation from the existing conventions, giving up social privileges and bearing the resulting risks. In order to 'educate' the public, to challenge them and thus to turn them into active participants, means are sometimes used to evoke in the passive spectators, who behave as in traditional theatre, the feeling of being superfluous, unadapted to the new circumstances. A characteristic solution of this difficult problem has been found by Tadeusz Kantor in his happening 'Koncert Morski' ('The Sea Concert'), 1967. The function of the public consists there in the rather passive role of the concert-audience. The passiveness of the public — the most frequent manner of its behaviour, to be changed only with greatest difficulties — is there intended and fitted into the structure of the happening. The public has been treated there as a 'ready made', an object — one of many objects used in this happening.

Besides happenings in which ambitious efforts are made to transform the public into fully fledged, active participants, there are spectacles where the role of the audience is much more modest. They carry out certain simple operations (e.g. move rolls of words, make phrases with rubber-stamps), and often are simply there to live through an experience in accordance with the established theatrical tradition. This is perhaps better, more honest than participation which can easily be turned into a worn out cliché.

The maximalistic stand toward audience participation as proclaimed in manifestos — a stand which, after all, cannot be fully realized — was counterbalanced by a more realistic attitude of those happeners who saw the limits of the possible, and who clearly differentiated the role and significance of the audience from those of the performers and the creator. Claes Oldenburg writes: "... I am very grateful to the audience for coming each weekend ... I cannot deny it is good to have an audience". However, he further states "... the audience is taken to differ from the players in that its possibilities are not explored as far as that of the players, whose possibilities are not explored as far as my own."[23]

C. *The Participation of Actors*

The majority of happeners are against the use of actors. They are not necessary, because in the happening there are neither roles, nor characters to be played as in stage theatre. In the happening — they say — one does not play a role, but is involved in an action in which every participant is just himself. It was also stressed that the actor's professional manner precludes the spontaneity of experiences and behaviour — features so essential in the happening. Also against the use of actors are those happeners who aim at a therapeutic effect, at evoking special experiences or psychical states (e.g. Lebel, Nitsch, Dine).

The statement quoted above asserts that in the happening the participants do not play any roles, but are just themselves. What is the methodological status of this statement? No doubts arise if it is taken to be a postulate suggesting a certain way of behaviour, for it is then an element of the declared program; this program can be accepted or rejected, but it cannot be said to be discordant with the facts. The doubts arise, however, as soon as the statement is interpreted as a description of facts. Do the participants in a happening always (or even only as a rule) manage to engage themselves so deeply, and in such a way, that all elements of acting or simulation are absent? Such a high degree of engagement and absorption is difficult to achieve, and is certainly not a rule. If this remark is justified, then there are in the happening elements of acting — an amateur, untrained acting, to be sure, but nonetheless 'playing a role'. Also, there arises the question whether it is psychologically possible for a participant to follow the script as well as the instructions received during rehearsals, and at the same time to be 'just himself'. These situations seem to conflict each other: the more detailed the script and the rehearsal-instructions, the less is the participant 'just himself', and more he becomes an actor playing his role. An actor not in the professional sense, of course, but in the sense of acting, of unspontaneous behaviour. Those are two different meanings, but they have an element in common, essential for the present discussion: acting, 'not being just oneself'. The final solution of this problem requires empirical research; not an easy task, for it refers to psychic states and processes which it is difficult to observe, describe or control.

An extreme stand toward the use of actors, widely differing from attitudes of other creators, has been taken by Salvador Dali, who in his happenings used exclusively professional actors.[24]

D. *The Semantic Function of the Happening*

Beside strict, systematic relations of the plot-type other forms of semantic representation are also considered, e.g. themes, symbols, metaphors, expression. They can be ordered on a scale; at one extreme is the plot — the most elaborate and consistent system of semantic representation, richly imbued with logical and causal relationships; the other extreme denotes the lack of any semantic function whatsoever. Activities and objects which neither present, symbolize or express anything, nor perform any other semantic function, are entirely devoid of semantic elements — are asemantic. Between these two extremes there are many intermediate alternatives: various more or less loosely shaped semantic relationships, depending on the intensity of chance-intervention in the structure of the happening.

The happening has no plot — this stand is unanimously represented by all happeners, in their manifestos as well as in their realizations; they are joined by theoreticians of happening. With reference to the other extreme the absolute lack of semantic functions in the happening — there is no uniformity of stand. Those authors who declare for the entirely asemantic happening stress that it does not represent or express anything, but is a 'real' action. Activities and objects used in a happening are not to present anything, but are just 'repetition' or 'extension' of real life. Some describe the function of the happening as 'visualizing' or 'quoting' life activities, and stress that these do not have semantic functions, but are 'ordinary acts'; in this connection the happening is sometimes described as a manifestation of the most consequent realism (H. Ptaszkowska). The asemantic view of the happening seems to follow from Kaprow's early works; it appears explicitly in Hanna Ptaszkowska's writings. I think, however, that it remained only a point in declarations and manifestos. As far as I know, none of the existing realizations is fully asemantic; perhaps Kaprow's early realizations, on the line between the happening and the environment, come nearest to this extreme.

Particular realizations are imbued to a greater or lesser degree with semantic elements. There are happenings which have a sort of residuum or para-plot. An example are Lebel's pieces or Dine's 'Car Crash'. The latter has a definite thread of at least psychological continuity. Also, the selection of objects is here not casual, but determined by their semantic function; they suggest a definite occurrence and express a specific atmosphere: something like bloodstained bandages, visceral organs and smashed machine-parts. The room had overtones of a hospital, even the floor was painted white. Dine at one point had thought of dressing the audience in white caps and overalls, to accentuate this atmosphere.

A dark-haired, white-faced girl . . . stood silent in the corner . . . Cut-out crosses, some white, some red or silver, hung from the ceiling. . . . a man dressed in silver, with two lights on his head, appeared. This was the car, played by Dine himself. Two other figures appeared holding two flashlights held like headlamps. . . . They proceeded to play a sort of hide-and-seek game with their lights. Whenever the lights struck the silver man he moaned loudly. . . . The girl starts a stream-of-consciousness monologue: The car is my hertz spot of love to zoom through the whole transmission of my lovely time. . . . The silver man is at a wringer which is fastened above a blackboard. As he turns the handle the word HELP appears painted on every piece of a paper towel-roll.[25]

The personal element in this happening is very strong: it could be described as a sort of group psychotherapy to cure Dine (and maybe the audience) of the experience of a real car crash.

Claes Oldenburg states too that in some of his pieces he set up events into a pattern, a pseudo-plot, based on associational rather than logical connections.[26]

Besides happenings with para-narrative threads of the type described above, there are happenings with more loosely patterned semantical relationships, e.g. a theme. An example is a series of Kaprow's realizations under the general title 'Fight'; the particular themes in this series: 'Combat', 'Money', 'Eating', 'Sex'. However, even with regard to those loosely patterned semantical relationships there are differences of opinion among happeners about the kinds of admissible themes. According to some of the happeners (e.g. Kaprow) a theme in a piece can be anything, but art; this is connected with the tendency to assimilate the happening to real life, and with the opposition to auto-thematic art. Nevertheless, there are happenings, mainly by Polish artists, whose theme is just art. It suffices to mention happenings of Kantor (e.g. 'The Raft of Medusa' – a live reconstruction of the picture by Garricault, performed by the audience; 'The Anatomy Lesson after Rembrandt' – a paraphrase of Rembrandt's picture, in the form of a clothes vivisection), or happenings by Jerzy Beres (e.g. 'Event', whose theme is the creative act).

Contrary to programmatic declarations about absence of expressive function, the happening used, as a rule, to express something, at least in the sense of evoking some more or less definite moods.[27] Even in those happenings, then, where one could not speak of para-narrative threads, or themes, there still remains an expressive function. Specific moods are expressed, for instance, in Dine's 'Car Crash' or Nitsch's 'Abreaktionsspiel'; other examples could easily be adduced.

Let us return to the difference mentioned earlier between representing and 'repeating' ('extending', 'visualizing', or 'quoting') real life. Happeners and theoreticians of happening attach great importance to this difference. They refer to it when they argue for the asemantic character of the happening. What does this difference consist in? Is the 'quoting' or 'visualizing' really devoid of semantic elements? The semantic relation is made up by at least the following five constituents: **1.** an object functioning as a sign; **2.** its denotation or meaning; **3.** the intention of the sender; **4.** the intention of the recipient; **5.** rules, at least in the form of habits, which establish the meaning of the sign, and thus bind together all the preceeding elements of the semantic relation. Depending on a particular conception of sign, all or only some of the above elements are taken to make up the sign relation. The following three elements appear in many current conceptions: **a.** an object functioning as a sign; **b.** its denotation or meaning; **c.** rules which establish (**a**) as a sign of (**b**). In other conceptions the stress is put on the intention of the sender or the intention of the recipient. The semantic attitude, the attitude an interpreter takes with regard to a certain object is then considered a necessary, sometimes even a sufficient, condition for this object's being a sign. If a similar semantic attitude with regard to a given object is taken by many members in a social group, there may arise in the group a habit of interpreting the object in a definite way. If verbalized, the habit turns into a semantic rule. In this way objects acquire a semantic function independently of the intention of persons who produced them or make use of them, for instance, in a happening. One of the significant features of the present time is the common presence of an attitude which I would call semantic universalism. It is of its essence to take instinctively, as it were automatically, an interpretative attitude toward all human activities and their products, independently of any possible semantic or communicative intention of the acting subjects. Such is especially the case in situations when objects, activities, or behaviour are claimed to be art. This tendency to take the interpretative attitude may give rise to certain ways of interpreting, characteristic not only of particular individuals, but of whole social groups. One can then speak of general rules which establish the interpretation of given objects (activities, behaviour). The existence of the attitude of semantic universalism is a social fact. The question then arises what sense can it have to distinguish between objects or activities which have a semantic function and the supposedly asemantic 'quoting' of real life. The fact that a happener has no semantic intention does not prevent his audience from taking an interpretative attitude towards his production. One can, of course, brand this attitude as a misunderstanding, but of what use would this be, in view of the universality of the attitude? The doubts remain when we look at the matter from the side of the happener. Is it not psychologically false to assume that a performer in a happening, especially in a spectacle in front of an audience, does not present, communicate, or express anything, but is 'just himself', carries out 'usual', 'real life' activities, without any semantic intention? The difficulties here adduced seem to speak against the possibility of wholly asemantic happenings, or, at least, make it very doubtful.

E. *Entertainment and Serious Purposes*

According to many authors, e.g. Vostell, Lebel, Nitsch, the aim of the happening is to assume an attitude toward serious matters: political or social problems, psychological or existential problems of the individual. Anyway, the happening should not simply afford entertainment, be amusing. However, there are happenings, for instance, by some English authors, whose aim is just this.[28] In the group of 'serious' happenings itself there are also divergencies with regard to the general attitude toward life and the existing social conditions. The attitude of defiance, of sharp criticism, frequent among European happeners, is opposed by the attitude of acceptance, characteristic of many American happeners affiliated with Pop-Art, or influenced by the philosophy of Zen-Buddism. Serious as well as entertaining happenings are opposed by a third alternative: spectacles dripping with dullness. These prolong themselves beyond endurance, as if their authors wanted to try out, how great a dose of boredom can yet be endured by the audience.

F. *Assimilation to Usual Life versus Extraordinary Occurrence*

The happening should be built of occurrences as similar as possible to those in everyday life — this postulate appears in declarations of many creators; sometimes it is really carried out. In Georg Brecht's piece the performer makes salad, or, if he prefers, he makes soup — this the end of the spectacle. In Mark

Boyle's 'Street', 1964, the audience is led into a small curtained auditorium. When the curtains are opened they find themselves looking through a shop-window into the street. The 'action' is the usual life of the street outside.[29] Happenings of this character are opposed by spectacles in which the presented life is condensed, intensified, and the occurrences shown are unusual. An example are Lebel's pieces, for instance, 'To Invoke the Spirit of Catastrophe', 1962, or Nitsch's 'Abreaktionsspiel'.

G. *Experiences of Participants versus Features Accessible to External Observation as Criteria of the Happening*

According to Lebel only the experiences of participants decide whether or not a spectacle is a happening. The absence of such specific experiences testifies that the spectacle cannot be counted as a happening, even though all features of the happening, accessible to external observation, are present. This stand is opposed by those creators who characterize the happening with reference to a definite set of externally accessible features. It is to be remarked that as a consequence of Lebel's stand the concept of happening is turned into a relative one: something is, or is not, a happening only relative to a given person, to the person's experiences. Strictly speaking, an additional time-relativization is here necessary; for, one and the same person may live through the required experience during one realization of a happening, but not experience it during another one.

H. *Repetition of Performances versus their Unrepeatability*

Happenings should be performed only once — this postulate has been stressed with great force.

> ... many of the happenings ... have been given four or five times — writes Kaprow — ostensibly to accommodate larger audiences, but this, I believe, was only a rationalization of the wish to hold on to theatrical customs. In my experience, I found the practice inadequate, because I was always forced to do what could be repeated, and had to discard countless situations which I felt were marvellous, but performable only once. ... to repeat a happening means to compromise the whole concept of change.[30]

Robert Whiteman's 'Flower' is one of the happenings most often performed; in March 1963, alone, it was performed twenty times.

J. Historical and Universal Concept of Happening

Michael Kirby asserts the historical character of the concept 'happening'. He states: "... the best thing to do is to use the term 'happening' in the historical sense, as a description of a certain theatrical form which presently belongs to the past ... happening is connected with a definite historical period."[31] The distinctive feature of the historical concept of happening is its space-time localization. Spectacles which do not belong to the specified period or place are not happenings by definition. The case is different with the universal concept of happening. Its definiens does not contain any space-time localization; and, consequently, does not preclude the appearance of happenings in any historical period. Neither, however, does it imply that happenings have in fact appeared or will appear in other periods. The question of their appearance in any particular epoch is an empirical problem to be solved by suitable research.

THE PROBLEM OF THE DEFINITION OF HAPPENING

I have presented the more important features ascribed to happenings, calling attention to the existing divergencies. The question arises whether in the face of such divergencies the term "happening" can at all be defined? It is, of course, not the trivial sense of this question I have in mind, according to which every term can be defined, if only its definition is formally correct. Rather, I think of a definition which adequately renders the existing usage of the term. Attempts at such a definition have, in fact, been made. Michael Kirby, for instance, defined happening as a purposefully composed form of theatre in which diverse alogical elements, including nonmatrixed performing, are organized in a compartmented structure.[33]

The following critical remarks come to mind.

The understanding of happening as a form of theatre prejudges the question of audience-participation in accordance with the conceptions prevailing in this domain of art. We have seen, however, that audience-participation has many forms: from passive observers through more or less intensive engagement up to full participation on equal terms. In the latter case the audience, as such, is entirely eliminated; there remain only partner-participants, sometimes prepared for their function in a happening by way of rehearsals and script-readings. I shall recall at this occasion the postulate — put forward by many happeners — to abolish the artificial line, as they say, between the actors and the public; also, no special talent is necessary to be able to participate actively in a happening.

Acting (nonmatrixed performing) is, according to Kirby, one of the definitive features of happening. However, the creators often stress that the participants should not play any characters or roles; they are to be just themselves, do things one ordinarily does everyday. To what extent this postulate can be carried out is another matter, as I have said, but it remains and important element in declarations and manifestos.

Kirby's definition is modelled on realizations resembling the theatre. However, there are happenings which mostly resemble other domains of art: the assemblage, the environment, painting, music.

Finally, there are happenings which are entirely devoid of artificially produced occurrences or activities — elements so characteristic of the traditional theatre. Such happenings are 'phases of reality itself' (Vostell), and the intervention of the happener is there limited to a certain pointing-differentiating gesture; it helps the audience to perceive a given fragment of reality in a fresh or critical way, to feel it more deeply (compare, for instance, Boyle's 'Street', or Vostell's happenings whose action takes place on many spots scattered throughout a city).

To conclude, if Kirby's definition is intended as an adequate rendering of the existing usage, it is unsuccessful. Equally unsuccessful are other known attempts, for instance, the definition put forward by D. Suvin, whose defects have been pointed out by S. Morawski.[34]

Should we conclude that the term 'happening' cannot be defined? Every ordinary definition, i.e. equivalence definition of the form $A =_{df} B$, establishes a certain assembly of features which is unique for the objects falling under the term being defined, that is, common to all those objects and only to them. We do not mean any unique assembly whatsoever, but an assembly of features which are interesting relative to a given domain of research or practical activity in which the term being defined is to be used. The divergencies considered above between features ascribed to happenings by various authors indicate that such an unique assembly of features does not exist. Consequently, no equivalence definition of the term 'happening' is possible in which the existing usage is adequately rendered. Should we conclude that the term 'happening' is ambiguous? Such a solution would not correspond to the existing usage; also, it would overshadow essential similarities between particular realizations, differing in some other respects. There are many indications that the term 'happening' has a family meaning.[35]

'HAPPENING' AS A TERM WITH A MEANING-FAMILY

The way the term 'happening' is used by creators and theoreticians of happening bears distinct symptoms characteristic of terms with family-meanings. 1. Many features of pieces called happenings admit of degrees; they appear in particular realizations with different degrees of intensity, including the intensity zero, i.e. complete absence. Here are some more important examples of such features: intervention of chance in the structure of the happening, assimilation to real life, audience-participation, extension of the spectacle in time or space, similarity to various domains of art, like painting, music, the assemblage, the environment, theatre, circus, psychodrama. 2. The divergencies listed under (1) point that there is no set of features which uniquely characterizes realizations called happenings. 3. Certain realizations — let us call them typical — undoubtedly fall under the term 'happening'; they exhibit in a distinct degree at least some of the seven typical features, distinguished earlier. The remaining pieces counted as happenings resemble the typical ones. 4. The extension of the term 'happening' comprises a number of subsets, each of which covers pieces which are uniform relative to an assembly of features. 5. Each of the subsets has some attributes in common with at least one other subset. 6. A definition of happening would, then, consist of a number of partial definitions; each of them specifies a partial criterion for the applicability of the term 'happening' or its negation.[36] 7. In the simplest case, a partial definition specifying a positive criterion of applicability may take the form of the following conditional sentence:

> If a realization x has the attribute A, then x is a happening.

On the basis of this definition certain realizations, namely those exhibiting the attribute A, can be counted as happenings. However, the definition does not provide us with any information on what other realizations, in addition to those exhibiting the attribute A, can be included in the extension 'happening'; to be able to do that we would have to introduce further partial positive criteria of happening. Also, the above definition does not give any negative criteria of happening, i.e. criteria which enable us to recognize certain pieces as non-happening. To do that, we have to introduce negative criteria which stipulate either a necessary condition of happening:

> If a realization x does not have the attribute F, then x is not a happening,

or else a sufficient condition for the application of the negation of 'happening':

> If a realization x has the property H, then x is not a happening.

8. All partial definitions taken together do not add up to a full equivalence definition of happening. The extension of this term remains open. This means

138   CHAPTER VI

that there are realizations, present or future, which are not covered by any of the hitherto assumed partial criteria; their eventual inclusion in the extension of 'happening' establishes further partial criteria.

Positive partial criteria for different variants of happening can be formulated in reference to the attributes mentioned in the literature, like the presence and role of the audience, the use of actors, the role of chance and the extent of its intervention, artistic, social or philosophic aims, etc. The presence or lack of these attributes, the way they are exhibited, and the degree of their intensity, can be used to formulate partial criteria, characteristic of particular elements of the family of subsets which belong to the extension 'happening'. The assembly of features registered in Kirby's definition can be used as one of such positive partial criteria. However, in Kirby's definition this assembly is used as an equivalence criterion: all pieces matching the criterion are happenings, non-matching ones are not. Within the present conception, instead, this assembly provides only a sufficient condition; it makes it possible to count certain realizations as happenings but does not, however, prejudge what other realizations could eventually be subsumed under 'happening' (this requires additional positive criteria), nor does it specify what happening is not. To decide the latter question, we would have to enrich Kirby's definition by negative criteria, with reference to which certain realizations can be acknowledged as non-happenings. It seems to be easier for the happeners to reach agreement on the negative than on the positive criteria of happening; this is so, I believe, because it is easier for them to agree on what they commonly reject, than on what they commonly accept.

Interesting material for further positive partial criteria can be found in the assembly of features set by Vostell. He describes happening as

... a pre-arranged or improvised occurrence; phases of reality; presentation of facts or dreams not in closed quarters, but on many places scattered throughout a city, on those namely, on which they usually occur: e.g. an airfield, car dump, slaughter house, or multi-storey car-park, etc. The spectator participates in the occurrence or even takes over the responsibility for the course of the happening.[37]

None of these features, I think, taken separately and in the form presented by Vostell, makes up a sufficient condition of happening. We can, however, obtain such conditions by working out the features and eventually joining them together. I should like to remark that the features made up by Vostell do not exhaust all variants of happenings, e.g. those approximating the assemblage or the environment. What is here meant are all hitherto known variants; that these features do not exhaust all possible variants of happenings already follows from the open character of the concept involved.

The scientific usefulness of concepts with meaning families is generally lower than that of ordinary concepts, defined by equivalence definitions. This follows from the logical structure of concepts with meaning families.[38] As a result of evolution such concepts may split into several distinct concepts; some of them may then take on the structure of the ordinary concept, definable by equivalence definition. Whether or not such a transformation takes place depends on the function of the newly formed concept in a theory into which it is to be incorporated. As theoretical reflection on the happening develops, and a theory of the happening, or at least an essential fragment thereof is formed, the corresponding concept may undergo the transformation described above. The family of subsets which presently forms the extension 'happening' would then be split up, and a set of realizations chosen, unique with regard to a certain assembly of features; this would make an equivalence definition of happening possible. However, such a transformation cannot be carried out on the strength of an arbitrary decision. It must be based on a theory of happening or at least essential rudiments thereof; (it could also be a more general theory of aesthetic phenomena); the aim of the theory being description and explanation of the artistic and social function of happening. The role of the newly proposed definition of happening in this theory justifies then why these and not other definitive features have been selected; it also vests this definition with the virtue of scientific usefulness.

CONCEPTUAL ELEMENTS IN THE HAPPENING

Happeners endeavoured to stimulate the audience to creative participation in the spectacle. This purpose was also to be served by the conceptual elements in the happening: those stimuli whose meaning and function were only shaped in the imagination of the recipient, who developed and enriched them, and attached to them a network of his own emotional-intellectual associations. An important role was here played by chance: the distinctiveness, and unexpected character of juxtapositions determined by chance; activities breaking the established conventions — all these factors stimulate the imagination, sometimes activating also the unconscious.

The number and the role of conceptual elements in the happening vary; sometimes they come to the foreground to determine the character of the entire spectacle.

Robert Filiou's 'No-Play in Front of a No-Audience', 1962, takes place without either audience or actors, and even without any objects whatever — and thus in the imagination. A photograph in Sohm's book shows the place of the spectacle: in front of a building are rows of empty chairs — they are the only objects used in the spectacle. In front of the chairs a man is standing still on a sort of stage; he is silent. The witty script suggests that the spectacle be announced through all possible media:[39]

> No one must be told not to come. No one should be told he really shouldn't come. No one must be prevented from coming in any way whatsoever!!! But nobody must come, or there is no play. That is, if the spectators come, there is no play. And if no spectators come, there is no play either. ... I mean, one way or the other there is a play, but it is a No-Play.[40]

In 'Wind Music' — a conceptual happening by Chieko Shiomi, the orchestra sits still, wind blows scores away; this is all that occurs in the happening.[41]

The function of conceptual elements was not only to stimulate the recipient to creative effort, but also to induce him to experiences of a more general, philosophic or political nature. So for instance, John Cage's known concert "4' 33''" (throughout the time the artist sits still in front of the piano) had, in the intention of the artist, to give the public a chance to live through the specific experience inspired by Zen-Buddism.

The observation of changes the conceptual music happenings have undergone makes one suppose that their creators were in doubt whether the scarce, ascetic stimuli, mainly silence, supplied in their happenings suffice by themselves to rouse the imagination of the recipient. So, they complemented them with other elements, like plastic effects, movements, etc. The wish to use recurrently the basic idea of conceptual music may have played its role, too; therefore they enriched silence with other elements, to avoid repetition. As a result the conceptual music happenings have become increasingly visual performances. This is clearly seen, for instance, in George Maciunas' '12 Piano Compositions':

> 1. Let Piano movers carry piano into the stage. 2. Tune the piano. 3. Paint — with orange paint — patterns over piano. 4. With a straight stick the length of a keyboard sound all keys together. 5. Place a dog or cat (or both) inside the piano and play Chopin. 6. Stretch 3 highest strings with tuning key till they burst. 7. Place one piano on top of another (one can be smaller). 8. Place piano upside down and put a vase with flowers over the sound box. 9. Draw a picture of the piano so that the audience can see the picture. 10. Write 'piano composition no. 10' and show the audience the sign. 11. Wash the piano, wax and polish it well. 12. Let piano movers carry piano out of the stage.[42]

* * *

Does the happening have an aesthetic program? In manifestos and declarations appear statements which deny that the happening should realize any aesthetic values. Actually, however, such values were assumed by happeners. In promulgating them and in combating values acknowledged earlier they availed themselves as a rule — perhaps unconsciously — of argumentations camouflaged as statements of facts, explanation, substantiation, etc. Take, for instance, the acceptance of chance as a possible artistic determinant. Apart from its purely negative aspect — destruction of the established values — it also has a positive one, the acceptance of values created by chance. However, chance was not proclaimed to be a source of new aesthetic values. It was admitted only because of the view that real life is also governed by chance, and that art should assimilate real life. Frequently, argumentation took on the character of persuasion in which advantage was taken of the emotive load of linguistic expressions to combat the established values or to preach new ones.[43] Consider, for instance, the slogan: 'Abolish the artificial borderline between art and life'. This slogan covers an entire aesthetic program, relating to various fundamental aspects of the happening, like the kinds of objects to be used in the spectacle, the function of the audience, the use of actors, etc. This slogan owes its persuasive impact to negative emotional associations connected with the word 'artificial'; as if the existence of a borderline between art and life was objectively something more artificial than its lack.

The creators of happening connected with it great hope of changes, in art itself as well as in the lives of individuals and of the society. This hope is based on various assumptions about the character of reality, and the laws which govern the individual and the social life. So, for instance, great significance was ascribed by happeners to chance: chance was supposed to help abolish the obsolete conventions binding freedom of artistic expression; to release psychic inhibitions that mutilate the individual; to loosen the authoritarian patterns in interpersonal relations. These are far reaching expectations. Are they justified? Even the short historical distance which presently divides us from the peak period of happening-realizations justifies the following general evaluation: the postulates and assumptions made by happeners, if taken literally, in their extreme, glaring, sometimes contradictory formulation, have turned out to be myths which replaced the older myths abolished by the happening. There is no doubt, however, that the happening essentially influenced art as well as socio-political attitudes and phenomena.

NOTES

[1] Michael Kirby, 'An Interview on the Happening'. *Dialog* 10, 1971.
[2] Ben Vautier, poster exhibited in the Gallery Amstel 47. Amsterdam 1964.

[3] M. Kirby, *The Art of Time*. New York, 1969.
[4] Cf. Udo Kultermann, *Leben und Kunst*, Tübingen, 1970.
[5] Cf. M. Kirby, *Happenings. An Illustrated Anthology*. New York, 1965; I quote H. Sohm, *Happening und Fluxus*. Materialien zusammengestellt von H. Sohm. Köln, 1970.
[6] Happeners return here to certain tendencies in earlier art, for instance, to Schwitters, or, generally, to dadaism.
[7] Allan Kaprow, *Assemblage, Environments and Happenings*. New York, 1968, p. 167.
[8] Cf. Hanna Ptaszkowska, *Happening w Polsce* (The Happening in Poland), Współczesność, 1969.
[9] This view was maintained e.g. by Kaprow; cf. *Urszula Czartoryska, Od pop-artu do sztuki konceptualnej* (From Pop-Art to Conceptual Art), Warszawa, 1973.
[10] For instance 'Landscape Gardening Versus Living Rooms' by Miller and Cameron lasts two weeks (cf. Adrian Henri, *Environments and Happenings*. London, 1974; the action 'Asamblaż zimowy' (Winter Assemblage), arranged by the Gallery Foksal, Warsaw, has no time limit nor did it envisage any end-effect; all that is left behind are disconnected traces of activities devoid of any compositional or plot bonds.
[11] Cf. M. Kirby, Happenings. . . ,
[12] Cf. H. Sohm, *op. cit.*
[13] An extreme instance of the application of chance understood as free decision is Higgins' 'Graphis 82'. The script allows every participant to do anything he wants, and as long as he pleases. The participants are unaware of each other's intentions; everyone determines for himself the way he moves in the space of the happening.
[14] Cf. M. Kirby, Happenings. . . .
[15] In informational aesthetics a frequency has been found with which a given feature should appear in an aesthetic object to produce on the spectator the maximal effect. Cf. the chapter on informational aesthetics in this book.
[16] One can, of course, adopt a separate probability mechanism to select the set of alternatives and the probability mechanism to be used to select from the selected set of alternatives. However, this does not solve the problem, but only shifts it by one step, whereupon the initial situation repeats itself.
[17] Cf. A. Kaprow, *op. cit.* p. 176.
[18] A. Kaprow, *op. cit.* p. 176 ff.
[19] Cf. E. Lucie-Smith, *Movements in Art Since 1945*. London 1975, p. 34.
[20] Cf. Urszula Czartoryska, *op. cit.*
[21] Cf. A. Kaprow, *op. cit.*
[22] op. cit. p. 195 ff.
[23] Cf. H. Sohm, *op. cit.*
[24] Cf. M. Kirby, 'An Interview on the Happening', *op. cit.* One can gather the impression that Kirby had some doubts about counting Dali's pieces as happenings. However, I have taken them into consideration, for it is my purpose to render adequately the existing usage of the word 'happening', and not to stipulate a new meaning.
[25] A. Henri, *op. cit.* p. 101.
[26] Cf. H. Sohm, *op. cit.*
[27] I analyse varieties of expressive function in another chapter of the present book (Interpretation of Art-Works); cf. also my: *Zum Problem der Interpretation und Wertung des Ästhetischen*. Paderborn, 1977.
[28] Cf. A. Henri, *op. cit.* p. 117.

[29] Cf. A. Henri, *op. cit.* p. 114.
[30] Cf. A. Kaprow, *op. cit.* p. 194. However, Kaprow admitted a special instance where more than one performance is justified: this is when the score is designed to make every performance significantly different from the previous one.
[31] M. Kirby, 'An Interview on the Happening', *op. cit.*
[32] Cf. my *Begriffsbildung und Definition*. Berlin 1980, on conditions of formal correctness of definitions.
[33] M. Kirby, *Happenings*...; I quote A. Henri, *op. cit.* p. 86.
[34] S. Morawski, 'Happening'. *Dialog* 9, 10, 1971.
[35] The logical structure and function of such terms is the subject matter of another chapter in this book. Cf. also my: *Normen der Begriffsbildung*. Paderborn 1977.
[36] The structure and function of partial definitions is explained in detail in my: *Begriffsbildung und Definition*. Verlag de Gruyter, Berlin 1980.
[37] Cf. J. Becker, W. Vostell, *Happenings*. Reinbeck 1965, p. 46.
[38] Cf. the chapter 'Concepts with Family Meanings in the Humanities' where this question is discussed in detail.
[39] The fact that the happener renounced the performance must be made public, if it is to have any sense – this stand was firmly stressed by Filiou and other conceptual artists.
[40] Cf. H. Sohm, *op. cit.*
[41] *op. cit.*
[42] *op. cit.*
[43] The persuasive function of language and its use in the humanities and in everyday language are discussed in a separate chapter of this book.

CHAPTER VII

INTERPRETATION OF ART WORKS

Some attempt at an interpretation is involved in any more attentive contact with an art work. Sometimes the understanding comes spontaneously, as if of itself, so that the interpretational efforts remain unnoticed. It is only when one encounters difficulties in comprehension, when various persons ascribe to an art work differing meanings, that the processes of interpretation become fully conscious. What is the nature of these processes? Are particular interpretations instances of the same kind of activity? Or do they rather form a non-homogeneous set which falls under closer analysis into several sets of differing character? These problems are the subject matter of this chapter which is conceived as a study of the more important methodological problems concerned with interpretation of art works.

Let us consider two examples of interpretation. One concerns a sculpture by Alina Szapocznikow entitled 'Dervish', 1960. In the other the author makes use of psychoanalysis to explain a particular instance of a certain literary motif—namely the death of Hamlet's father. In the former case, A. Zielinski writes:

The sculpture by Alina Szapocznikow has much in common with the painter's conceptions of space, both being interested in unveiling the structure of matter. We have the impression of looking at a primitive material form which has not yet received its final shape, but is still being shaped while rotating in space and changing itself in this motion.[1]

Discussing the ways in which Shakespeare modifies a motif already known in earlier English literature, Ernest Jones states:

To the unconscious, 'poison' signifies any bodily fluid charged with evil intent, while the serpent has played a well-known role ever since the Garden of Eden. The murderous assault had therefore both aggressive and erotic components, and we note that it was Shakespeare who introduced the latter [serpent]. Furthermore, that the ear is an unconscious equivalent for anus is a matter for which I have adduced ample evidence elsewhere.... Hamlet himself, as Freud pointed out long ago, was unconsciously identified with Claudius, which was the reason why he was unable to denounce and kill him. So the younger brother attacking the older is simply a replica of the son-father conflict, and the complicated poisoning story really represents the idea of the son castrating his father.[2]

Jones further asks why in Shakespeare's drama an old simple story of envious ambition has been given such an extraordinary shape. In his answer he maintains that homosexual elements can also be found in other Shakespeare's plays as well as in Shakespeare's personality; that Shakespeare wrote Hamlet to give outlet to tremendous emotional tensions which were aroused in him as a result of betrayal on the part of persons whom he loved.

The above examples of interpretation differ in several important respects. In the first example, directly observable qualities and structures in the art work and their similarity to some processes in the material world are taken as the grounds of interpretation. In the second example, qualities directly observable in the interpreted art work—strings of inscriptions or sounds—do not play the same role as in the case of sculpture, and their interpretation is based on a principle different from that of similarity of appearance to some external phenomena. In the interpretation of sculpture, no reference is made—at least explicitly—to the intention of the artist; such reference is especially important in this interpretation of Shakespeare's drama. To come to his conclusions Jones has to assume psychoanalysis, i.e. a certain scientific theory. No such theory is assumed in the interpretation of sculpture, or, even if some theoretical conception is alluded to, it plays only a marginal role, not to be compared with the role psychoanalysis plays in the interpretation of Hamlet. The interpretation of sculpture contains no reference to the situation of the artist or to his needs; this, however, occurs in the interpretation of Hamlet. The interpretation of Hamlet contains also an attempt at an explanation, i.e. at finding causes which brought about changes in the known literary motif; no such attempt is present in the interpretation of the sculpture.

The two examples here adduced, chosen from many other, methodologically similar examples, show that the set of activities named as interpretation is non-homogeneous.

In what follows, the process of interpretation in the sense considered here as the fundamental one is analysed. Three constitutive elements of this process are distinguished: 1. the formal, 2. the semantic, and 3. the emotional. Further, procedures used to substantiate interpretation are discused. Attention is also drawn to some other uses of 'interpretation'; among others to the causal one. Also, some methodological problems which arise in this connection are discussed.

Before we proceed further it is well to notice that certain constituents of interpretation may not be present in the interpretation of some contemporary art. This is a consequence of recent changes in the very conception of art. Thus, for example, some creators of happenings, environments, or assemblages deny that their compositions are to form homogeneous, unique structures. On the contrary, the order of their constitutive elements can be changed, some of the elements can be omitted or new elements added, without any detrimental effect on the work. Similarly, some contemporary authors declare that their works do not have any semantic or emotive functions. Of course, the interpretation of such art-works lacks the corresponding elements. The above remarks show that both the concept of art and the concept of art-interpretation have undergone a parallel evolution which has turned them into concepts with family-meanings. The extension of such a concept does not comprise a homogeneous set of objects characterized by an assembly of properties possessed by all elements of the set and only by them. On the contrary, it consists of a number of subsets bound by only partial similarities, due to which they form a family of extensions. Such concepts can often be found in the humanities. Their logical structure and function is a subject of discussion in a separate chapter of this book.[3]

INTERPRETATION OF ART WORKS IN THE FUNDAMENTAL UNDERSTANDING OF THE WORD

The phrase 'interpretation of an art work' in the sense which can be acknowledged as the fundamental one refers to a complex psychic process by way of which the subject becomes aware of values contained in the work, arrives at an understanding of it and lives through a specific emotional reaction. The same phrase is alternatively used to denote the verbal expression of this process. There arises then the difficult question of whether it is possible to find an adequate language counterpart for all elements of the psychic process. Of course, the above loose description is not a definition of interpretation; no attempt at a definition is here intended. Instead, constitutive elements of the process of interpretation will be distinguished which can provide a starting point for future definition. As stated above, the process of interpretation contains three elements: the formal, the semantic and the emotional. Such differentiation is possible only by way of intellectual analysis. Actually, these elements are plaited closely together and always occur simultaneously.

THE FORMAL CONSTITUENT OF INTERPRETATION

An art work consists of stimuli to sensuous perception. Inscriptions, lines, spots of colour, lights, surfaces, solid bodies, sounds, rhythms, motions are the simplest elements of which art works are constructed. It is not an easy task to say precisely what basic elements constitute a work of art. The answer depends upon such factors as the kind of art to which the work properly belongs, the historical period in which it was made, its style, its semantic or expressive functions, etc. So, for instance, depending on such circumstances we might consider the basic elements in a musical composition to be its themes, or motifs, simpler than themes, or dodecaphonic series, or even—e.g. in contemporary music—other elements, including individual sounds. A systematic analysis of factors which we take into account in the process of interpretation—while decomposing an art work into its basic elements or, inversely, constructing of those elements complex wholes—has not yet been carried out.[4]

The role the basic elements play in those arts which operate mainly with language signs is different from their role in plastic and visual arts, in ballet or music. Strings of inscriptions or their phonetic counterparts have an aesthetic value of their own, independently of their eventual meanings, as it was clearly manifested in Dadaist poetry. However, the main source of their aesthetic value lies in their semantic function. In other branches of art those basic, sensuous elements are a very important—sometimes the sole—underpinning for aesthetic values. Independently of this difference, the factor present in the interpretation of all kinds of art works consists in discerning their basic elements and the rules of joining them into complex structures. As examples of such structures, composed in accordance with rules characteristic of various styles, one could instance a dadaistic poem, a sonata in the classical style, an impressionistic painting.

In joining[5] the basic elements into complex wholes we assume definite presuppositions and rules. The problem why these and not other assumptions have been made does not, however, belong to interpretation itself, but to its substantiation. I shall later have occasion to return to this question. At this point it suffices to indicate that the operation of forming complex structures out of the basic elements may be governed by assumptions relating not only to the form of the art work, but also to its contents. However, the latter kind of assumptions are taken into account only in so far as they determine the form of the work rather than its semantic function. This can easily be seen from the previously given examples of complex structures. On the other hand, to identify certain complex wholes such as a realistic novel, a symphonic poem, or an impressionistic landscape, we would have to refer to some semantic rules as factors which determine the contents of those wholes.

With regard to contemporary art works the reconstruction of a complex structure from the basic elements is often not a unique operation; its results vary with particular realizations of a given work. A similar phenomenon of formal ambiguity is well known. For instance, individual performances of a symphony by Brahms under different conductors will differ, although all are in accordance with the score. However, the differences result here from the fact that musical notation does not provide means for a unique prescription of the way of performing. In contemporary art, instead, some aspects of an art work are purposely left undetermined by the artist, and are thus intentionally ambiguous. As an example we can point to some compositions by Witold Lutoslawski in which the composer applied a technique described by him as the loosening of time-relations between sounds, and later known as limited aleatorism. This technique provides for a margin of freedom in execution of certain details, mainly rhythmical ones, within the framework of a precisely composed whole. Because of this, each performance of an aleatoric composition can be enriched by additional artistic effects: for instance the irregularity and complexity of rhythmic details which evoke the impression of richness, so characteristic of Lutoslawski's aleatoric compositions.

These artistic effects are achieved without increasing the complexity of the score or the difficulty of performance. Similar examples of formal ambiguity can also be found in other branches of contemporary art. Such art abounds in changeable compositions of various kinds whose changeability has a certain margin of freedom, sometimes generated by a probabilistic mechanism.[6] Examples of such art works can be found in collections of modern art. They include also works of graphic art. The Swiss journal *GRAPHIS* once reproduced a poster designed in blacks and whites with round holes scattered irregularly throughout the surface. These holes turned into spots of varying colours, depending on the background against which the poster happened to be placed. Thus with every change of the background the poster is transformed into a different graphic-colouristic whole.

THE SEMANTIC CONSTITUENT OF INTERPRETATION

In semantic interpretation we strive to read the message carried by an art work. The following are the most often mentioned semantic functions of art work: meaning, denoting, depicting, symbolizing, expressing. An art work performs these functions on the strength of certain relations which refer the work to some objects, phenomena, or experiences. These relations are of a varying character. They may consist in a similarity of some directly perceptible features; or else in more complicated correspondences between proportions, or between certain aspects of an art work and some experiences or dispositions. All these bonds may be supplemented by a convention which stipulates a relation between the sign and the represented object. Depending on the kind of the relation, various types of signs are differentiated, e.g. iconic signs, symbolic signs, language signs.

An art work or its constituent often functions as a sign on the strength of several relations simultaneously. An example is the above quoted interpretation of Hamlet in which, in addition to their usual sense, language signs carry the meanings given to them within the framework of psychoanalytic theory. Good examples are also supplied by surrealistic art. Another kind of ambiguity can be found in situations when a given sign is repeated in many art works and each time receives a different meaning depending on the contex, on the character of a larger whole in which the sign appears. The image of a rose exemplifies such ambiguity in painting. Depending on the age, sex, or facial expression of the person represented in the painting, a rose painted beside the figure may symbolize beauty, love, or friendship; but may also signify the transience of life.[7] The meaning of the sign changes because each time different features of the rose are selected as the basis of relation between the sign and the represented object. And each time the selection is determined by the context in which the sign appears.

Much has been written about methodological problems which arise in connection with the interpretation of art works; and unquestionably results have been achieved in this field.[8] However, the problem is far from being exhausted. Thus, for instance, the typology of various relations holding in art between signs and the represented objects or phenomena should be systematically worked out. This would provide grounds for a new classification of signs useful for purposes of semantic analysis of art. General theory of signs (semiotics) can be of great help in carrying out this task.[9] With the aid of semiotics it will be possible to show that all types of relations which in art works connect sign with their denotations are particular cases of the relation described within this theory by the general definition of sign. Those concepts will also serve to differentiate within the semantic layer of an art work its various constitutive elements and to analyse their function in the work. They may likewise help to solve the still controversial problems of semantic interpretation or at least to give those problems a more precise formulation.

There seem to exist important analogies between the formal and semantic constituents of interpretation and the science of logical syntax and semantics. The application of concepts and methods of this science to the problems of art interpretation may bring interesting results.

In discussions of those problems reference is frequently made to the concept of artistic expression. This concept happens to be used in different meanings which are often mixed.

1. One speaks of expression when the artist avails himself of artistic means in order to communicate to the recipients either his own experiences or the experiences of the characters presented in his art work.

2. Sometimes 'expression' refers to an unintended and often even unconscious revealation in an art work of the emotions, dispositions, or needs of the artist. As a rule certain general interdependencies of a psychological or sociological type are here explicitly or tacitly assumed. It is only with regard to such assumptions that an art work can be said to express something in the sense here described. Without these assumptions such a statement would be unfounded. The interpretation of Hamlet can here again be used as an illustration.

3. The word 'expression' has yet another meaning when it refers to the use of artistic means to evoke in the recipients definite experiences. The word 'impression' or perhaps 'evocation' seems in this case to be more suitable.

4. Sometimes an artist is said to have expressed something when he has communicated his experiences to the recipients in order to evoke in them similar experiences. 'Expression' so understood connects in itself the first and the third of the above differentiated meanings.

5. The term 'expression' refers, finally, to the ability of an art work to evoke in the recipients certain experiences independently of whether or not this was intended by the artist. Here also the term 'impression' seems to be more appropriate, or perhaps some other term might be employed to differentiate the present meaning from the sense registered under point (3). Under the present meaning the ability of an art work to evoke certain experiences does not depend on the intention of the artist. This ability follows from some general, empirically testable causal relationships which govern the effects produceable in the recipients by the form and contents of art works. It is, of course, possible that such effects can be modified by changes in psychological, social, or historical conditions. Appropriate researches may help to discover the general laws of this changeability.

Numerous pronouncements by art critics, art theoreticians, and by artists themselves testify how important and topical is the problem of expression. These pronouncements are often controversial. It is worth while to refer here to an interesting opinion of Paul Hindemith on the subject of musical expression. Hindemith decidedly rejects the conviction that music expresses emotions. He explains the origin of this conviction by reducing it to a collective mystification whose mechanism he describes as follows. The composer notices that various juxtapositions of sounds evoke in the listeners definite emotions. By repeating such juxtapositions he reinforces his initial perception until finally he himself begins to believe that the experiences evoked by his music are his own experiences. The performer in his turn hears about emotions with which the composer has allegedly filled his music. However, having analyzed the composition he is unable to find any. He therefore considers it his duty to fill up the gap and strives to cram into the composition the world of emotions roaming in his mind. The listener, at last, who does not know of the composer's illusions or of the performer's manipulations, and who thus believes that music expresses emotions, finds it proper to experience them.[10]

In this argument the term 'expression' is used in several of our formerly differentiated meanings, but these meanings are not kept distinct. The various premises and the conclusion of this argument may turn out to be true when one sense of 'expression' is assumed, and false when another is employed. To make the argument logically correct, one would have to decide clearly in which sense the word 'expression' is to be used and then stick to it throughout. Let us add that if this were done, the statements contained in the argument would turn into empirical hypotheses testable by way of suitable research.

With reference to Hindemith's argument the following additional remark suggests itself. Contrary to Hindemith's intention, empirical facts presented in his argument can be used to support the conclusion that music is expressive. Namely, by observing the emotional experiences which repeatedly occur as reactions to given juxtapositions of sounds composers and recipients of music would gradually arrive at a conscious decision to ascribe these juxtapositions the function of expressing those emotions. By so doing they would pass from the purely causal understanding of 'expression'—the fifth of the differentiated meanings—to the first or the third sense, each of which contains the element of conscious intention of expression. This kind of passage can be found in all cases when a constant relationship discovered between some two phenomena is later turned, on the strength of convention or custom, into the indicator relation.

In the realm of science the ambiguity of statements is looked upon as a deficiency which should rather be avoided. It is not so in the arts. Here the ambiguities and reticences which leave room for varied interpretations of the semantic layer of an art work and stimulate the recipient to such interpretative efforts are counted among values of high rank, characteristic of a good work. Ambiguities and reticences contained in an art work create for the recipient a barrier. In order to overcome it, he is compelled to a greater intellectual effort which deepens and enriches the meanings he is able to bring out in his act of interpretation. There are, however, art works in which the ambiguity is misused. This occurs, for instance, in some films of low artistic value; by resorting to a complicated montage technique the directors strive to create the impression of deepness and richness of content. Such montage technique makes it difficult to grasp even the simplest facts. When in the end the recipient succeeds in ordering the scattered scenes into a whole, it becomes clear to him that these formal complications cover the poverty of substance. Thus, one of the important achievements of contemporary film—a specific montage technique—is reduced to a caricature of itself and used for purposes discordant with its original intention.

Ambiguity contributes to the richness of meanings carried in an art work. However, this value is in conflict with the work's clarity and its comprehensibility. It seems to be impossible to indicate the optimum between these two extremes, unless one is ready to pay the price of an arbitrary stipulation. It is an interesting task, instead, to discern those types of ambiguity which are credited with high artistic value.

The foregoing remarks testify that the recipient has, in a sense, his share in the creation of the perceived art work. For, the final shape of the work as moulded by his act of perception has the stamp of his personality, depends on the richness of his experiences, on his dispositions, on the amount of effort put into the understanding. Marcel Proust writes:

After a certain age all our associations interweave so closely that the object of which we think or the book we read are of no importance any more. We imbue everything with ourselves, everything is fruitful . . . and soap commercials can induce us to discoveries equally precious as those induced by Pascal's *Pensées*.[11]

THE EMOTIONAL CONSTITUENT OF INTERPRETATION

Two constitutive elements of interpretation have hitherto been distinguised: the formal and the semantic. We shall now proceed to discuss the third element which consists in the proper emotional response to qualities and values present in the perceived art work.[12] By including this element the author takes sides with that conception of interpretation which sees it as an act of double cognitive-emotional character and not as a purely cognitive one.[13]

This conception is supported by insights gained through reflection on cases in which the understanding of art, and especially of contemporary art, has met with difficulties. An average recipient of asemantic compositions in contemporary painting, sculpture or music often declares that he does not understand them. When asked, he readily acknowledges the formal qualities and values contained in such compositions, however, as he says, they do not appeal to him, they leave him indifferent. The absence of proper emotional reaction is here the cause of his inability to understand.

Artists themselves repeatedly stress the important role played by emotional reaction in the understanding of art. Here is a characteristic pronouncement which originates with August Endell, an eminent artist of the Art Nouveau period.

Forms and colours produce in us without mediation . . . a certain emotional effect. . . . Whoever has learnt to yield completely to his impressions, without any associations, any accompanying thoughts, he who has but once sensed the emotional impact of forms and colours, will find them to be a never failing source of extraordinary and unanticipated pleasure. It is, indeed, a new world that reveals itself. And it should be an experience in everybody's life when his comprehension of these things begins to awaken. It is like an intoxication, like a craze, coming over us. Joy threatens to destroy us. He who has not experienced this, will never grasp the meaning of art.[14]

Reflection on the social reception of art leads to the conclusion that it is more difficult to develop the ability to grasp the formal qualities present in an art work, and to respond to those qualities with proper emotional reaction, than the ability to read the message carried by the work. This holds not only with reference to the general public, but to art critics as well. As a rule, in their reviews they discuss only the content of art works, their social and moral function, etc., neglecting wholly their formal aspects and the artistic craftsmanship. The difficulties people experience in grasping the formal qualities of art come to light especially clearly in contacts with contemporary asemantic art.[15] His contacts with such art bring to a less cultivated recipient little satisfaction; for he is unable to take delight in the beauty of form, and he does not find the meanings which he was accustomed to look for in his former contacts with Old Masters. The inclination to seek, above all, the content of art works, an inclination acquired from earlier experiences, creates an additional hindrance to a fully developed aesthetic satisfaction. This difficulty does not appear, or is not so great, in such domains of the arts as music, which has always, historically as well as today, abounded in works of asemantic character. The proper understanding of contemporary music has been made difficult mainly by the extreme difference of formal and sound qualities in earlier and in present day music.

Obstacles of a different kind hinder the understanding of contemporary art works with semantic elements. The cause lies mainly in the abstract character of the ideas expressed in those works. Space constructs and space relations, time and movement, are often themes in present day art. The very titles of such compositions: 'Rotation', 'Penetrations', 'Microstructures', 'Forms in three-dimensional space'—to mention only a few—indicate their abstract character.

One might end the foregoing remarks with the following conclusion. Contemporary art develops much faster than the ability of the general public to understand it. This is one of the very many undesirable consequences of growing specialization. It creates a real problem for the artist as well as for the society as a whole.

INTERPRETATION AND ITS SUBSTANTIATION

The conclusions we arrive at as a result of formal and semantic interpretation are based on two kinds of data: internal and external. The first derive from the observation and analysis of art works themselves. In the second we make use of certain accepted rules and assumptions. In what follows I shall discuss the external evidence and the methodological problems which arise in this connection.

When formal interpretation of an art work leads us to conclude that the work exhibits a structure with definite stylistic features, we take for granted—tacitly or explicitly—a number of assumptions. It is only when these assumptions are added to observations of the work itself that our conclusion is justified. These assumptions characterize the basic elements of which the work consists and the rules of joining them together into a complex whole. Here are some examples: The impressionist rules of how to lay on the paints; The neo-impresionist principle of splitting the local colour into contrasting points—it is only in the eyes of a perceiver that these points mix together to form a homogeneous colour; The relevant statements of the physics of colour and the psychology of colour, on which the above principle is based; The rules of linear perspective; The rules of cubist space; The characteristic of figurative variations in music; The principles of montage technique in the films of the French 'New Wave'.

Sometimes these assumptions are formulated explicitly by the artist himself, as is the case with dodecaphonic music whose principles were laid out by its creator, Arnold Schönberg. Most often, however, it is the task of critics and theoreticians of art to reconstruct them by way of analyses and comparison of particular art works, supported by remarks and commentaries made by the artists themselves, and by any other relevant knowledge. The process of reconstruction consists of a series of attempts at an interpretation. On the basis of initial observations, hypothetical assumptions and rules are formulated which are subsequently verified and corrected by the procedure of trial and error. This is undoubtedly one of the most fascinating tasks in the theory of art. And one of the most difficult, too. It is well to remember that many artists have never accepted such reconstructions made with regard to their works. Pablo Picasso is here an expressive example.

Let us now turn to the semantic interpretation. Its assumptions have diverse methodological character. They include, first of all, semantic conventions, or less explicit customs, due to which various aspects of art works function as signs. Reconstruction of these is not an easy task at all. They have to be traced in customs prevailing in a given epoch, milieu, or social group. They may be characteristic of a single artist or only of a single art work. It is then necessary to take into consideration all works by a given artist and also all information which could possibly help us to understand the message contained in this work.

Those assumptions which arise from statements of various scientific disciplines like biology, psychology, or sociology have a different methodological status. In the quoted interpretation of Hamlet the assumptions derive from psychoanalysis. They ascribe to certain words or acts the additional function of psychoanalytic symbols.

Another kind of assumption is formed by theorems of philosophic or religious systems. Such assumptions have played an important role in establishing the semantic function of art works in many epochs and parts of the world. The most elaborate system of meanings developed along these lines can be found in the religious art of the Middle Ages.[16]

A separate group is made up of assumptions which refer to the intention of the artists, meaning those intentions which relate to the work itself and not to external circumstances, such as the pursuit of profit or fame. To find out what were in fact the intentions of an artist is usually a difficult task, even with regard to the present, not to mention the past.[17] The empirical grounds for such conclusions are supplied primarily by art works themselves; however, they have to be supplemented by external sources, e.g. remarks and commentaries stemming from artists, or information about artists preserved in documents. We have to remember that there are no simple, infallible methods of reasoning which lead from the above mentioned data to conclusions about the artist's intentions. On the contrary, the methodological structure of such reasonings is complicated and their character as well as their conclusive force are still a matter of controversy. Besides, there arises the question of what purpose is served by this difficult enterprise. If its purpose is simply to help us to understand art works, then the following critical remark suggests itself with regard to the usefulness of such help. The understanding of meanings, and the reconstruction of intentions, are both based on the same empirical data. The ascertaining of intentions brings, therefore, no information which could not be deduced directly from those data, and thus seems to be dispensable. Of course, the situation is different when we can ask an artist for additional information, other than that contained in his work or in his earlier pronouncements.

There exist two conflicting views as to the possible interpretations of art works. According to one of them, only interpretations which accord with the intention of the artist are admissible. The followers of the other view maintain that this limitation deprives the work of such content-elements which, although present in the work, have not been consciously recognized by the artist, or else have been projected into the work by tradition. "Asking us to interpret Hamlet only in terms of what the very hypothetical views of Shakespeare or his audience were is asking us to forget three hundred years of history. It prohibits us to use the insights of a Goethe or Coleridge, it impoverishes a work which has attracted and accumulated meanings in the course of history.[18] Let us leave as an open problem the question of whether the diversity and changeability of interpretations is admissible only within the bounds marked by ambiguities and reticences present in the work, or whether it can transgress those bounds. Are interpretations discordant with the style, the epoch, or the alleged intention of the artist admissible? In what sense can they be qualified as 'correct' or 'faulty'? What are the bounds of arbitrariness?

SOME METHODOLOGICAL PROBLEMS

An act of interpretation may give the interpreter the feeling of having understood. However, such feeling does not always appear. On the other hand, a superficial contact with an art work, although deviating widely from the proper interpretation, may nonetheless evoke the impression that one has understood, an impression which is sometimes registered with great force. A critical observer may be prone to remark that this is only an illusory feeling and not a result of real understanding. This opinion, however correct it may be, does not change the facts. The existence of such situations provides grounds for differentiating between two kinds of interpretations: pragmatic and methodological. The first refers to a procedure which gives the interpreting person the feeling of understanding. This concept of interpretation is a relative one, for it contains a relativization to the interpreting person. The course of interpretation and its constitutive elements may in each particular case be different. It is also obvious that a procedure which brings one person the feeling of understanding may not give it to another one.

On the other hand, the methodological concept of interpretation is not a relative one. The content of this concept remains the same for all possible interpreters and forms an ideal model of conduct. The concept of interpretation which has here been discussed—interpretation in the fundamental sense—has the character of an ideal methodological standard.

Particular examples of interpretations often deflect from the ideal model. The deviation may consist in omitting a particular step in interpretation, or in its superficial and incomplete realization; or else some conclusions may have been drawn without proper substantiation, on the basis of only vague feelings, etc. In this connection some authors differentiate between amateur and specialist interpretations; the latter being carried out with the aid of research procedures which secure the maximum possible fulness, precision and justification.[19] In view of the universality of amateur interpretation it is an interesting and socially important task to analyze its structure and to ascertain its methodological value.

More attention must also be paid to the linguistic problems of interpretation.[20] It is urgent and important task to improve on the conceptual apparatus of aesthetics and art theory. This, in turn, will make it possible to formulate the problems of those disciplines in a better and more precise way, and will thus help to solve them.

In describing art works we often use terms in their metaphorical and analogical sense. We speak, for instance, about the colour of an orchestral composition, about dry and rich sounds or colours, we perceive some colours as quiet or aggressive, as flat or deep. In addition to purely descriptive terms like red, curved, dismembered, we use expressions of purely evaluative or descriptive-evaluative character: beautiful, magnificent, colouristically refined, softened, rich in content, gloomy, repellent, obsolete, etc. It would be an important and theoretically interesting task to carry out a semantic analysis of expressions used in methaphorical and evaluative senses, to ascertain their empirical content, and to formulate more precise criteria for their application.[21] Also, the possibility of using ostensive definitions to establish the meaning of words which refer to directly observable features of art works should be considered.[22]

What is the relation between interpretation of an art work and its evaluation? A complete interpretation carried out in accordance with the standard outlined here seems to supply sufficient grounds for a justified value judgement[23] Is such interpretation also a necessary condition, or should we rather recognize certain other procedures as leading to justified value judgements, too?

It is an interesting empirical problem to find out whether there is an interdependence between an evaluative attitude taken with regard to an art work and the course of the subsequently undertaken interpretation of this work. Also, the relation between interpretation and aesthetic experience requires scrutiny. Is such experience always a part of an interpretation, or may it also appear independently?

OTHER CONCEPTS OF INTERPRETATION

In addition to the meaning which has been here characterized as the fundamental one, the term 'interpretation' has also some other meanings.

Some authors tend to limit the content of this concept to its semantic constituent. They seem to presuppose tacitly that only the content of art work can be the subject of understanding; at the same time they reduce interpretation to understanding.[24] This view does not seem to be justified. For one thing, the processes of understanding play their role in perceiving not only the content, but also the form of an art work. Besides, the exclusion of the emotional constituent from among the definitive features of interpretation would make this concept inapplicable to the analysis of art reception. This holds especially true with regard to the reception of contemporary asemantic art. As was stated earlier, with regard to such art the lack of understanding often has its source in the absence of emotional response.

According to another conception the content of the term 'interpretation' should include not only the three constituents here differentiated, but in addition also the substantiation of interpretation. This view seems likewise to be untenable. When we undertake an interpretation of an art work, we strive to find out what formal, semantic and emotional qualities are contained in the work. The justification of our findings does not belong to interpretation, but to its substantiation.

The last differentiation is associated with another distinction, sometimes to be found in aesthetic texts, namely that between internal and external interpretation.[25] The first has its grounds exclusively in the qualities present in the work itself; the second has recourse to some external factors. However, this division is not sufficiently clear or consequent. For, after a closer scrutiny the examples quoted as allegedly internal interpretation turn out to be operations in which reference is made not only to the properties of the work itself, but also to certain assumptions, e.g. to semantic or formal rules. To be sure, those rules are accepted in the milieu where the work has arisen, but they are not present in the work itself. The possibility of differentiating precisely between internal and external interpretation, as well as the scientific usefulness of such a division, require further methodological analysis.

Let us in turn consider a meaning of 'interpretation' which can be referred to as causal interpretation. To interpret an art work causally means to point out causes which conditioned its formal and semantic features. To explain various properties of art works recourse has been made to factors of a psychological nature as well as psychiatric, social, economic, biological, geographic, meteorological and physical factors. The controversies among the followers of those theories are well known. Likewise known is the dispute between the monistic stand which reduces causation to only one factor, considered as the only, or the 'most important' cause, and the pluralistic stand in which many 'equally important' causes are admitted. The resolution of this controversy is made more difficult through the ambiguity of the term 'cause'. It may denote a sufficient or a necessary condition, a necessary constituent of a given sufficient condition, a condition which causes the effect with a certain probability, or still other kinds of conditions.[26] These complicated and difficult problems are far from receiving a satisfactory solution. Their solution in the future depends on the introduction of new research methods which can cope with the variables involved, variables which are both numerous and difficult to grasp.

One cannot omit from these remarks the conception of interpretation as performance—performance of a musical composition, of a drama or ballet, etc. This meaning of interpretation seems to diverge widely from those considered earlier, yet there is a close connection between them. For, performance must be preceded by and based on interpretation in the fundamental sense here distinguished. Interpretation of an art work discovers and enhances its formal and semanic values which are subsequently rendered in the performance.

I shall always remember the experience I once lived through when listening to Shostakovitch's First Violin Concerto: Roshdestvensky was conducting. He conceived the final fragment of the composition as a dialogue, full of dramatic tension, between the violin and the tuba with the muffled orchestra in the background: the despairing, spasmodic lamentation of the violin defied the gloomy, massive, menacing roar of the tuba.

NOTES

[1] A. Zieliński, *O widzeniu artystycznym*, *(On Artistic Vision)*, p. 90. Warszawa, 1966.
[2] E. Jones, 'The Death of Hamlet's Father'. In: W. Phillips (ed.) *Art and Psychoanalysis*, p. 148 ff. Cleveland, 1963.
[3] Cf. the chapters: 'Concepts with Family-meanings in the Humanities'. Features of happenings and the structure of the corresponding concept are discussed in the chapter: 'The Concept of Happening'.
[4] What is here meant is not the physical process of joining or decomposing, but the intellectual one which takes place in an act of interpretation.
[5] Compare the remark in note 4.
[6] Various functions and uses of probability in the arts are differentiated in the chapter: 'The Concept of Happening'.
[7] Cf. Goran Hermeren, *Representation and Meaning is the Visual Arts*, p. 16. Lund, 1969.
[8] In the Polish literature various methodological aspects of art-interpretation have been discussed by, among others, R. Ingarden, S. Ossowski, W. Tatarkiewicz and M. Wallis. The world literature on the subject comprises a vast number of books.
[9] There is a large number of papers in the world literature of the subject. In the Polish literature see e.g. J. Kotarbińska, 'Pojęcie znaku' (The Concept of Sign), *Studia Logica*, VI, 1957. J. Kmita, *Z metodologicznych problemów interpretacji humanistycznej (Some Methological Problems of interpretation in the Humanities)*, Warszawa, 1971; J. Pelc, 'Meaning as an Instrument'. In: J. Pelc (ed.) 'Studies in Functional Logical Semiotics'. Janua Linguarum, Series Minor, 90, The Hague–Paris, 1971.
[10] Paul Hindemith, 'Musik–keine Gefühlskunst'. *Melos*, nr. 1, 1960.
[11] M. Proust, *Remembrance of Things Past*.
[12] It seems warranted to distinguish between proper and improper emotional reactions to an art work. Compare in this respect the chapter: Beauty and its socio-psychological determinants.
[13] Compare, however, the earlier remarks (p. 145) on recent changes in the conception of art and the parallel changes in the concept of art interpretation.
[14] August Endell, *Um die Schönheit*. 1896.
[15] The question of whether there exist art works entirely devoid of semantic elements is controversial. However, even one who acknowledges the existence of such purely asemantic works may nonetheless argue that interpretation of these works contains a certain cognitive act, different from the acts which serve to grasp the formal aspects of art; this act amounts to the statement that there are no semantic elements in such works.
[16] Cf. e.g. M. Wallis, 'Sztuka średniowieczna jako język' (Medieval Art as Language). *Studia Estetyczne*, 1965.

ART INTERPRETATION 161

[17] Compare the remarks on intentional kitsch contained in the chapter: 'The Concept of Kitsch'.
[18] René Wellek, *Concepts of Criticism*, p. 16 ff. New Haven 1963.
[19] With regard to the differentiation between amateur and specialist interpretations compare: H. Lützeler, 'Die außerwissenschaftliche Kunsterfahrung'. *Jahrbuch für Ästhetik und allgemeine Kunstwissenschaft*, VII, 1962.
[20] Some of these problems are discussed in the following books: *Aesthetics and Language, a collection of papers*, Oxford, 1959; Nelson Goodman, *Languages of Art*, London, Oxford Univ. Press, 1959.
[21] The inquiries into the metaphoric function of language are only in their initial phase. Here are some of the papers relevant for the aesthetic use of metaphor: J. J. A. Moij, *A Study of Metaphor*, Amsterdam 1976; M. B. Hesse, 'The Explanatory Function of Metaphor'. In: Yehoshua Bar-Hillel (ed.) *Logic Methodology and Philosophy of Science*, Amsterdam, 1965; M. Black, *Models and Metaphors*, 1962; J. Kmita, 'O wartości poznawczej dzieła literackiego' (On the Cognitive value of a Literary Work), *Studia Filozoficzne* No. 1, 1963; M. Przełęcki 'O metaforze w filozofii' (On Metaphor in Philosophy), in: *Moralność i społeczeństwo. Księga Jubileuszowa dla Marii Ossowskiej* (Morals and Society. Papers Dedicated to Maria Ossowska), Warsaw, 1969;
[22] Cf. e.g. J. Kotarbińska, 'On Ostensive Definitions'. *Philosophy of Science*, 27, 1960.
[23] A Thorough understanding of an art work seems to be the foundation of a justified evaluation of it. This holds especially with regard to such conceptions of aesthetic value judgments which ascribe to them truth value. Compare in this respect the chapter: Beauty and its socio-psychological determinants.
[24] It would take a separate paper to analyse the concept of understanding—one of the fundamental and at the same time very vague and ambiguous concepts of social and cultural sciences. Classical analyses of this concept can be found in the works of Dilthey, Rickert and Spranger. This concept continues to draw the attention of contemporary researchers; cf. e.g. Dina Sztejnbarg, 'Rozumienie i wyjaśnianie w doktrynach Diltheya i Sprangera'. (Understanding and explaining in the doctrines of Dilthey and Spranger), *Kwartalnik Psychologiczny* VII, 1935; S. Ossowski, *Die Besonderheiten der Sozialwissenschaften*, Frankfurt-am-Main, 1973; cf. also: H. Albert, E. Topitsch, (Hrsg.), *Wissenschaftslehre und Gesellschaft*, Darmstadt 1971; H. Albert, *Plaedoyer für krytischen Rationalismus*, München 1973; 3. Aufl.; E. Topitsch, *Vom Ursprung und Ende der Metaphysik*, Wien 1958.
[25] Cf. e.g. Ingo Seidler, 'The Iconolatric Fallacy: On the Limitations of the Internal Method of Criticism', *Journal of Aesthetics and Art Criticism*, 26, 1967.
[26] For explanation of these concepts see. T. Kotarbiński, *Paraxiology*, Oxford, 1965.

CHAPTER VIII

BEAUTY AND ITS SOCIO-PSYCHOLOGICAL DETERMINANTS

Aesthetic experiences sometimes find their external expression in value judgements. It is a fact that these are changeable and differ widely. It often happens that a particular listener or viewer changes his evaluation of an art work under the influence of various factors. Divergency of opinions also occur among different members of an audience. This diversity in appreciation is the ground for two opposing views on the nature of aesthetic value judgements, known as subjectivism and objectivism. Until recently the dispute between them was conducted mainly on philosophical grounds, with occasional reference to some general observations of a psychological or sociological character.

Now a certain stock of knowledge has been collected which makes it possible to view these questions in a new light. One should mention here, first of all, the achievements of the psychology and sociology of art and also studies of the psychological and physiological phenomena of perception.

Everyday observations gathered over the years, and supported by the results of present research, allow us to isolate a series of factors which influence the course of aesthetic experiences and the evaluation of beautiful objects.[1] Among these factors are biological, psychological and cultural ones. Frequent contacts with and knowledge of art, as well as the mood of an audience, and their being rested or tired, are all of immense importance; and so are the immediate conditions of perception and the quality of performance, in the case of music, theatre or ballet. The list of factors is not exhaustive and I doubt whether an exhaustive list could ever be completed. For it is not a problem to be solved by merely logico-semantical analyses, no matter how penetrating they may be. It is only on the basis of empirical investigations that such a list could gradually be elaborated without, however, the certainty of completing it. In what follows I discuss chosen examples of how such factors influence our perception and evaluation of art works, limiting myself to examples taken from the psychology and sociology of music. I shall only sample the results and data which we possess in this area, a complete presentation is neither necessary nor possible. I will also omit any critical analysis of these results. Instead I will consider what bearing they may have on the dispute between subjectivism and objectivism in the question of aesthetic value judgements. Finally I will present my own conception of aesthetic value judgement.

PSYCHO-SOCIAL CAUSES OF THE VARIABILITY OF VALUE JUDGEMENTS

Training

One of the main themes in contemporary psychology is the process of learning and its role in the life of the individual and the society. The importance of these processes for cognition is emphasized in psychology:

> ... one must first reject the widely held though incorrect conception that the human mind reflects external phenomena in a way similar to that of a mirror. The human mind is incapable of receiving and registering anything without the appropriate introductory training. One could paradoxically say that we are capable of seeing only that which we have once seen and of doing only that which we have once done.[2]

The cognitive processes form an important constituent of any aesthetic experience. Thus it is understandable that researchers strive to ascertain their influence on the perception and evaluation of works of art, and upon the development of aesthetic experience. An essential element of the learning process is frequent repetition of a given stimulus. I am here interested in the consequences of repeated contacts with an object of beauty and in particular with a work of music.

The perception of a musical composition, the achievement of aesthetic pleasure, depends among other things on the ability of the listener to descry the variations in the basic qualities of tones and series of tones such as volume, duration, colour, rhythm and melody. To persons incapable of swift recognition of subtle changes in those tone qualities, a contact with musical composition will bring little aesthetic satisfaction, and may even be utterly deprived of it. The perception of a musical composition is, in such cases, incomplete and somehow deformed, while the aesthetic evaluation must be inaccurate. This was the experience of some European missionaries in Africa who claimed that Black percussion music sounded discordant and was without aesthetic value, because Africans had no sense of rhythm. In fact the opposite was true: the rhythm of the African music was too complicated and too refined to be appreciated by listeners brought up on European music, which at that time was rhythmically much less refined.[3]

Until recently it was believed that the various abilities involved in descrying variations in basic tone qualities are inborn and cannot be perfected by exercises. Today this opinion has undergone change. Experiments have shown that many of these abilities, including that of absolute pitch discrimination, can be improved.

Both casual observation and formal experiments reveal that perception as well as evaluation of a musical composition change with the number of hearings. One can observe a certain regularity in these changes. A difficult, valuable musical composition heard for the first time is often disliked. Only after further listenings, sometimes after a good many, does there develop an aesthetic experience and then the evaluation changes from negative to positive. Proper time intervals between listenings are of great importance. Intense concentration can be wearing and cause the process of maturation to the composition to be forced. Nonetheless the intervals between the first few listenings have to be short. As in all learning processes, what is characteristic is the leap-like growth in understanding. A friend of mine described how his first contact with Bartók, which began with the string quartets, in particular the Fifth Quartet, evoked bewilderment caused by the mass of complicated sounds. His reaction did not change appreciably during the course of the next few listenings. Utterly resigned, he lay the record aside and did not return to it for a longer period of time. When during the course of a conversation on Bartók's music he played the record again he suddenly experienced an aesthetic dazzlement. The same friend described the experiment he undertook in order to introduce his little daughter to music. His intention was not to give her the rudiments of musical notation, or to teach her sing naive songs and plunk away on the piano – which is often considered, goodness knows why, to be an education in music appreciation. Rather, his intentions were to develop in her a need for good music and for the deep aesthetic experiences which this music is capable of producing. With this in mind he changed his own pattern of listening to records at home. This was not a change in program; he continued to listen to 'adult' music – music which can bring aesthetic satisfaction to persons of a certain musical sophistication. The change consisted mainly in that he adjusted his listening time to those hours in which his daughter was at home, and that he more frequently repeated the same works. He also consciously avoided all suggestions which might influence her aesthetic judgement, all encouragement of the sort: Wouldn't you like to listen? It's such good music! His intent was to let the repeated musical stimulus act by itself.[4] Over a certain period of time he did not observe any changes in her reactions. Later she gradually began to exhibit interest, asking what was being played and who composed it, studying the record sleeves and the illustrations on them, putting various questions concerning the composition, the composer or other matters concerning music. Once she requested that he play one composition which, as she said, she enjoyed most. It was Handel's 'Water Music'. Later she began to put on records of her own choice. She is a teenager now, with a level of musical culture rarely equalled even among adults. She listens frequently and with great pleasure to complete concert repertoires, including the more difficult 20-th century compositions. At present she is captivated by Bartók, his 'Piano Concertos', 'Concerto for Orchestra', and particularly his marvellous 'Music for Strings, Percussion, and Celesta'.

In connection with the role of repeated listening in producing an aesthetic experience, the following remarks suggest themselves with regard to concerts of the kind that are arranged to encourage music appreciation. The conception of some such concerts, those at which musical compositions are performed only once, contradicts what is known of the psychology of music, and especially the principle of repeated listening. In consequence such concerts usually are of little value to their listeners. It seems that a music appreciation concert should include a discussion — suited to the level of the audience — of the formal structure of the composition to be performed, and of its peculiar qualities and values. All the main concepts and descriptions used should be illustrated with suitably selected fragments of the composition. After the discussion the composition should be performed at least twice. Exaggerating a little we could say that a music appreciation concert should rather resemble a rehearsal than a performance. For, the aim of such concerts is not primarily to produce immediate aesthetic experience, although such experience can undoubtedly arise, but to prepare the listeners for their future unaided listening and for independent experience of music.

The learning process is characterized by two basic elements: repetition of the stimulus and its reinforcement. But what, in the above mentioned experiment, functions as stimulus reinforcement? Is it the development of aesthetic satisfaction? What other factors might be significant? One of them could be the approbation of the learner by the person conducting the experiment. In such a case one is faced with the difficult problem of determining the form of approbation which would serve to reinforce the stimulus and yet would not suggest an evaluation of the composition. Such a suggestion would disturb the proper conditions for perception of art works. I shall return to this subject later on.

A fully developed aesthetic experience demands a certain amount of intellectual endeavor, thanks to which the elements and qualities present in an art work can be woven into a whole and be perceived in their entirety. However, such an effort, if it is too intense, destroys the emotion which is an essential part of aesthetic experience. Previous training, in the form of frequent contact with the work of art, makes it possible to distinguish all the elements without an excessive effort and thus releases a perfect aesthetic experience. However, this does not mean that richness of an aesthetic experience and satisfaction brought about by perception of a composition will continue growing with repeated listenings. The opposite is true; repeated listenings will reach an optimum point, which differs with the type of work, after which the listener is satiated and aesthetic pleasure lessens. Tests have shown, as one might expect, that the curve of aesthetic satisfaction is steep for popular music (including in that category all music which is easily assimilated) and flattened for the more difficult serious music. This indicates that compositions of the first type require fewer listenings to bring full aesthetic satisfaction and to evoke satiety; these processes occur more slowly and with greater difficulty in the case of serious music. Satiation with a given work of art leads us to other works in search for new aesthetic experiences. This state of satiety can arise with respect to an entire class of works created in the same style or according to the same general rules of composition. In such cases there arises a need to go beyond the received schemata and to discover new values. It is clear that in the creation and satisfaction of this need the main role is played by the composer. As an example one can point to Arnold Schoenberg's dodecaphonic music, which was an attempt to break through the conventions of the tonal system in order to create a music which did not evoke the feeling of tonality. Nonetheless his success was incomplete and temporary. Many people became so satiated with Schoenberg's dodecaphonic music that even there they began to detect a certain minimum of tonality. Independently of what Schoenberg himself believed, the psychologically understood atonality is relative and changes with the process of learning.[5]

Cultural Conditioning

This is a factor which has serious influence on aesthetic experience and evaluation. As is well known, whether the same work is judged positively or negatively depends very often on how the evaluating person was culturally conditioned. For example, works of African art are often unattractive to Europeans. Similarly comparative studies of American and Chinese students' reactions to music revealed that the Americans did not like Chinese music while European music was not valued by the Chinese. That aesthetic value judgements vary with cultural differences is generally understood. But the fact that cultural conditioning can influence perception of such qualities as dissonance and consonance, melody and tonality caused amazement and disbelief. Until recently it was assumed that these qualities were completely and exclusively determined by the tones themselves and did not depend on the listener. However, observation has shown that a series of tones recognized by members of one culture as melody may be seen by persons from another culture as a loose, unconnected succession of tones. Similarly a chord received as consonant by some, may sound dissonant to others.[6]

To end these remarks on cultural conditioning I want to emphasize that it largely reduces to frequent repetition of stimuli, and thus to learning processes. This confirms once again the great usefulness of learning theory as a means of explaining and predicting social and psychological phenomena.

Snobbery

Another factor which influences reactions to a work of art is snobbery. This is a powerful factor, as it is loaded with emotion. Its essential constituent is at least partially insincere imitation of persons, considered in certain circles as refined aesthetes, arbiters of taste — in short: persons of high standing. It is not difficult to find examples of attendance at certain concerts, or appreciation of certain works or of their performance, caused not by sincere liking but rather by the need to align one's behaviour with that of persons of prestige. Witold Gombrowicz describes in his Journal an experiment in snobism. A selected group of guests were invited to a reception at which, they were informed, a recital of contemporary piano music would take place. The host together with the pianist cleverly gave the impression that this was a serious concert of music which, however difficult and avant-garde, was nonetheless of highest quality. Actually, the pianist did not perform any composition, but rather drummed on the piano in a random manner. Nonetheless when he finished he was bravoed and congratulated on such an excellent performance of such exquisite music. In his commentary on this experiment Gombrowicz speaks ironically about both snobs and snobbery. The irony is understandable yet it should not screen the fact that snobism can serve a positive role in strengthening the desire for perfection, and to improve one's own abilities, among them the capacity for intelligent perception of valuable art works. Such art is difficult on the whole, and to fully grasp in an aesthetic experience all the elements and values it contains, requires previous training. Such training, like every learning process, involves repeated efforts, and the promise of future aesthetic satisfaction may prove too weak a stimulus to assure a lasting effort. Now, snobism, an attitude loaded with strong emotion, may help one to pass through the early period of contact with difficult art works by supporting the then weak stimulus of aesthetic emotion with emotion of a different sort.

It is worth mentioning that unequivocal appraisal of the above experiment is complicated by the role played by chance and probability in contemporary art.[7]

Snobism may, however, have a harmful effect in keeping us away from worthy art works about which the opinion has grown that they are not deep, not sufficiently refined, or are too easy. This sort of snobism is an important constituent of an attitude which V. Jankielewicz describes in his book *Ravel* in the following manner: "Among the reasons which can explain Masenet's disfavour is not only our well-grounded dislike of flat things, but also a complex resentment towards that which brings us pleasure, a masochistic infatuation with boredom, a cult for spurious profundity and a sort of frivolity in reverse which is so fashionable in certain circles today".

Suggestion

Differing from snobbery, yet often appearing in conjunction with it and forming our aesthetic reactions, is suggestion. We are all susceptible to suggestion and often it requires a special effort to withstand it. Social psychology and sociology contain numerous experiments on suggestion, two of which we shall present below.[8]

The opinion arose among concertgoers that Heifetz's performances were lacking in warmth, that they sounded cold. It was suspected that this impression was not caused by the artist's manner of playing but rather by some other factors, above all by the suggestion evoked by a certain stiffness in his posture and movements as well as by the lack of 'expression' on his face. In an attempt to ascertain if this supposition was correct the following test was conducted. A group of persons who considered Heifetz an extremely cold performer of violin music listened to two different recordings of the same composition one of which was performed by Heifetz. Of course, the listeners were not informed which recording was by Heifetz. The result was that the other recording was judged to be the colder of the two. The experiment thus confirmed the initial supposition.

In another experiment the purpose was to ascertain what suggestive effect the title of a radio programme may have on its listeners. On a programme of serious music broadcast by Danish Radio the title 'Serious Music', which is often associated in listeners' minds with boredom and erudition, was replaced by the title 'Popular Music', while the program remained the same. As a result the number of listeners doubled.

SUBJECTIVISM AND ITS VARIANTS

The facts and interdependencies which have been presented are among the more important factors which influence aesthetic experience and judgement. Let us now consider whether, and in what way, these facts can bear on the problem of objectivity of aesthetic value judgements. At the outset we ought to realize what we have in mind when we say that an aesthetic value judgement is subjective or that it is objective.

A. In one view, the subjectivity of an aesthetic value judgement, e.g. of the expression "This symphony is beautiful", consists in that it only spuriously refers to the musical composition, while in fact it refers to the aesthetic experience of the listener. An aesthetic value judgement is thus identified with a certain psychological proposition. The correctness of this stand is supposed to be corroborated by the changeability of value judgements, their dependence on a momentary disposition or mood. Within this stand opinions differ as to what particular form value judgements should have. Consider for example the statement "This landscape is beautiful." Some feel that the proper form of the sentence ought to be: "This landscape is pleasing to me." Others, more radical, and, let us add, more consequent, believe that the sentence should contain a time relativization: "This landscape is pleasing to me now."

A closer analysis of this version of aesthetic subjectivism reveals that its particular followers differ in their understanding of the phrase: "a given statement refers in fact to such and such an object". Sometimes they mean that an expression having the grammatical form of a sentence ascribing aesthetic value to an object, is an abbreviation consciously substituted for a statement which refers to the aesthetic experience of the person making the statement. At other times their idea is that although the person making an aesthetic value judgement of an object does not realize that he is speaking instead about his own experiences, he would nonetheless unavoidably arrive at that conclusion if he only critically considered the content of this statement. This 'unavoidability' sometimes carries normative, axiological colouring to the effect that person making the value judgement would, after consideration, have to admit that in fact he was speaking about his own experiences if that consideration was performed in the 'proper' or 'correct' manner. Thus the solution of the question is here influenced by assumptions of non-descriptive, axiological nature. This is not the only case when the axiological factor intervenes in the matters now under discussion. I shall return to this point later. It is worth noting that within the framework of this version of subjectivism the problem of incompatible value judgements disappears. For the disagreement between two persons appraising a given work of art turns into a spurious one, as each person is speaking about something else, namely about his own experiences.

B. A second type of subjectivism sees its essence in the fact that aesthetic value judgements, unlike descriptive statements, cannot be substantiated. In any case, no procedure exists, similar to the procedures used in the mature empirical sciences, which could be used to substantiate aesthetic value judgements in a way convincing to anyone who cared to consider the supplied arguments and evidence. This view often associates with a conviction that aesthetic value judgements are not sentences in the logical sense of the word, that they are neither true nor false, and thus, ex definitione, cannot be either corroborated or falsified.

C. The third version of subjectivism declares that there does not exist any empirically testable property of objects the possession of which would make them beautiful. If such a property did exist it would have been already identified; and an intersubjective, empirical procedure for substantiating aesthetic value judgements would have been found. The beauty of an object, they say, does not depend on the object's properties, but on the person who perceives it.

D. The last of these versions of subjectivism contends that unrelativised value judgements, if taken literally, are meaningless utterances. They should be treated as abbreviations for statements which contain relativisation to a person or a group of persons. Thus, for instance, "That picture is colouristically refined" is an abbreviated form for: "That picture is colouristically refined relative to a person p (group G)". Subjectivism so conceived is, therefore, a variant of relativism.

AN OBJECTIVE CONCEPTION OF AESTHETIC VALUE JUDGEMENTS

The adherents of these versions of subjectivism contend that the variability of aesthetic value judgements — the way one person's appraisals will change, intercultural differences, the changes effected by learning processes — all speak for the correctness of the subjectivist stand. Are there any arguments which might oppose the subjectivists? I think such arguments do exist. I shall present them together with a certain conception of beauty which I treat as a working hypothesis. My conception credits aesthetic value judgements with objective value. Let us first consider what should guide us in choosing one and not another definition of beauty. Are we free from any restrictions or do we have to observe certain rules? Of course I do not have in mind the logical rules of definition which assure its formal correctness and whose observance is necessary. What I do mean are the non-formal considerations for the usefulness of the constructed definition.[9] In determining a definition of beauty one can have in view at least two different tasks. First, one can attempt to reconstruct the colloquial meaning of the term 'beauty' and thus to give it an analytic definition.[10] Unfortunately the meanings associated with the word 'beauty' in colloquial language are neither clear nor unified enough, to ensure success in an attempt at analytic definition. However, a definition does not have to aim at an exact reconstruction of the received meaning of the term being defined. One can also aim at a concept of beauty which — however different it may be from the received one — will prove useful in formulating and solving the theoretical, the psychological and the sociological problems of art. I believe that such a definition is possible. Of course, in constructing it one should attempt to capture those current insights into the meaning associated with the word 'beauty' which are sufficiently clear and coherent.

My conception ascribes an objective validity to aesthetic judgements, which objectivity consists in the existence of some empirically testable properties whose appearance in an evaluated object corroborates the value judgement. Such properties include: colours, forms, proportions, lights, movements, sounds, signs with expressive or semantical functions, etc. In those arts which primarily make use of language signs the semantic function of these signs is the main source of aesthetic value and not their visual or sound qualities. Though in some kinds of art, e.g. in concrete poetry, these qualities of words move onto the first plane. The view which sees the beauty of an object in its possession of a certain set of empirically testable properties is, it seems in agreement with many current insights. What also supports this conviction is much introspective evidence: when we live through an aesthetic experience while perceiving a work of art, our attention is intensely concentrated on the object observed, discovering its various qualities and the relations between them. This act is accompanied by the feeling that it is thanks to these qualities that the observed object is beautiful. In music, for instance, if we listen to the beginning of the third part of Bartók's 'Sonata for Two Pianos and Percussion', the content of our experience is this: the rich, energetic ringing of the piano and above this the dry, rhythmically refined sounds of percussion.[11] At the same time we feel the composition is beautiful; its beauty is just this arrangement of qualities.

CHAPTER VIII

The Demand for Unified Conditions of Perception and Evaluation

I have pointed out that the objectivity of an aesthetic value judgement depends upon the appearance in the evaluated object of a certain set of empirically testable qualities. The problem is, however, that aesthetic value judgements are not always passed or accepted in conditions which I would here define as the proper ones. It is in this deficiency that I find the cause for the variability of judgements. I do not yet possess a completely satisfying and totally worked out solution to this problem, yet I believe I can point out an accurate direction for research.

As a matter of fact, the variability of aesthetic judgements so much appealed to by the subjectivists, forms an argument of questionable value. I view this variability as spurious, because it is effected by the diversity of conditions under which perception and aesthetic evaluation of objects occurs. Let us imagine two persons listening to a difficult composition; one is a person of high musical culture and has already heard the composition several times, while the other is hearing the composition for the first time and has only just begun to develop his musical taste. One may expect the judgements of these two persons to differ. More than that, a complete agreement of opinions scarcely ever occurs in such cases, at least, if both are sincere. The situation is in some respects similar to that in which two persons report their observations on the colour of an object which each of them has seen in differing light, or when one of them has normal eyesight and the other is Daltonist.

I propose to unify the conditions under which the perception and aesthetic evaluation of objects takes place. Accordingly, two aesthetic judgements of the same object are comparable only when the acts of perception, on the basis of which the judgements were made, occurred in conditions unified with respect to factors able to bear upon the judgements. Uniformity of conditions should cause the variability of evaluation to disappear, proportionately to the degree to which the factors were actually unified. It is obvious that uniformity of certain factors, such as temperament or personality, cannot be realized. But it can be achieved with regard to factual knowledge and previous experiences, the external conditions of perception, freshness or fatigue, etc. It is well to remember that a similar demand for unifying the conditions of observation is put forward in all kinds of empirical research.

The unification of the above factors is only one step toward the solution of our problem. One can choose many unified sets of factors, but not all of them will be equally 'good' or 'correct'. The selection should be made in such a way that the course of the aesthetic experience is optimalized. But optimalization is a relative concept which can be determined only in relation to certain characteristics or parameters. The choice of the appropriate set of such parameters makes the aesthetic experience 'full', 'rich', and 'proper'.[12] Whatever optimal conditions we choose for aesthetic perceptions they will form an ideal pattern. Particular acts of perception will only approach this ideal to a greater or lesser degree.

Let us add that the whole complex of problems connected with the concepts: 'an optimal set of parameters' and 'a proper aesthetic experience' still awaits a detailed and exact analysis.

THE METHODOLOGICAL CHARACTER OF THE CONCEPT OF BEAUTY

Those who seek a criterion for beauty in certain properties of objects believe more or less consciously that in its methodological aspects the concept of beauty is very similar, if not entirely identical, to concepts denoting directly observable properties. But there is a real difference between the two types of concepts. How do we arrive at a properly substantiated opinion that a given work of art is beautiful? A simple act of direct observation, to which we have recourse when we want to ascertain whether a given object is red, round or sweet, is not enough. To come to a substantiated conclusion about the beauty of an art work we have to perceive it as a whole and to supplement this perception with numerous observations of its various qualities and the relations between those qualities. The perception of an art work with semantic functions involves in addition the multileveled processes of interpretation. We have to conclude that there is a basic difference between simple observations and value judgements. A value judgement might be more aptly compared to a sentence reporting an interpretation of a complicated X-Ray. The concept of beauty is thus removed from the level of sensory data with which it is connected by more direct relationships. If we had at our disposal some more elaborate empirical theory of aesthetic phenomena, the concept of beauty would not belong to its elementary concepts but to its theoretical ones.[13]

Another significant property of the concept of beauty which has not been noticed until now is its only partial definability. All attempts to find a criterion of beauty in the properties of beautiful objects have been aimed at discovering a set of properties which would make up an equivalent condition of beauty. Behind those attempts there was a belief in the concept's full definability, i.e. in the possibility of formulating a definition in the form of an equivalence. Having such a definition, we would be able to decide with regard to every object not only the question 'How can I tell that the object is beautiful?', but also the question 'How can I tell that the object is not beautiful?' I think that a full definition of beauty is not possible. This concept is only partially definable, by way of many partial definitions. Such definitions may stipulate various kinds of conditions as the criteria of beauty: a sufficient condition, or only a necessary one, or else the so called necessary component of a sufficient condition.[14] Thus a definition which determines a sufficient condition includes certain objects in the class of beautiful objects, while a definition determining a necessary condition excludes certain objects from that class. Nonetheless all partial definitions accepted at a given moment do not taken together form a full definition of beauty. There will always remain objects, actually existing or possible ones, e.g. future works of art, which on the basis of the then accepted definitions cannot be either included in or excluded from the class of beautiful objects. This conception of partial definability of the concept 'beautiful' agrees, I think, with the facts of art history as well as with the phenomena of aesthetic valuation. In particular, the creation of new works of art, based on hitherto unknown principles can be interpreted as supplementing the existing criteria of beauty. This conception is also in agreement with the pluralistic theory of aesthetic values developed in Poland by S. Ossowski, W. Tatarkiewicz and M. Wallis. This theory acknowledges the existence of many differing aesthetic values. In my conception each of these values can be interpreted as the basis for a separate, partial criterion of beauty. There is, of course, nothing in the conception which would force us to admit that the aesthetic values known so far exhaust all possible ones. It is not excluded that partial criteria will in future be reduced in number and replaced by more general ones. Detailed morphology of art is one of the ways to achieve this aim.[15]

Not all Objects are Beautiful

The objective conception of beauty outlined above will now be supplemented by one further assumption to the effect that not all objects are beautiful, or, in other words, that there exist objects which are not beautiful. This assumption is indispensable in that it eliminates such an interpretation of the partial definability of beauty which would allow one to subsume under this concept practically any object by way of perpetually introducing newer, arbitrarily chosen partial criteria. Such interpretation would give the concept of beauty a universal extension, thus stripping it of any usefulness. I believe this assumption is true and in agreement with generally held opinions. It is, of course, possible by the use of appropriate methods such as teaching, suggestion, persuasion, etc. to make some people believe that certain objects are beautiful while in fact they are not. No one has proved, however, that this can be done with regard to every person and any freely chosen object. However, even if it were possible, which I seriously doubt, one would have to note that the perception of an object under such circumstances would violate the requirement of optimal conditions. Thus, the evaluation of the object would be groundless.

Beauty and Aesthetic Experience

One of the essential properties of beautiful objects is their ability to evoke aesthetic experiences and emotions. Is it, then, not necessary to include this ability in the definitional properties of beauty? Would it not be improper to define this concept with reference only to the properties of beautiful objects, irrespective of their ability to evoke aesthetic experiences, and would this not cause an undue separation between these two spheres of beauty? Let us consider two possible solutions to this problem. First, the ability to evoke aesthetic experiences would be acknowledged as one of the definitional properties of beauty. If now the perception of an object under appropriate conditions does not call forth an aesthetic experience, then the object, *ex definitione*, is not beautiful. This consequence holds only on the assumption that it is every perception of a beautiful object under appropriate circumstances which by definition evokes an aesthetic experience, and not only the majority of them. Within the framework of the second solution the capacity to produce an aesthetic experience is not a definitional attribute of beauty, but pertains to beautiful objects on the strength of an empirical regularity of a universal or a statistical character. Let us now assume that a perception of an object has not evoked an aesthetic experience. This does not prove that the object is not beautiful; it only falsifies the above mentioned empirical regularity, and only on condition that it is a universal one. It would take further analyses and research to choose one of the two solutions. Each of them has its merits and demerits. Thus a certain capriciousness in aesthetic emotion suggests that we should eliminate the ability to produce aesthetic experiences from among the definitional attributes of beauty. Inclusion of this factor however, would help us to specify the criteria of beauty in a way more concordant with the facts of human perceiving and experiencing.

Which solution would better fit the insights most in vogue? Let us first say that these insights are not sufficiently clear or unified. Nonetheless a certain type of commonly encountered reaction seems to support the second choice.

CHAPTER VIII

People sometimes say that a given art work must obviously be beautiful, since critics praise it, yet that they do not like it. Such a statement often serves as a polite way of expressing a disagreement. Sometimes, however, it reveals an understanding that the ability to appreciate an art work and to live through an aesthetic experience depends on suitable preparation as well as on appropriate conditions for the perception itself. It may also happen that a given art work does not produce an aesthetic experience in an aesthetically refined person, but such a person will be inclined to blame improper conditions of perception rather than any lack of aesthetic value in the work itself. These and like cases disclose the existence of a current view according to which the beauty of an object does not in itself guarantee an aesthetic experience upon each perception of that object. Following this view, I shall not include the capacity for evoking aesthetic experiences in the definitional properties of beauty. This ability can be ascribed to beautiful objects on the basis of an empirical regularity which, moreover, is of a statistical rather than universal character. Instead, I shall recognize this regularity as one of the important criteria for the scientific usefulness of the concept 'beautiful'. That is, I refute as useless any definition of beauty incompatible with the empirical hypothesis that the perception of a beautiful object, in the appropriate conditions, and in the majority of cases, produces an aesthetic experience.

The conception of beauty presented here may awake opposition in those readers who are not willing to identify the beauty of an object with its having a set of empirically ascertainable qualities. To those readers I should like to suggest a compromise solution. Basically, it would involve the acceptance of only some of the statements which make up the above conception. These would comprise first of all the hypothesis asserting the existence in an art object empirically ascertainable sets of properties, whose perception in unified, optimal conditions calls forth in the majority of cases an aesthetic experience and a positive aesthetic evaluation of the objects perceived. The existence of such sets of attributes forms the basis for the objectivity of aesthetic value judgements. The question whether the beauty of an object consists in possessing such attributes would remain unresolved.

I shall conclude my analyses with a remark which is perhaps in conflict with the objective tendencies revealed here. Namely, the problem of beauty cannot be resolved solely by empirical research supported by suitable conceptual analyses. An essential role is also played by axiological assumptions contained in the concepts: 'the optimal conditions of perception', 'the properly developed aesthetic experience', 'the scientifically useful definition'. The attitude of the researcher is thus not purely descriptive, but also evaluative.

NOTES

[1] The term 'beauty' is here used as equivalent with 'positive aesthetic value'. This term is also used, particularly by authors who recognize many aesthetic values, to describe a specific type of aesthetic value. Cf. M. Wallis, *Aesthetic Experience and Value*, (Polish), Kraków 1968.

[2] J. Reykowski, 'Personality', in: *Psychology as a Study of Man*, (Polish), Warsaw 1967, p. 95 ff.

[3] The examples mentioned here come from the following books: P. R. Farnsworth, *The Social Psychology of Music*, New York 1958; R. W. Lundin, *Objective Psychology of Music*, New York 1953; C. W. Valentine, *The Experimental Psychology of Music*, London 1962; F. Winckel, *Phänomene des musikalischen Hörens*, Berlin 1960.

[4] It is possible that the very authority of the father, his emotional relationship to his daughter had a disturbing effect on the conditions of the experiment, thus influencing the aesthetic judgments of the daughter. In a similar experiment under laboratory conditions one would have to take these factors into account.

[5] P. R. Farnsworth, *op. cit.*, p. 46. One should emphasize that what is here under consideration is one's sense of tonality and atonality, that is, the psychological understanding of these terms. Tonality and atonality in the musicological sense is, of course, something independent of cultural conditioning as here discussed.

[6] P. R. Farnsworth, *op. cit.* Here also the psychological understanding of the terms is meant.

[7] The role of chance and probability is discussed in the chapter on happenings; cf. also: M. Bense, *Aesthetica*; J. Reichardt, *The Computer in Art*.

[8] P. R. Farnsworth, *op. cit.*

[9] Compare my *Begriffsbildung und Definition*. Some remarks on the problem can also be found in the present book; cf. the chapter on meaning families.

[10] The concept of analytic definition is discussed in Begriffsbildung und Definition; compare also: T. Kotarbinski, *Gnosiology*, London 1966.

[11] This description contains terms used in a metaphorical sense. The analysis of metaphorical expressions, the regaining of their empirical sense is an important task for aesthetics. Authors on the subject include: J. J. A. Moij, *A Study of Metaphor*, Amsterdam 1976; M. Przelecki, 'On Metaphor in Philosophy', in: *Morals and Society. Papers dedicated to Maria Ossowska* (Polish), Warsaw 1969; M. Black, *Models and Metaphors*, 1962.

[12] Compare: R. Ingarden, *Aesthetic Experience, Work of Art, Value*, Krakow 1966 (Polish); M. Wallis, *op. cit.*; these works contain analyses of 'proper' and 'full' aesthetic experiences.

[13] For a differentiation of elementary and theoretical concepts see R. Carnap, *The Methodological Character of Theoretical Concepts*.

[14] The concept of a necessary component of a sufficient condition can be explained in the following way. Let the factors A, B, C, D together form a sufficient condition for the factor X. Then the factor C is a necessary component of the whole set A, B, C, D if the smaller set A, B, D ceases to be a sufficient condition for the factor X.

[15] Morphological analyses of this type can be found in Thomas Munro's *Toward Science in Aesthetics*.

PART TWO

APPLICATIONS

B. Social Sciences

CHAPTER IX

THE CONCEPT OF INDICATOR IN THE SOCIAL SCIENCES[1]

THE PROBLEMS. INTRODUCTORY REMARKS

Frequently, the aim of social research is to find answers to questions concerning various attitudes, character traits, opinions, general characteristics of individuals or social groups. In such questions reference is often made to such concepts as religious strictness, modernity of attitude, tolerance of deviance, alienation, frustration, authoritarian personality, social status, effectiveness of communication within a social group, low (high) morale in an individual or in a social group. Many more examples could be quoted without difficulty. If we consider such concepts more closely, we find two characteristics which they have in common and which are of great methodological importance.

1. They refer to entities which are not accessible to direct observation and and can be reached only by way of some indirect procedure.

2. Without such a suitable indirect procedure, it is very difficult to decide in particular cases whether those concepts are applicable to these entities or not.

In this connection the requirement of operationalization is put forward which postulates formulating empirically accessible indicators for those directly inaccessible entities. Thus, for instance, in one of the Turkish peasant surveys[2] the concept of politicisation is used. This directly inaccessible attitude is provided with an indicator based on specific features of external behaviour, namely on answers to the following questions:

1. Have you ever voted in a national election?
2. Can you name the main political parties in Turkey today?
   (here follows a series of names denoting political parties; the parties may be named correctly, not named, or named incorrectly).[3]

Here is another example of an attempt at operationalization. In his paper 'The Birth and Growth of Variates' P. F. Lazarsfeld states: " ... what is an efficient worker — one who works quickly, one who makes few mistakes, or the optimal combination of both? How about an efficient organization? It does not consist of efficient people only; ease of communication among its members, the absence of internal conflicts, and many other features come to mind".[4]

As the above examples show, an indicator gives empirically testable criteria for entities which are further removed from the level of direct observation. The question then arises, what are the formal characteristics of the relation between an indicator and the indicated property? This question is scarcely ever put in sociological texts, although it has great methodological significance. Thus, for instance, we may ask whether a given set of answers makes up an equivalent condition for politicization? Or rather a sufficient, or only a necessary one? Or, if none of the previous universal relationships occur, is the relation of the probabilistic type? The answers to the above questions determine important methodological aspects of the relation between an indicator and the indicated property. Thus, for instance, if the relation is that of a sufficient condition, we can conclude the presence of a property from the presence of its indicator; however, the absence of the indicator does not then authorize us generally to infer that the indicated property is also absent. Such a statement would be a logical mistake.[5] If, on the other hand, we assume that the relation is that of a necessary condition, the lack of the indicator permits us to assert that the indicated property is also absent. However, the presence of the indicator does not now give grounds for concluding that the property it indicates is present.[6]

I want now to call attention to another important methodological aspect of the indicator relation. Suppose we have formulated an indicator for alienation. Suppose further that the indicator constitutes a sufficient condition for alienation. Those stipulations do not yet entirely specify the relation between the indicator and alienation. On the contrary, they leave an important aspect of this relation undetermined. Namely, the indicator may be formulated for the purpose of predicting the presence of alienation, or else to define the concept 'alienation'. In the first case I shall speak of a factual indicator; in the second − of a definitional one. There are essential methodological differences between these two types of indicators; they will further be discussed in detail.

In international and in comparative social research the problem often arises of finding a property which could be used as an indicator for the existence of the same attitude, or another directly unaccessible entity, in some two or more social groups. Upon closer consideration the problem so formulated proves to be ambiguous and can be analysed into its component problems. Some questions which arise in this connection will also be the subject of discussion.

INDICATOR, INDICATUM, SENTENCE INTRODUCING AN INDICATOR

Social research is often directed at finding facts and regularities relating to phenomena inaccessible to direct observation. Examples of such phenomena have been previously quoted. To preserve the empirical character of social science, one has to find directly accessible indicators by way of which those hidden phenomena could be approached. As examples of such indicators various objects, properties or phenomena are adduced: behaviour traits, including verbal ones such as answering questions in an interview or questionnaire; ownership of an apartment and its equipment; number and character of regularly read magazines and journals; the kind of education obtained; the number and character of offences committed in a given social group within a given period of time, etc.

From these examples it can be seen that not all indicators are really directly accessible properties. However, as a rule they are accessible more directly than the objects for which they serve as indicators. To make one property an indicator for another one it is necessary that they are connected by a kind of bond upon which the indicator relation is based. This bond is sometimes described as a causal one; at other times it is referred to as a diagnostic one. Thus, the authors of *Authoritarian Personality* write: "The task was to formulate scale items which, though they were statements of opinions and attitudes, would actually serve as 'giveaways' of underlying trends in the personality" ... "For every item there was a hypothesis, sometimes several hypotheses, stating what might be the nature of its connection with prejudice".[7]

After these remarks and examples I can procede to formulate the following description of the indicator relation: A property F is an indicator for a property H if they are linked by a universal or a statistical connection. This connection allows conclusions about the existence of one of the properties from the presence of the other one. Moreover, F is a property directly — or at least more easily — accessible to observation than property H. Of course it is not necessary that both properties F and H appear in the same object. On the contrary, they may be features which characterize two different objects, as is for instance the case when the quality and equipment of an owned apartment is used as an indicator for the social status of its owner.

This fairly describes the meaning which is most commonly connected with the word 'indicator' in social research. In what follows the description will be further elaborated and evolved. In sociological research a distinction is made between an indicator and an index — an index being something more complex, composed of or built on the basis of several indicators. For the methodological purposes of this chapter this distinction is not relevant. It can be seen that both index and indicator — in the narrower sociological sense — are instances of 'indicator' in the broader sense here defined. Let us now assume that a property F is an indicator for a property H and that the relation holding between F and H can be expressed with the aid of the following sentence

(1) For every object x: if x has the property F, then x also has the property H.[8]

Under this assumption I shall speak of H as the indicatum of F; the sentence (1) will be referred to as the sentence introducing the indicator F. It is, of course, possible that one and the same sentence introduces more than one indicator. Thus, for instance, the sentence

(2) For every object x: x has the property F if and only if x also has the property H.[9]

Introduces F as an indicator for H, and at the same time non-F as an indicator for the absence of H.[10] On the other hand, a sentence like

(3) For every object x: if x has the property T, then if x has the property F, it also has the property H.[11]

introduces the conjunction of two properties T and F as an indicator for the property H.

LOGICAL STRUCTURE AND METHODOLOGICAL CHARACTER OF THE INDICATOR RELATION

The analysis of numerous examples of sociological indicators shows that the connection binding indicator with indicatum can vary in two important respects: its logical structure and its methodological character. The first comprises a wide range of variations: from simple conditional sentences (implications) which give either a sufficient or a necessary condition for the presence of the indicatum; through more complicated universal sentences of an implicational or an equivalent type; to sentences which give the relative probability for the presence of the indicatum or the reverse probability for the appearance of the indicator. In what follows I shall discuss examples of indicators illustrating some of the variations.

However, I should like to stress that those who formulate indicators do not see the problem of logical structure clearly enough. They are usually satisfied with formulating an indicator for a given indicatum, leaving the logical structure of the indicator relation undefined. In nearly all the examples discussed below the reconstruction of the indicator relation is my own responsibility. Of course, in doing this I have tried to make use of all suggestions found in the authors' texts.

Analysis shows that the methodological character of the indicator-introducing sentences varies. They can have the character either of empirical statements or of meaning postulates. In the first case their validity depends on empirical data; in the second – on semantical stipulations. Let me explain this methodologically essential difference in detail.

Suppose we have constructed an indicator for tolerance of deviance.[1][2] Let the indicator be denoted by the term I and the attitude of being deviance tolerant by the term T. Let us further assume that the connection between the indicator and the indicated attitude can be expressed with the aid of the following statement

(4) For every person x: if x has the property I, then x also has the attitude T.[1][3]

The methodological status of the sentence (4) is thereby not yet determined. There are two different interpretations open to us. First, we can understand it as an empirical statement which makes it possible *to predict* the existence of deviance tolerance Tx from the presence of indicator Ix. The truth value of (4) depends now on empirical data. It is corroborated by every concrete case of a person who while having the property I (the indicator), has also been found to possess the attitude T (deviance tolerance). It is falsified by any case of a person x who has the property I, but does not have the attitude T. It is essential to note that the meaning of the term T and the criteria of its application have now to be determined entirely independently of the term I. In other words, what term T means cannot now be defined with the aid of the term I; this has to be done by reference to some other terms which neither contain I nor are definitionally dependent on I. In such cases I shall name I *a factual indicator* for the attitude T. However, we can see in (4) not an empirical statement, but a meaning postulate. The function of statement (4) is now not to provide grounds for predicting the presence of the attitude T, but *to define* the meaning of the term T with the aid of the term I. In such cases I will be referred to as a *definitional indicator* for T.

I have said above that term I defines the meaning of the term T. This statement requires further elaboration in view of the specific features of the relation which binds a definitional indicator with its indicatum. What are those features? Do sentences introducing definitional indicators differ from regular definitions? In a regular definition, definiendum and definiens are connected by the equivalence relation. Thanks to this, the definiendum is fully defined by the definiens; i.e. criteria are given for the application of the definiendum as well as for the application of its negation.[14] Although equivalence cannot be ruled out, the relation which binds a definitional indicator with its indicatum is usually of a weaker type. It is often an implication which gives either a necessary or a sufficient condition for the application of the indicatum. Still weaker is the probabilistic relation which is also frequently met with. Definitions of non-equivalent type, i.e. which do not define their definienda fully, are called partial definitions. Consequently, we have to classify the majority of sentences introducing definitional indicators as partial definitions of terms denoting indicata.

The concept of partial definition originated with Rudolf Carnap. He first called attention to the fact that there are notions which cannot fully be defined, i.e. every attempt at a full definition must end in failure.[15] He used the expression 'dispositional concepts' (i.e. denoting dispositions, such as attitudes, etc.) to refer to such notions. The terms denoting indicata are mostly dispositional terms, and therefore only partially definable.

I shall now consider a few examples of indicators; they are not fictitious indicators devised for the special purpose of illustrating the foregoing theoretical analyses, but have been taken from actual social or socio-psychological work. I have already said that the authors of indicators are often satisfied with formulating their indicators for the corresponding indicata leaving the logical structure of the indicator relation undefined. The same holds true with regard to the methodological status of indicator-introducing sentences. Usually, the authors do not clearly see the difference between definitional and factual indicators. Consequently, it is often not certain whether they aimed at a definitional indicator, to define the term denoting the indicatum, or rather at a factual indicator, to make possible the prediction of the indicatum. The interpretation of the examples analyzed below is my own. I am fully conscious that it may run counter to the authors' intentions.

Factual Indicator for Religious Strictness[16]

The indicator is based on the following five questions: **1.** Does hanging pictures in one's house conflict with religion? **2.** Does translating the Koran into Turkish conflict with religion? **3.** Does drinking raki and wine conflict with religion? **4.** Does lending money at interest conflict with religion? **5.** Does using drugs to prevent conception conflict with religion? The answers to these questions are given numbers ranging from 0 to 5; the higher the score received, the greater the religious strictness. The authors do not declare whether they consider their indicator a factual or a definitional one. However, judging from the general content of the work it was not their intention to give definitional criteria for the term 'religious strictness' — they accepted its colloquial meaning. Rather, they wanted to formulate clues in relation to which one could empirically ascertain the degree of religious strictness.

What is the logical structure of the relation connecting the indicator with the indicatum? The answer which first comes to mind sees it as the following equivalence:

(5)   For any two persons x and y: the religious strictness of x is greater than (equal to) that of y if and only if the score obtained by x is higher than (equal to) that obtained by y.[17]

However, the contents of questions on which the indicator is based show that they can meaningfully be put only to members of the Turkish community or at most to the followers of Islam. The indicator-introducing sentence should, therefore, contain some relativization to this social group:

(6)   For any two persons x and y: if x and y are both Muslims, then the religious strictness of x is greater than (equal to) that of y if and only if the score obtained by x is also greater than (equal to) the score obtained by y.[18]

It can be seen that this indicator permits us to ascertain the degree of religious strictness only in relation to persons who meet the condition described in the antecedent of the above conditional sentence; for members of other social groups separate indicators would have to be constructed.

With regard to metrical indicators — and the indicator now discussed belongs in this category — there arises the question of the scale type upon which they are based. Theoretically, there exists a non-denumerable infinity of scales, but only a few of them have found practical application. In the social sciences the so-called ordinal scale is used most frequently. Measuring objects on this scale we assign numbers to them in such a way as to give isomorphic representation only to the relations of equality and precedence holding among those objects. This is a weak type of scale and, consequently, the variety of admissible sentences stating quantitative relationships among the data obtained with the aid of this scale is very limited. The interval and the ratio scales are examples of stronger scale types. It is, however, difficult, although not impossible, to build such scales within the realm of the social sciences.[19]

The type of scale upon which the indicator for religious strictness is based was not specified by its authors. Nor do they give any justification or explanation with regard to the problem of scale. In fact, they do not consider this question at all; however, the future meaningful use of the indicator to formulate quantitative sociological statements depends heavily upon determining the type of scale for religious strictness. In the above formulation (6) it is assumed that this scale is of the weak ordinal type — only the relations of equal and stronger religious strictness are introduced. This is in accordance with the authors's comment which accompanies the indicator: 'Higher score = greater strictness of religious interpretation'.

A Definitional Indicator for Prejudicial Attitude[20]

The authors wanted to find out if there exists a relationship between prejudicial attitude toward an ethnic group (e.g. Negroes, Chinese) and the appearance of the galvanic skin response. The galvanic skin response was to be used as an indicator for the prejudicial attitude which was also independently ascertainable with the aid of a specially constructed questionnaire. The authors did not take any explicit stand with regard to the methodological status of their indicators. One can, however, suppose that the galvanic skin response was conceived by them as a factual indicator for the prejudicial attitude. At the same time this attitude was partially defined by an indicator based on the above mentioned questionnaire. Let me reconstruct the sentence introducing this last indicator. The following two possibilities suggest themselves.

(7) For every person x: if x has been tested with the questionnaire A (which contains items assumed by the authors to indicate a prejudicial attitude toward a given ethnic group), then x has a prejudicial attitude toward that group if and only if the test has ended with such and such a result.[21]

(8) For every person x: when x has been tested with the questionnaire A (which contains items assumed by the authors as relevant for prejudicial attitude toward a given ethnic group), then if the test has ended with such and such a result, x is prejudiced against that group.[22]

The authors of this indicator give in their paper neither the contents of the questionnaire nor the results of the test needed to qualify a person as prejudiced. Consequently my formulations include such expressions, as:

'questionnaire A', or 'the test has ended with such and such a result'. However, the explicit description of the questionnaire or of the required test result is not essential for the purpose of the present analysis.

Both formulations (7) and (8) give partial definitional criteria for the term 'prejudicial attitude toward a given ethnic group'. They are partial, because they are determined only with regard to persons who can meaningfully be tested with the questionnaire constructed by the authors. With regard to persons to whom this questionnaire cannot meaningfully be applied, the term remains undefined.[23] There is, however, an essential difference between (7) and (8). The first gives a positive as well as a negative criterion for 'prejudicial attitude', whereas the second specifies only the positive one. This means that with (7) we are able to ascertain that a person tested has the prejudicial attitude or that the person is free from prejudice — depending on the result of the test. With (8) only the first is possible. With the symbols used in footnotes (21) and (22) we can describe this difference in a concise way as follows: According to (7) the conjunction Ax and Rx forms the criterion for the application of Px; the conjunction Ax and non-Rx — the criterion for non-Px. On the other hand (8) specifies only the conjunction Ax and Rx as a positive criterion for Px.[24]

Probabilistic Indicators

In the examples discussed so far, the relation binding an indicator with its indicatum was of a universal type, although the logical structure of this relation was in every case different. Besides universal indicators, probabilistic indicators are also often used in the social sciences. It would take a separate paper to give a detailed and full analysis of such indicators. I shall concentrate here on some problems of a general methodological nature.

The structure of probabilistic indicators varies depending on the situation. However, the simplest and commonest form can be presented in the following way:

$$P(A/I) = p \quad \text{or} \quad P(I/A) = q \quad \text{where} \quad 0 < p, q < 1.$$

The first formula gives the probability for the presence of indicatum A (e.g. of an attitude) relative to the presence of indicator I; the second gives the reverse probability for the presence of indicator I assuming the presence of indicatum A. The difference between the two forms corresponds to the difference between a sufficient and a necessary condition for the appearance of an indicatum. An example is the indicator for family solidarity formulated by L. T. Jansen.[25] He saw this indicator in the frequency of joint house work.

This is only a probabilistic indicator and not a universal one. For, according to to the author the fact that house work is frequently carried out jointly does not always indicate the existence of family solidarity; conversely, the lack of such activities does not always speak for the absence of family bonds. It is difficult to discern whether, according to the author's intentions, this indicator should be interpreted as a definitional or rather as a factual one. Some of the author's statements suggest the first alternative.

The form of probabilistic indicators is different in cases where the indicated attitude or property admits of gradations. In such cases the probability of presence of the indicated property is usually different for every degree of this property. The indicator must then take the shape of the probability distribution function which determines the probability for every degree of indicatum. As an example we can adduce indicators formulated by P. F. Lazarsfeld in connection with his Latent Structure Analysis:

$$p_g^s = \frac{n_g^s}{n^s} \quad \text{and} \quad r_g^s = \frac{n_g^s}{n_g}.$$

The first of these indicators determines the probability for the answer-pattern g on the assumption that the answering person has the latent attitude in degree s. The second gives the reverse probability for the latent attitude in degree s on the assumption that the answers given form the pattern g.

In connection with probabilistic indicators there arise a number of methodological questions which have not so far found satisfactory solutions. Thus, for instance, how is the term 'probability' to be understood: as a frequency distribution or in some other way? In relation to what set of objects or phenomena is this probability defined: relative to some set which is empirically given or rather hypothetically assumed? Because of these methodological difficulties it is sometimes suggested that the use of probabilistic indicators of the definitional type should be abandoned in favour of universal ones. Such a decision would, of course, have to be accompanied by suitable changes in the sociological generalizations in which those indicators appear. At least some universal statements would have to be reformulated as probabilistic ones. The problem is still far from its final solution.

THE TRANSFERENCE OF INDICATORS FROM ONE SOCIAL GROUP TO ANOTHER

Sometimes indicators used in research on one social group G_1 are transferred to research on another social or ethnic group G_2. These two groups may be quite different, i.e. they may have no elements in common, but it is possible that G_2 contains G_1 as its proper subset. In the last instance, the application of indicators is extended to cover cases contained in the broader group G_2. The need to transfer indicators may arise in connection with research of a comparative type, but it is by no means restricted to such cases. Sometimes it is motivated by a tendency to economize effort. It usually takes a lot of work to construct concepts and indicators needed in a particular research. The possibility of using this conceptual apparatus in research concerned with other social groups or with other social problems than those for which it was initially constructed would save all that effort.

However, such transfer of indicators, if it is to be scientifically useful, cannot be done in an arbitrary way, but has to obey certain rules. The aim is to guarantee that the indicators represent the same concepts in both (all) social groups in which they are to be used. The problem is by no means trivial. First, we have to observe that the expression: 'the indicator should in both social groups represent the same concept' is usually understood in a vague and ambiguous way. With the aid of the concepts which were previously introduced we can distinguish between representation in the definitional and the factual sense. An indicator represents its indicatum in the definitional sense if it is a definitional indicator for that indicatum; similarly, it represents its indicatum in the factual sense if it is a factual indicator for that indicatum. The requirements needed to secure representation are different in the two cases.

Let us first consider representation in the factual sense. Suppose a property F is used as a factual indicator for an attitude A in a social group G_1. We want to know if F can also be used as a factual indicator for the same attitude A in another social group G_2, where G_1 is contained in G_2 or where they have no elements in common, i.e. are two entirely different social groups. To do this in a sound way it is necessary that in both groups there is an empirically testable connection between the indicator and the indicated attitude.

Let us consider an example. Suppose galvanic skin response is used as an indicator for prejudical attitude. If the tested person shows high galvanic skin response, he is prejuciced against a given ethnic group. The formulation of the indicator for the two social groups G_1 and G_2 is as follows:

(9) For every person x: If x belongs to G_1 and shows high galvanic skin response when confronted with a statement praising an ethnic group, then x is prejudiced against that group.

(10) For every person x: If x belongs to G_2 and shows high galvanic skin response when confronted with a statement praising an ethnic group, then x is prejudiced against that group.

Statement (9) is accepted as a result of empirical research carried out with regard to the group G_1. Statement (10) can initially be accepted as a hypothesis concerning group G_2 and suggested by results of research into group G_1. However, this hypothesis can be accepted only after it is corroborated by suitable empirical research among group G_2. In carrying out this research the sociologist has to remember that in both (9) and (10) galvanic skin response appears as a factual indicator for the prejudicial attitude. This means that the term 'galvanic skin response' cannot simultaneously be used as a meaning criterion for the term 'prejudicial attitude'. An attempt to use the first term as a meaning criterion for the second would immediately lead to contradiction; for it would change the methodological status of the sentence (10) turning it into meaning postulate for the term 'prejudicial attitude', contrary to the initial assumption according to which this sentence was to introduce a factual indicator. It follows that to be able to ascertain empirically the truth value of the sentence (10) the sociologist must have some other criteria, independent of the galvanic skin response, for the application of the term 'prejudicial attitude'. These criteria have to be identical for both social groups G_1 and G_2; or, if they are different, they have to be such as to guarantee the meaning identity of the term 'prejudicial attitude' in both (9) and (10). Otherwise galvanic skin response would not serve as an indicator for the same attitude in two different social groups, but rather as an ambiguous indicator for two different attitudes.

In (9) and (10) the same universal implicational relation is assumed between indicator and indicatum in both social groups. One can, however, imagine a situation when this relation is universal in G_1, say of the type (9), and has the probabilistic character in group G_2. It is an open question whether in such cases one should speak of two different indicators, or rather of one and the same indicator which in group G_1 has a 'stronger' and in group G_2 a 'weaker' connection with its indicatum.

Let us now consider the transfer operation in the case of definitional indicators. We assume that some property D is a definitional indicator for an attitude T in a social group G_1. The question is whether D can also be used as a definitional indicator for the attitude T in another group G_2. We admit, as before, that G_1 is either a proper subset of G_2 — in which case the application of indicator D is to be extended to a larger social group G_2; or else that G_1 and G_2 have no elements in common, i.e. the indicator D is to be transferred to an entirely different group G_2. When would such a transfer be justified? Would the existence of an empirically testable correlation between indicator and the indicated attitude in both groups G_1 and G_2 be a sufficient justification? The answer has to be in the negative. For, with any attitude T, or – more generally – with any indicatum T, there usually correlate many properties D, but only a few of them function as definitional indicators for T. A definitional decision is necessary to transform property D into a definitional indicator for an attitude T. Due to this decision the methodological status of the sentence introducing the indicator D is not that of an empirical statement, which can be corroborated or falsified by observation, but that of a meaning postulate, which partially defines the sense of the term T with the aid of the term D.

In transferring a definitional indicator from one group G_1 to another group G_2 we can choose one of the following two courses: analytic definition, and synthetic definition. I shall discuss each of these briefly. Suppose the sentences introducing D as a definitional indicator for T in both groups G_1 and G_2 are of the following simple form

(11)   For every person x: if x belongs to G_1, then x has the attitude T if and only if x has the property D.

(12)   For every person x: if x belongs to G_2, x has the attitude T if and only if x has the property D.[26]

We assume that (11) has already been accepted as sentence introducing property D as an indicator for the attitude T in group G_1. Now, we can justify the acceptance of (12) by pointing out that:

1. in both groups G_1 and G_2 term T is understood in an identical way, and

2. sentence (12) is a true, partial, analytic definition of the term T with the aid of the term D. Analytic – with regard to the language spoken by members of the social group G_2. As is well known, a definition of the term T is analytic with regard to a given language L if it strives to render the existing meaning of T in the language L.[27] Of course, the abovementioned justification of (12) must be based on some insight into language-habits in the social groups G_1 and G_2. Such knowledge can, for instance, be gained by surveys of the socio-semantic type.

Sometimes it may be very difficult or even impossible to prove that a partial definition is a true, analytic definition in a given language L. The cause of the difficulty may lie with the extreme vagueness of the term T. Or, on the other hand, an analytic definition of T may be possible, but its construction would be scientifically useless, because the phenomena referred to by T – as it is understood by members of the group G_2 – make up the so-called 'linguistic class', i.e. they do not correlate with any other sociologically interesting phenomena, and are therefore useless as tools for stating such correlations. In such cases the sociologist may choose the second of the above alternatives — the synthetic definition. He can now justify transferring the indicator D to group G_2 by pointing out that:

1. independently of how the term T is understood in group G_2, its meaning, as partially defined by (12), is identical with its understanding in group G_1 as defined by (11) and

2. sentence (12) is a scientifically useful synthetic, partial definition of the term T with the aid of the term D. Let me explain this more fully.

In defining synthetically the term T, we neglect its existing sense in the language L (in our case the language spoken by members of the group G_2), but give it, instead, a new meaning determined by our own semantic decision. This decision may, in principle, be wholly arbitrary, i.e. we can define T in any desired way. However, to make our semantic decision something more than a mere play with words, we have to define T in such a way as to make it scientifically useful. This means we have to prove that the phenomena denoted by T are connected by way of empirical statements with many other phenomena of sociological interest. By stating and corroborating those empirical statements we prove that term T is scientifically useful. If these statements have the character of sociological generalizations, they may be used to explain and possibly also to predict some of the phenomena with the aid of the others. Thus, if the sociologist chooses this way of justifying his transfer of indicators from one social group to another, he has to carry out a difficult task of building a corroborated network of sociological statements in which relations are stated among the transferred indicators, their indicata, and other variables of sociological interest. In building up this network of statements he may be helped by the insights he gained from his research over social phenomena in group G_1. In international comparative research there arises the need to translate questions, or other items used to build indicators, from one ethnic language into another. It often happens that these items cannot be translated literally, since literal translation would change their original meaning. For instance, the question: "Are you in favour of a national health service?" is interpreted differently in the United States and in Europe: in the United States an answer to this question is tantamount to a declaration of support for a certain political party, which as a rule is not the case in Europe.[28] This raises the issue of what is called functional translation, i.e. one which, while not being a literal translation, would yield a semantic equivalent. This problem is not easy to solve. It is said that functional translation of a question or of another item yields an equivalent which grasps the same attitude or disposition. But this relation is too loose to be called translation. Consider, for instance the following two questions: 1. "Are you for or against integration?" and 2. "Czy zgadza się Pan(i) z opinią że zawsze będą istniały na swiecie narody wyższe i niższe, i że w interesie wszystkich zainteresowanych jest, by kontrola nad biegiem spraw świata spoczywała w rękach narodów wyższych?"[29] Answers to both questions may be taken as indicators for a racist attitude, but the latter is in no way a translation of the former. The problem of translation, and especially that of functional translation, in international comparative research still awaits adequate, satisfactory solution.

NOTES

[1] The work on this paper has been sponsored by the Science Centre, Berlin.
[2] F. W. Frey, A. R. Kessler, J. E. Rothchile: 'Index Construction and Validation. Report No. 2, Rural Development Research Project. Massachusetts Institute of Technology, 1967.
[3] Cf. the above mentioned Report.
[4] In: P. F. Lazarsfeld, A. K. Pasanella, M. Rosenberg (eds): *Continuities in the Language of Social Research*. The Free Press, New York, 1972, p. 17.
[5] The reasoning would in that case follow a logically false formula: if p, then q, therefore if non-p, then non-q; symbolically:

$$(p \to q) \to (-p \to -q)$$

[6] In an attempt to draw such a conclusion we would reason according to a logically false formula: If non-p, then non-q, therefore if p, then q; symbolically:

$$(-p \to -q) \to (p \to q).$$

[7] T. W. Adorno et al.: *Authoritarian Personality*. Harper, New York, 1950, p. 223 and 225. Of course, we have to remember that answers to questions or, for that matter, any other items of external behaviour, can be used not only to express an internal attitude, but also to hide it. That is why answers have to be corroborated by other items. The difficulties which arise in connection with using answers as indicators for internal dispositions and attitudes have been discussed in the relevant literature.
[8] In formal notation: $(x)[Fx \to Hx]$ [9] $(x)[Fx \equiv Hx]$
[10] This follows from the logical connection which holds between equivalence and implication, namely: equivalence $Fx \equiv Hx$ is equivalent to the conjunction of the following two implications: 1. $Fx \to Hx$ and, 2. $Hx \to Fx$. The first implication (1) introduces F as an indicator for H; logical transposition of the second implication (2) introduces non-F as an indicator for non-H. As is known, according to the law of transposition implication $Hx \to Fx$ is equivalent to the implication non-$F \to$ non-H.
[11] In formal notation: $(x)\{Tx \to [Fx \to Hx]\}$

¹² The concept 'tolerance of deviance' was used in the above mentioned Rural Development Research Project where an indicator for it was also constructed.
¹³ Formally: $(x)[Ix \to Tx]$. The range of variable x may be restricted by additional criteria to a given social group, e.g. to contemporary Turkish peasant communities.
¹⁴ For instance, let one-place predicate Ax be fully defined by the expression S; the definition has then the form of the following equivalence: $Ax \equiv S$. This equivalence is equivalent to conjunction of the two implications: $S \to Ax$ and $Ax \to S$. The first implication gives a sufficient condition for the application of the term A; the transposition (see explanation given in note (10)) of the second implication non-$S \to$ non-Ax establishes non-S as a sufficient condition for the application of non-Ax.
¹⁵ For a presentation of R. Carnap's conception see his 'Testability and Meaning', *Philosophy of Science* 1936 and 1937. Partial definitions and their applications in the social sciences and the humanities are analyzed in: T. Pawlowski, *Begriffsbildung und Definition*. See also W. Stegmüller: *Das Wahrheitsproblem und die Idee der Semantik*.
¹⁶ Example taken from the already quoted 'Rural Development Research Project'.
¹⁷ $(x)(y)[Rx \geqslant Ry \equiv Sx \geqslant Sy]$
¹⁸ Formally: $(x)(y)\{Mx \cdot My \to [Rx \geqslant Ry \equiv Sx \geqslant Sy]\}$
¹⁹ A fuller discussion of the measurement problem is given in another chapter of this book.
²⁰ Example taken from a study by I. B. Copper, D. Pollock: 'The Identification of Prejudicial Attitude by the Galvanic Skin Response'. *Journal of Psychology* 1959, 50, 241–245.
²¹ $(x)[Ax \to (Px \equiv Rx)]$
²² $(x)[Ax \to (Rx \to Px)]$
²³ Compare in this respect the questions upon which the above given indicator for religious strictness was based. They can be put meaningfully only to members of a Turkish or at most of a Muslim community.
²⁴ This difference results from different logical bonds which connect the prejudicial attitude with test results: in (7) this bond is an equivalence, in (8) only an implication. Compare in this respect remarks given in notes (10) and (14).
²⁵ L. T. Jansen: 'Measuring Family Solidarity'. *American Sociological Review*, XVII, 1952.
²⁶ Symbolically: $(x)\{G_1 x \to [Tx \equiv Dx]\}$ and $(x)\{G_2 \to [Tx \equiv Dx]\}$
²⁷ For a fuller explanation of the concepts of analytic and synthetic definitions cf; T. Kotarbiński: *Gnosiology*, Pergamon Press London 1966. Cf. also: T. Pawlowski, *Begriffsbildung und Definition*.
²⁸ An example taken from: E. K. Scheuch, 'Progress in the Cross-Cultural Use of Surveys'. International Social Council Round Table on Comparative Research. Theme III: Comparative Sample Surveys. Mimeograph, 1965.
²⁹ "Do you agree with the opinion that there will always be superior and inferior nations, and that it is in the interest of all concerned that the destinies of the world be guided by superior nations?"

CHAPTER X

SEMIOTIC THEORY OF CULTURE

The application of linguistic, or, more generally, of semiotic concepts and methods, in the realm of cultural research is today in vogue. Such applications are sometimes referred to as 'the semiotic theory of culture', especially when they encompass the broader domain of human behaviour and its products. What are the advantages which the followers of the semiotic approach hope to gain by the transference of linguistic concepts and methods to the realm of cultural phenomena? Linguistics is the most advanced and precise of all the humanistic disciplines—or so the practitioners of semiotics say—and the transference will make it possible to achieve in the field of cultural research results as fruitful as those gained in linguistics. However, the subject matter of linguistics is languages, i.e. certain systems of signs. Therefore—the argument continues—in order to be able to apply linguistic concepts in cultural research, we have to extend the existing usage of the concept 'sign' in such a way, as to subsume under it all or nearly all cultural phenomena.

Is such a procedure justified? Will it bring the expected results? In what follows I consider these problems in detail. Also, I make use of the conceptual apparatus of modern logic to analyse what it means to apply concepts of one science in another science.

The semiotic approach to art and culture has brought some interesting results. However, as often happens with methodological innovations, the advantages which the applications of semiotic concepts are supposed to bring are in some points exaggerated or are anticipated on the basis of unfounded assumptions. In my analyses I shall concentrate on these defective aspects of the semiotic approach; a full discussion of its achievements is here not intended.[1] To give a few names of authors whose works are here taken into consideration, one can mention Claude Lévi-Strauss, Roland Barthes, or Umberto Eco.[2] According to so called pansemiotism—an extreme stand which is probably never adhered to consistently—all cultural phenomena are signs. This is opposed by a more moderate attitude which sees the functioning of signs only in some areas of behaviour; although even here the concept of sign has a much broader extension than it has in its common usage.

Let me cite a few examples of objects or phenomena considered as signs by both the extreme and the moderate variants of semiotism. First come language expressions which, of course, are claimed to be signs, and, moreover, the most perfect ones. Also, they usually mention figurative painting, programme music, road and railway signals. Rules of kinship relations in a social group are held to constitute a collection, and even a system, of signs; as are also genes, whose exchange in the process of reproduction is looked upon as 'communication'. A sun tanned face in winter is considered a sign of affluence, or a sign of predilection for a specific type of sports and entertainment. Various foods and ways of cooking them are signs, because they inform us about the religion, wealth, or social status of the persons involved. For the same reason many other objects, such as clothes, cars flats and their equipment, are interpreted as signs.

Are the above mentioned objects really signs? How is the term 'sign' to be understood to encompass all those examples? Would the term so defined prove to be useful in scientific discussion and research? To find answers to these questions, let us reflect on what relation should bind two objects A and B to turn one of them into some kind of sign for the other. The existing usage distinguishes several possibilities; they can be arranged according to the degree to which particular relations are determined by psycho-cultural factors.

The most all-embracing variant is the *indicator relation*.[3] This holds between two objects A and B when they are connected by a universal or a statistical bond which makes it possible to infer the presence of B from the presence of A. No further requirements are postulated in regard to the nature of the indicator relation. In particular, it can have the character of any natural connection between phenomena; that, for instance, which allows to recognize illness from its symptoms, or to predict rain from the presence of dark clouds. It is obvious that all examples of 'signs' listed earlier are indicators in the sense defined.

The cultural indicator relation is a specific type of indicator relation. This holds between two objects A and B when one can infer the presence of B from the presence of A because of accepted conventions or customs. Not all of our examples belong in this category. Certainly, neither genes, nor, usually, sun tanned face can be counted as examples of cultural indicators. On the other hand, an army uniform, or the kind of meal taken on Christmas Eve, do function as cultural indicators. Because of received customs or conventions we can infer from these the profession or religion of the persons involved.

Let us now ask under what conditions an object A can really be said to be a sign—in the strict sense—of another object B. Of all the three relations the sign relation is to the largest extent determined by factors of psycho-cultural nature. I shall not set out a strict definition, for such definitions vary from author to author. Instead, I shall expound those properties of the sign relation which bear on the main problems discussed here.[4] An object A is the *sign* of an object B only when there exists a cultural convention C which makes A suitable to express a definite thought about B.[5] The sign relation between A and B does not usually hold (according to some authors, never does so) solely because of convention C. It also depends on the existence of a natural or a cultural bond which turns A into an indicator of B. If, for instance, this bond consists in a similarity between A and B, then A is called an iconic sign of B.

Only some of the quoted examples are signs. Language expressions, road and railway signals, as well as some works of art, are, of course, signs. But what about clothes, foods, cars, or flats? Are they also signs? Now, it is true that due to certain known correlations we can infer from those objects various characteristics of their owners. However, this fact alone does not make signs of the objects; it only turns them into indicators. They can take on the function of signs only in situations when the received customs or conventions confer on them the function of expressing certain definite thoughts about some other objects. From the above it can be seen that one and the same object can function as a sign or only as an indicator, depending on the circumstances. In papers propagating the semiotic approach to culture these two different functions are often confused or insufficiently distinguished. A source of difficulty which contributes to this mistake lies in the fact that the existing customs or conventions are not always clear enough to make it possible to decide whether the relation they establish between some objects is of the sign type, or only of the indicator type.

In order to include all the cited examples under the category of signs one would have to broaden exceedingly the received extension of that concept, so that the extension 'sign' would become indentical with the extension 'indicator'. Such a solution is accepted more or less consciously by practitioners of the semiotic approach. What are the motives for this decision? They seem to believe that otherwise they would not be able to use linguistic concepts and methods in cultural research. The concrete advantages which they hope to gain by this transfer of linguistic methods to cultural research can be reduced to three points. 1. Uniform treatment of all cultural phenomena with the aid of precise linguistic methods will be made possible. 2. It will allow one to draw a scientifically justified demarcation line separating cultural phenomena from natural ones. 3. It will provide for a scientific theory to explain cultural phenomena.

Is the above reasoning correct? Does the application of linguistic methods in the realm of cultural research really entail the necessity to broaden the concept of sign? The answer must be in the negative. The application of semantics, a branch of linguistics,[6] is, of course, possible only in regard to those cultural phenomena which are signs in the third sense here differentiated. In this case it is unnecessary to broaden the concept of sign; nor would such operation bring any useful results. However, those who favour the use of linguistic methods in the realm of culture have usually in mind the methods of phonology and not those of semantics. Thus, for instance, as far as I can ascertain, Lévi-Strauss in his papers on kinship relations or cooking habits has recourse only to the concepts of phonology. Now, with phonology the situation is quite different. Today the reconstruction of the phonetic system of a language can, in principle, be carried out without taking account of the semantic function of its expressions.[7] The basic concepts, of distinctive features, of phonemes, of phonologic equivalence, can be defined without reference to the meaning of language signs. It follows that the concepts and methods of phonology can be usefully applied in research into a domain of phenomena which are not signs at all and do not have any semantic function; in particular, any asemantic cultural phenomena. It is only necessary that there is some structural similarity between the domain in question and the phenomena which form the subject matter of phonology. If this is so, then the intention to use phonological concepts in the realm of cultural phenomena does not by itself imply the need to extend the concept of sign, nor, in fact, does it require any declaration as to how this concept should be defined.

What I have said above will become even more obvious if one realizes that the application of phonology in cultural research to date, never consists in the literal transference of its concepts or statements, but in the use of their analogical counterparts. Are there any rules of forming such equivalents? Making recourse to the methods of mathematical logic, we can describe this procedure as interpretation. A cultural interpretation of a phonological statement S consists, generally speaking, in the substitution of suitable cultural concepts for the concepts of S. Such an operation is possible and meaningful only when the two domains are related by some structural similarity. Let me illustrate the operation of interpretation with the aid of Boolean algebra. This is an abstract theory whose symbols can be given various interpretations. Those interpretations differ with regard to the contents, but are identical in their formal structure. Depending on the chosen interpretation the theorems of Boolean algebra may be turned into statements of sentential calculus, or set theory, or a theory of electronic systems, or else some other theory.

The fact that all these theories are obtained by interpreting one and the same Boolean Algebra does not, of course, imply their mutual identity. The maximal similarity consists, at best, in the isomorphism of their models, i.e. their proper domains of phenomena.

As an example of interpretation let us consider one of the formulae of Boolean Algebra:

$$X \circ Y = Y \circ X$$

Here are some of the possible interpretations of this formula which we obtain by substituting various symbols in place of the variable '$\circ$':

1. $X \vee Y = Y \vee X$ Sentential calculus, law of commutation for disjunction
2. $X \cdot Y = Y \cdot X$ Mathematics, law of commutation for multiplication
3. $X \cup Y = Y \cup X$ Set theory, law of commutation for the union of sets

All these interpretations are formally identical, they all meet the same formal condition stated in the Boolean formula, although their contents are different. In a similar way statements of phonology can be given cultural interpretation, in replacing phonological concepts which appear in those statements by suitable cultural concepts. The question arises, what do we gain by such a procedure of interpretation?. Well, reinterpreted phonological statements supply us with a collection of hypotheses which state relations between cultural phenomena. Which does not mean that such hypotheses are automatically true. To find out if they are true, we have to undertake suitable empirical research.

The existing applications of phonology to cultural research differ widely from the procedure used in the interpretation of Boolean Algebra. And the difference lies not only in the degree of precision. As far as I know, in no instance of such research has a systematic interpretation of the complete phonological system been carried out. What one finds are but fragmentary interpretations in which use is made of selected theorems and concepts of phonology. However, even this is an overstatement. Their claimed application of phonology usually consists in the derivation of some loosely described methodological rules. Here is an example of such a rule: Try to decompose the examined phenomenon into its component parts, and take the opposition of distinctive features as your criterion of division. The analyses of kinship relations and cooking habits supply illustrative examples. The use of the label 'semiotic theory of culture' in reference to such research seems a little exaggerated, and can even be misleading. The term 'phonologic theory of culture' would be more suitable, provided the applications of phonology were to go beyond the use of loosely described rudiments and take on a more systematic character.

We said above that it is not necessary to broaden the concept of sign in order to be able to apply linguistic concepts and methods in cultural research. This statement was substantiated by reference to the structuralist thesis according to which the reconstruction of the phonetic system of a language can, in principle, be carried out without taking account of the semantic function of its expressions. Some authors express doubts as to the correctness of this thesis, and some reject it. To meet these objections I shall presently show that my statement can be defended without recourse to the structuralist thesis. It is enough to point out that there is strucutral similarity between cultural and linguistic phenomena which makes possible cultural interpretation of at least some linguistic statements. In practice we assume such similarity hypothetically, on the basis of the fragmentary knowledge or insights we possess. Then cultural interpretation of some linguistic statements is carried out and the reinterpreted statements are checked for their truthfulness.

It remains to consider whether the applications of phonology based on the extended concept of sign can produce the results expected by those who accept the semiotic theory of culture.

The possibility of a uniform theory of cultural phenomena built with the aid of linguistic methods is still far off. More than that; it is difficult to see how this aim can be achieved. Cultural phenomena are too varied and too complicated to be fully amenable to linguistic methods.

Furthermore, the broadened concept of sign does not seem to provide a suitable tool to be used for making a consistent and scientifically justified division between culture and nature. Indeed the contrary is the case, for the extension of that concept becomes so far-reaching that both cultural and natural phenomena are subsumed under it.

Can phonology be expected to supply a scientific theory which would explain cultural phenomena? I think this question should be answered in the negative. Noam Chomsky seems to be right when he maintains that phonology does not explain its phenomena, but only classifies them.[8] However, a classification of a domain of phenomena does constitute an important initial step toward their explanation. Actually, it is difficult to explain something which is but shapeless, structureless fog. In that sense the use of phonology in cultural research may bring useful results.

I said at the beginning that this chapter is not intended as a full discussion of the semiotic approach, but as a critical analysis of some of its central methodological problems. So attention has been concentrated on works in which the aspects criticised above revealed themselves. I should like to conclude by giving some additional bibliographical data on works in which those problematical aspects do not appear, calling attention mainly to some Polish works on the subject. Exact bibliographical data on these works are given in the bibliography at the end of the book.

Two series under the general editorship of J. Pelc are devoted to the problems of semiotics, one dealing with logical semiotics: *Studia Semiotyczne* (*Semiotic Studies*), and the other with semiotic studies in Poland: *Semiotyka Polska* (*Polish Semiotics*). Various basic concepts of semiotics ('sign', 'symbol', 'indicator', 'representation', etc.), are analysed by J. Kotarbińska, J. Kmita, J. Pelc, T. Pawlowski, B. Stanosz, S. Żółkiewski deals in his works with problems of cultural semiotics. A. Kłoskowska, A. Piotrowski, M. Ziółkowski are concerned with the application of semiotics in the social sciences. The use of semiotics in the history and the theory of art is discussed in the works of R. Ingarden, S. Ossowski, M. Wallis, W. Ławniczak and G. Sztabiński.

I should also like to mention in this context the works of J. Lotman and his collaborators.

NOTES

[1] I concentrate on works in which the methodological problems here discussed arise. Additional bibliographical information on the subject is given at the end of this chapter.

[2] Cf. e.g. Claude Lévi-Strauss, *Anthropologie Structurale*, Paris, 1958; Roland Barthes, 'Eléments de sémiologie', *Communications* nr. 4; Umberto Eco, *La Struttura Assente*, Milano 1968; *Einführung in die Semantik*, München 1972.

[3] For further explanation of the indicator relation compare another chapter in this book: 'The Concept of Indicator in the Social Sciences'.

[4] In differentiating these aspects of the sign relation I make reference to the formulations of such authors as C. S. Peirce, J. Kotarbińska, J. Kmita, W. Ławniczak, J. Pelc. For bibliographical data see Bibliography.

[5] This stipulation gives only a necessary condition for being a sign.

[6] I should like to call attention to the two different meanings of the term 'semantics' which are here involved: 1. semantics as a branch of linguistics and 2. semantics as a branch of semiotics, i.e. the general theory of signs as defined by Ch. Morris.

[7] Cf. e.g. Z. S. Harris, *Structural Linguistics*, Chicago 1963; T. Batóg, *The Axiomatic Method in Phonology*, London 1967.

[8] Cf. N. Chomsky, *Aspects of the Theory of Syntax*, Cambridge, 1965.

CHAPTER XI

THEORY OF QUESTIONS AND ITS APPLICATIONS IN THE SOCIAL SCIENCES

PRELIMINARY REMARKS

Communication by questions and answers is a research procedure which is frequently used in the social sciences. Questions and answers are essential elements in any investigation by means of a questionnaire or an interview. However, if one wants the investigation to yield the optimum result, one has to consider many other related elements, namely: **1.** the person who is to answer the question, **2.** the person who is to ask the question, **3.** the goal of the investigation, **4.** the situation in which the investigation is made, which covers psychological, sociological, political, and other factors. It is only when all those elements are taken into account that a good interview or questionnaire can be worked out. Scientific theory concerned with the study of communication by questions might be termed general theory of questions. The logical theory of questions, the subject matter of which is confined to questions themselves is merely an indispensable part of the general theory. It is obvious that in such a general theory the knowledge gathered by many other disciplines, such as psychology, sociology, information theory, logic, methodology is assumed. As is known, such a general theory unfortunately does not exist. There are only fragments of one, scattered throughout books and papers in the form of analyses of examples of ill-formulated questions or mishandled interviews. Those fragments also include various practical recommendations. The logical theory of questions is the only part of the general theory that has been worked out in a systematic way.

The present chapter outlines the main concepts used in the logical theory of questions and the classification of questions based on those concepts. These concepts will later be applied to analyse ill formulated questions in sociological questionnaires or interviews. Results achieved by several authors will be made use of, above all those presented by N. Belnap in his *Analysis of Questions*, which includes a review of many basic concepts and also a classification of questions.

In ordinary parlance a question may perform several functions. The person who asks them may seek information, or may want to check the amount of information the respondent has. The latter situation is very common in the process of teaching and also in sociological research, when the knowledge of certain facts or the possession of certain information may serve as an indicator of the respondent's interest in the issue to which the question refers. A question may also serve as a specific stimulus intended to evoke a sequence of verbal responses which would reveal the respondent's psycho-social attitudes and dispositions.

Despite this plurality of functions, questions met in every-day life and in science share the same outward structure, namely the grammatical form of a question. That form may, obviously, vary according to the type of question which it expresses. But, in ordinary parlance it is possible to formulate one and the same question both as a sentence which has the grammatical form of a question, and as a sentence which is declarative in form. There are also questions which are formulated in an abbreviated form that often prevents us from comprehending them exactly. Another difficulty stems from the syntactic or semantic ambiguity of questions encountered in every-day speech. All these difficulties make it necessary to base the logical theory of questions on an artificial language, defined with precision as to its syntax and semantics. This is not to mean, however, that no useful recommendations for an analysis of questions formulated in ordinary parlance can be derived from the logical theory of questions. On the contrary, that theory provides a useful instrument of analysis, examples of which will be given below.

The general theory of questions makes a distinction between two important types of questions: closed and open.[1] Here are examples: 1. Do you live in a town of more than 10 000 inhabitants? (a closed question); 2. What are the interhuman relations in a socialist enterprise? (an open question). Closed questions determine strictly the form of those sentences which are possible direct answers to such questions: 'I live in a town of more than 10 000 inhabitants' or the negation of that sentence, are direct answers to question (1). It should be pointed out that in every-day language closed questions are often formed in an abbreviated way, which may make it difficult to reconstruct the precise form of possible direct answers to those questions. Precise and complete forms of closed questions of different kinds are provided by the logical theory of questions; these forms can be used in the analysis and reconstruction of closed questions formulated in every-day language.

In the case of open questions it is not known exactly what a particular question is about, and hence it is not known exactly what the answer is to be like. An answer to an open question may take on different forms, depending on various factors — psychological, sociological, etc. — that determine the verbal behaviour of the respondent. Open questions leave the respondent a wide margin of freedom in his choice of the answer. This property of the open question may, according to circumstances, be an advantage or a disadvantage; it is a disadvantage always when we want the respondent to understand us precisely and to give a strictly defined answer. But it is an advantage in all those cases in which it is not advisable or possible strictly to determine the form of the answer.

The meaning of open questions is often analogous to the role of vaguely general titles which indicate roughly what problems are dealt with in the book, article or lecture bearing that title. It is only later, when the content is expounded in detail, that problems are formulated in terms of a number of closed questions. For instance, the open question, 'What was the course of the electoral campaign in Britain?' may be replaced later in the text by a series of closed questions, e.g. 'What percentage of those entitled to vote did actually vote?' 'Was the percentage of the voters the same in all electoral districts?'. 'Was Mr A. elected?'. 'Were there any political demonstrations near the polling stations?'. 'At what time was the last vote cast at the X. polling station?'. 'Which social group (out of those listed explicitly) had the greatest percentage of abstentions?', etc.

But it often happens that the vaguely general formulation of a problem in terms of an open question is not just a headline that provides general information to be later specified with concrete closed questions, but represents all we can afford to ask about in a given discipline at its given stage of development. For, it is obvious that in order to be able to formulate problems in the form of closed questions we must have at our disposal an adequate set of concepts and a certain knowledge of the field in question, which indicates that the discipline concerned with the studies of the facts involved has achieved a certain stage of development. It might also be said that an important aspect in the evolution of science consists in replacing problems vaguely expressed by means of open questions, by problems couched in precise closed questions.

THE LOGICAL THEORY OF QUESTIONS

In my analyses I shall make use of concepts introduced in the abovementioned book by N. Belnap. The discussion will, however, be confined only to concepts which are indispensable for the presentation of Belnap's classification of questions. In particular, Belnap's analysis of the syntactic and semantic structure of the language of the logical theory of questions will be omitted. Belnap's analysis, while very interesting and important for a full understanding of his theory, is of less significance to those applications of that theory with which we are concerned in this chapter.

Belnap sees the task of the logical theory of questions in defining the relation between question and answer. Every question presents a set of alternatives, and an answer selects a certain subset of that set. The same set of alternatives can be used to construct different questions, depending on the manner in which that selection is to be made. Consider the following two questions: **1.** Which of the following films: 'The Barrier', 'The Red Desert', 'Sunset Boulevard', 'The Pastoral Symphony', have you seen? **2.** Name one film you have seen from among the films: 'The Barrier', 'The Red Desert', 'Sunset Boulevard', 'The Pastoral Symphony'? Both questions present the same set of alternatives, but they are different questions since each of them makes a different selection request. In his answer to question (1) the respondent has to name all the films he has seen and in the answer to question (2) only one of those films. Of course two questions may differ as to selection request not only in cases when they present the same set of alternatives. Such a difference may occur between any two questions.

So far two factors have been indicated which determine the type of questions: the set of presented alternatives, and the selection request. They will be supplemented by a third one — the completeness claim request.[2] The completeness claim defines how many of the true alternatives presented by the question have been selected by the respondent. Consider the following two questions: **1.** What is an example of a prime number in the interval [2, 10]? **2.** Which of the following factors is, in your opinion, the most frequent cause of divorce: marrying too young; adultery; people marrying without having a sufficient knowledge of the character of the other party; marriage as an institution does not suit people nowadays; alcoholism of one of the spouses; marrying without taking financial conditions into account; sexual maladjustment of the spouses; gainful employment of women and their resulting financial independence.[3] Question (2) requires that the respondent in his direct answer lists all the presented alternatives which he believes to be true — which in this case reduce to one. Thus this question includes the maximal completeness claim. The case is different with question (1); it makes the minimal completeness claim, which in fact renounces all claim whatever. By selecting certain alternatives the respondent does not state what part of the true presented alternatives he has selected. It is worth-while noting that questions (1) and (2) are identical as to selection request — direct answers to both questions should select exactly one of the presented alternatives; but they differ as to completeness claim: the former includes the minimal and the latter the maximal completeness claim.

There is a gamut of intermediate cases between the maximal and the minimal completeness claim. Consider a situation in which the task is to find out the effectiveness of advertisements in a periodical. Suppose further that this requires interviewing a number of subscribers to that periodical. It is, of course, irrelevant which subscribers are selected, provided that they form a random sample of sufficient size, e.g. 1 per cent of all subscribers. In such a situation the question: Who are 1 per cent of your subscribers? is an example of a question in which the completeness claim is neither maximal nor minimal but lies between these two extremes.[4]

It follows from the above that only those questions which make the maximal completeness claim demand "the whole truth", i.e., demand the specification of all the true alternatives from among the alternatives presented by a given question. Why should the respondent be asked for less than the whole truth? Now, it is not always possible or necessary to demand the whole truth. It is not possible when the respondent knows only some of the true alternatives, or when the set of the true alternatives to be specified is very large or infinite. It is not necessary when partial information given by the respondent is sufficient for given theoretical or practical purposes, and at the same time the full information would be too expensive. The costs may be interpreted broadly so as to cover not only monetary expenses, but other values as well. By 'costs' we may mean the large amount of time needed to answer a long questionnaire covering 'the whole truth', which may discourage the respondent. In all such cases we usually resort to questions which make less-than-the maximal completeness claims.

Consider now the ways in which a question presents its alternatives. First, they may be explicitly mentioned in the question. Here is an example of a question presenting its alternatives in his way: 'What is your education: elementary, secondary, or higher?' Belnap calls them whether-questions; in the Polish literature of the subject (Ajdukiewicz, Giedymin) they are called decision questions.

Consider now the question: 'Which natural number equals $7 + 5$?'. The alternatives presented by this question are not explicitly mentioned in the question, but we can construct their general form. Each alternative can be obtained by substitution from the sentential function $7 + 5 = x$. In order fully to define the set of the alternatives we need a function determining the range of the variable x. The information contained in the question suggests the function: x is a natural number. It defines which type of names of objects is to be substituted for the variable x. This type of questions is called by Belnap which-questions. The corresponding term in the Polish literature of the subject is complementation questions.

When asking a question correctly we always presuppose something. For instance, the question: 'When did John die?' presupposes that John did die. Such an implied statement made when we ask a question is called a presupposition of that question. The issue of presuppositions is treated in different ways by different authors. In Belnap's theory, every question has only one presupposition, namely that at least one direct answer to that question is true. In this connection the issue arises how, in Belnap's theory, are we to treat answers such as 'None' 'nobody'. I shall revert to this later on.

Assuming the three mentioned properties of questions – selection request; completeness claim; and the way of presenting alternatives – as his principle of division Belnap classifies questions into six basic types. These types will be discussed now, although Belnap's formal definitions will be omitted.

1. *Unique-alternative whether-questions.* 'Are you a member of a housing co-operative?' 'Do you attend religious services regularly, occasionally, on special occasions (prenuptial confession, baptism of children etc.), never?'[5] The former question is a two-place whether-question, and the latter is a four-place whether-question. The content of the questions indicates that each requires the respondent to select exactly one of the alternatives presented by the question, and the alternative thus specified is to be the only true one. The maximal completeness claim is here combined with the selection request which calls for specifying exactly one of the presented alternatives. Thus the respondent states that the alternative he selects is the only true one.

2. *Unique-alternative which-questions.* 'Which of the films you have seen within the last three months do you like best?' 'Which natural number equals the sum 7 + 5?' Questions of this type are identical with the unique-alternative whether-questions as to selection request and completeness claim. The difference consists in the manner of presenting alternatives: in the case of which-questions they are not presented explicitly, but can be obtained by the appropriate substitution from the sentential function defined by the question.

3. *Complete-list whether-questions.* 'Have you: a telephone at home; a typewriter; a camera; a tape-recorder; a bicycle; a motorcycle; a car?'[6] 'In your opinion, should the court deprive the parents of their parental rights in the case of: continued alcoholism of the parents; prostitution of a parent; utter poverty of the parents: ill-treatment of the children by the parents; commission of a crime by the parents; grave mental disease of the parents; total neglect of the children by the parents?'[7]

Questions of this type present the alternatives by enumerating them explicitly. In that respect they are identical with the unique-alternative whether-questions discussed above. The difference is in the selection request and the completeness claim. They require that a direct answer should select all the true alternatives. For instance, the full formulation of one of the possible direct answers to the first question above would be 'I have a telephone at home, a typewriter, and a tape-recorder, but I have neither a camera, nor a bicycle, nor a motorcycle, nor a car.'

4. *Complete-list which questions.* 'Which contemporary French authors do you know?' 'Who has successfully climbed Mount Everest?' A direct answer to a question of this type should select all those alternatives which are true in the opinion of the respondent. Thus questions of this type are identical with the complete-list whether-questions as to the selection request and the completeness claim. They differ in the way they present their alternatives, which in this case are not mentioned explicitly in the question, but can be obtained by the appropriate substitution from the sentential function defined by the question. One of the possible direct answers to the first question could be: 'I know Sartre, Claudel, and Butor, and these are the only contemporary French authors I know.'

5. *Non-exclusive whether-questions.* 'Is John a sociologist or a mathematician?' 'Can you speak fluently any of the following languages: English, French, German, Russian (please underline one item)?' The selection request made by such a question calls for a direct answer to mention one of the true alternatives only, although it is not excluded that other alternatives, not mentioned in the answer, may also be true. These questions make the minimal completeness claim. A direct answer does not declare anything with regard to the truth value of the alternatives not mentioned in the answer and hence it consists of one element only, namely the only selected alternative. The second example above has a parenthesized explanation that only one true alternative should be mentioned in the answer. Such explanations sometimes occur in sociological questionnaires, and they are very useful since they help to identify the type of the question.

6. *Non-exclusive which-questions.* 'Who was one of the foreign conductors who performed this season in the Cracow Philharmonic Hall?' 'Which of the Polish university centres is, in your opinion, a suitable place for a modern research establishment for experimental psychology?' These are examples of this type of questions. They require a direct answer to select only one of the alternatives presented by the question, and at the same time they make the minimal completeness claim.

Questions formulated in every-day language cannot always be classed unambiguously as whether-questions or which-questions. In particular, not every question that begins with 'which' must necessarily be classed as a which-question. Consider, for instance the question: 'Which of the persons listed below is the author of *Adolphe*: Proust, Constant, or Stendhal?' Now two interpretations of this question are plausible. According to one of them it is a which-question, and the various alternatives can be obtained by substitution from the sentential function 'x is the author of *Adolphe*'.

But another interpretation seems equally plausible, and perhaps even more natural. It sees it as a whether-question, and the use of 'which' at the beginning of the question is only a matter of formulation, intended to make the question as short as possible. The full version would be: 'Is Proust the author of Adolphe, or is it Constant, or Stendhal?' It can easily be noted that in the latter formulation all the possible alternatives are stated explicitly, so that we have to do with a whether-question.

Very many questions encountered in scientific texts and in every-day life can be interpreted in the two ways described above. But such a double interpretation is possible only if the set of the alternatives presented by a question is small. If that set is very large or infinite the question presenting that set can be interpreted only as a which-question, since a whether-question presents its alternatives by specifying them explicitly, which is practically not possible in the case of a very large set, and by definition impossible in the case of an infinite set.

It has been said above that when formulating a question we state something which is the presupposition of that question. In Belnap's theory, the truth of at least one direct answer is presupposed for any question, regardless of its type.

In this connection it is worth-while to reflect on the answers such as 'none', etc., which are sometimes given to which-questions. Consider an example given by T. Kubiński.[8] The teacher asks his pupils: 'Who has solved the arithmetic problem?' The abbreviated answer may be: 'None of us'. This is a complete-list which-question, and a direct answer to it should be a conjunction of sentences each of which mentions a pupil of the given class, who has solved the problem. The answer 'none' does not satisfy this condition and hence, in Belnap's theory, is not a direct answer. Belnap calls such answers corrective, since they cancel the presupposition of the question involved.

In current parlance, and in sociological research as well, we often come across statements which, while being answers to certain questions, are not direct answers. They are what is called indirect answers. Since an analysis of this type of answers may be useful for a sociologist, we shall discuss them briefly by drawing formulations from a book by J. Giedymin.[9]

Indirect answers can be described in a general way as answers which are linked with direct answers by relations of logical consequence. Because of those relations, statements which are not direct answers provide a certain amount of information and may thus be treated as answers to questions posed. Those relations of consequence may be of two kinds, which accounts for the distinction between complete and partial indirect answers. A non-contradictory sentence S is a complete indirect answer to a question if a direct answer to that question is a logical consequence of S; it is further required that S is different from any direct answer to that question. A sentence S is a partial indirect answer to a question if it is a logical consequence of a direct answer to that question, also with the above proviso that S must be different from any direct answer. In every-day language the relations of consequence which hold between direct and indirect answers occur very often in elliptic form, i.e., they hold on the strength of certain statements which are tacitly assumed. In such cases we shall speak of a relativized concept of indirect answer, i.e., relativized to that tacit assumption. Thus a non-contradictory sentence S is a complete indirect answer to a question with respect to a statement E if a direct answer to that question is a consequence of the conjunction of the sentences S and E. Likewise, a sentence S is a partial indirect answer to a question with respect to a statement E if S is a logical consequence of the conjunction of E and a direct answer. The proviso that S be different from any direct answer also applies to relativized definitions. Below are some examples illustrating various kinds of indirect answers. The sentence: 'He is a Pole' is a complete indirect answer to the question: Is he a European?' since a direct positive answer is a logical consequence of that sentence (in conjunction with the definition of the term 'Pole'). The sentence 'This is made of copper' is a complete indirect answer to the question: 'Does this conduct electric current?'; it is an indirect answer with respect to the empirical statement: 'Copper conducts electric current' since a direct positive answer to the question' 'Does this conduct electric current?' is a logical consequence of the conjunction of the sentences: 'This is made of copper' and 'Copper conducts electric current.' The sentence: 'This is attracted by a magnet' is a partial indirect answer to the question: 'Is this made of iron?' As in the previous case, we have to do with an indirect answer with respect to the empirical statement: 'Iron is attracted by a magnet'; the sentence: 'This is attracted by a magnet' is a logical consequence of the conjunction of that statement and a direct positive answer to that question.

The above definitions of indirect answers are slightly modified formulations of those given by J. Giedymin. They are very useful in the analysis of various kinds of answers with which a sociologist has to do. This is why it is worth-while to point to some of their shortcomings which we ought to realize.

It has been mentioned that whether a statement is an indirect answer to a question depends on the relations of logical consequence holding between that statement and a direct answer to that question. Now, the weak point of the definitions given above is that the relation of logical consequence is not close enough to exclude those statements which in view of current intuitions we would be unwilling to accept as indirect answers. Further analysis should accordingly strive to impose additional restrictions on the concept of indirect answer, so that this concept would cover those statements only which are sufficiently closely related to a given question.

Here is an example. The sentence: 'Two times two makes four, or it is not true that two times two makes four' would have, by definition, to be accepted as a partial indirect answer to the question: 'Will Mr A. be re-elected?', since that sentence, being a substitution of a logical tautology, is a logical consequence of any sentence, and hence also of any direct answer to this question. But to accept it as such would contradict current intuitions. since there is no sufficiently close relation between that sentence and the question involved.

APPLICATIONS

Theory of questions makes it possible to formulate a typology of major errors which may occur in the construction and use of questions. Some hints are provided by the logical theory of questions itself; they concern issues which can be described in terms of concepts used by that theory, i.e., the recognition of the type of a given question and its correct formulation. Other useful indications can be provided only by the general theory of questions.

Distinction is made above all between two categories of question defects: those characteristic of questions as such, and those of a more general nature. In the light of Belnap's theory, the first category includes: 1. defects of the alternatives presented by a question; 2. defects of the selection request; 3. defects of the completeness claim. The second category of defects, which are not characteristic of questions as such, but may occur in various sentences and phrases, includes obscurity or vagueness of terms, lack of empirical meaning, faulty syntax, etc. The nature of these two categories accounts for the fact that they have been mainly studied by logicians and methodologists. The attention of sociologists has been attracted by defects of a third category — defects which appear in the very process of communication by questions, i.e., in making interviews and in collecting data by means of questionnaires. In analysing these defects it does not suffice to take into account the question and the language in which it is formulated; other factors must also be considered, and these include: the interviewer, the respondent, the circumstances — psychological, sociological, political, etc., — under which the interview takes place. In the present chapter I am mainly concerned with defects belonging to the first two categories.

First, consider a number of questions relative to the first category of defects (the questions have been taken from sociological questionnaires). Both in every-day language and in sociological texts, questions and answers are usually formulated in a manner which makes them incomplete with regard to the requirements of the logical theory of questions. This makes it difficult to identify the type of question. Hence it may happen that the interpretation of some questions, as here assumed, does not fully comply with the intentions of the authors who have formulated these questions.

In this question it is not clear what set of alternatives is presented: 'Are you for or against pensions and benefits for the unemployed?'[10] It would seem that this is a unique-alternative whether-question, but it is not clear what alternatives are presented by it. Let P and B stand respectively for the sentences: 'I am for pensions for the unemployed' and 'I am for benefits for the unemployed', and let the negations of these sentences be symbolized by the corresponding capital letters preceded by the '—' symbol. The two interpretations of the question under consideration which suggest themselves might by symbolized as follows: '$[PB, -P-B]$?' and '$[PB, -(PB)]$?' But the case '$-P-B$' is of course different from '$-(PB)$'. In the former the respondent is against both pensions and benefits, which is not necessarily the case with the latter interpretation: here merely the respondent's opposition to the joint payment of pensions and benefits is expressed, and this is equivalent to his opposition either to pensions or to benefits. But a third interpretation is possible, in which the question is treated as a concretion of two questions of the form '$[P, -P]$?' and '$[B, -B]$?' and these are two unique-alternative whether-questions. Each of the above three interpretations constructs a different question, and an answer to each of these questions provides different information on the respondent's attitude towards pensions and benefits for the unemployed. The most detailed and complete information is provided by answers to the two questions determined by the third interpretation' these answers also determine answers to the questions '$[PB, -P-B]$?' and '$[PB, -(PB)]$?' but not conversely.

In connection with questions of the type 'Are you for or against pensions and benefits for the unemployed?' we often encounter in relevant sociological texts the rule that in interviews, questionnaires, etc., a question ought to refer to a single issue only. It is believed that the question quoted above infringes that rule since it refers to two issues.

Is this rule justified? First of all, the rule is not clear, and it would be difficult to formulate it precisely in such a way that we always know whether a question refers to a single issue, or to more than one issue. For instance, how are we to interpret the following question: 'Are you in favour of a joint admission to the United Nations of the German Democratic Republic, the German Federal Republic, the Korean People's Democratic Republic and Spain, or against a joint admission of these countries?' Does this question refer to a single issue only, or to a number of issues? At any rate, it is a correct two-place unique-alternative whether-question:

'[G.D.R. · G.F.R. · K.P.D.R. · S., ─(G.D.R. · G.F.R. · K.P.D.R. · S.)]'.

It seems that the point is not so much that one should ask about one issue only, as that one should ask in such a way that the respondent can clearly see what alternatives are presented by a given question.

These comments do not mean to deny that under certain circumstances it seems advisable to avoid complex questions, concerned with 'more than one issue' each, for the fear that the alternatives each such question presents may, because of complexity, be misunderstood by respondents. For instance, in the examples quoted above the alternatives '─(PB)' and '─(G.D.R. · G.F.R. · K.P.D.R. · S.)' are equivalent to the alternatives '─P or ─B' and '─G.D.R. or ─G.F.R. or ─K.P.D.R. or ─S.', respectively, but many respondents may not know that the negation of a conjunction is equivalent to a disjunction of the negated elements of that conjunction (and not, e.g. to the negation of each of the elements), and so they may not comprehend clearly the meaning of the complex alternatives, and hence the meaning of the entire question.

The following is an example of a question defective with regard to selection request: A questionnaire included in A. Podgórecki's book quoted above has the following two questions: 'Have you had an opportunity to discuss the upbringing of children?' 'If so, did you discuss it with: your friends, at a public meeting, at school, with a priest, with other persons?'[11]

It seems natural to interpret this example not as two separate questions, but as a single whether-question. Recorded in such a form the question would look rather clumsy. Have you had an opportunity to discuss the upbringing of children with your friends? At a public meeting? At school? With a priest? With other persons?[12] Podgórecki's formulation is stylistically more elegant, and also it simplifies the answer of those respondents who have never had an opportunity to discuss the upbringing of children.

Nevertheless it is not clear what is the selection request of this question: it is difficult to say whether the respondent in his answer has to specify one of the alternatives presented by the question, or rather all the true alternatives. The formulation seems to indicate that one alternative is to be specified, but, on the other hand, the alternatives are not incompatible, which might suggest that the respondent is expected to list all the true alternatives. The respondent's position could be made easier by a comment like those added to many other questions in the same questionnaire. Such comments indicate the number of alternatives which the respondent ought to mention in his answer. In the case now under consideration this might be the instruction: 'Please, specify one alternative only (or all the true alternatives)', according to the selection request intended by the author of the questionnaire.

An example of a question in which the completeness claim is not clearly defined: 'Should the Polish Youth Union in your opinion bring up its members to be: **a.** exemplary citizens, **b.** supporters of the socialist system, **c.** communists, **d.** "don't know"?'[13]

The identification of the type of this question is made more difficult by the occurrence of the item 'don't know'. An analysis of questions containing such an item will be attempted below. If this item is disregarded, a whether-question is obtained. The question is ambiguous as to selection request: it is not clear whether the respondent is expected to mention one of the presented alternatives only, or more than one. The authors' comments in their article concerned with that questionnaire suggest that the respondent was expected to specify one alternative only, but in fact many respondents understood the authors' intention differently and listed in their answers a number of alternatives. The question is also not clear as to the completeness claim. As a result, it is not known whether a respondent, when specifying one of the alternatives, declares that in his opinion this is the only true alternative, or that it is only one of the many true alternatives presented by the question.

Concerning those questions which present sets of many alternatives certain sociological texts recommend that the alternatives be mutually exclusive.[14] On the whole this recommendation is not correct, and is applicable only to two types of questions: unique-alternative whether-questions and unique-alternative which-questions.

As mentioned above, the *presupposition* of every question is that at least one direct answer to that question is true.

Here is an example of a question which is defective in that respect: 'Do you think that members of the Polish Youth Union are superior to non-members: a. in political horizons, b. in social activeness, c. in honesty, d. in manners, e. as book readers, f. as good colleagues, g. in striving for better professional standards, h. as good workers, i. in concern about public property?'[15] How is this question to be classed? Its formulation does not enable one to identify it. At least two interpretations suggest themselves. In the first interpretation it is a nine-place complete-list whether-question. A direct answer to such a question ought to specify all those respects in which members of the Polish Youth Union are superior to non-members, and at any rate it must specify at least one respect, since otherwise the presupposition of the question would not be satisfied. But in their comments the authors state that some respondents thought that none of the alternatives presented by the question occurs. In such a case the respondents were advised not to mark any item. But this proved unsatisfactory since apparently there were respondents who would have marked the item 'they are not superior in anything', should such an item be included, and as it was missing they believed they had to mark one item of those listed.[16]

According to the second interpretation we do not have here to do with a single question, but with an abbreviated formulation of nine questions. Each of these questions is a two-place whether-question based on a couple of mutually contradictory sentences. Thus, item (c) is an abbreviated formulation of the question: 'Do you think that members of the Polish Youth Union are superior to non-members in honesty?'. Such a question admits two direct answers: in the affirmative and in the negative. The same would hold for other questions, corresponding to the remaining items. This indicates that the interpretation now under consideration does not presuppose that members of the Polish Youth Union are superior to non-members in one of the respects listed above. Since, if a person answers in the negative all the nine questions, the presupposition of each of these questions is satisfied (at least one direct answer to each question – namely that in the negative – is true), but this does not amount to the opinion that members of the Polish Youth Union are in some respect (out of those listed) superior to non-members. In this interpretation, the introductory part of the question, treated as an abbreviated formulation of nine questions, should be couched in a different way, e.g.: 'Do you think that members of the Polish Youth Union are superior to non-members in any respects listed below?'.

An example of a question whose meaning is ambiguous; this is caused by vagueness of the terms 'many', 'almost everything'. This question was put to respondents in the United States:

'Would you like many changes and reforms to take place in this country, or would you prefer almost everything to remain as it was before the war?'

Sociological questionnaires often include questions one entry of which is: *'Other items – specify which'*. Here is an example:

'Suppose your salary is raised by 25 per cent. On what would you spend that extra money in the first place: **a.** food, **b.** clothing, **c.** housing, **d.** furniture, **e.** entertainment and travel, **f.** home appliances, **g.** other items – specify which.'[17] How is such a question to be interpreted? 'Other items' sometimes simply stands for a full specification of all the remaining alternatives, which would be inconvenient because of their large number. Such abbreviated formulations can make a given question difficult to comprehend, and in particular to grasp what is the set of alternatives presented by the question. Moreover, such abbreviations are admissible only if the respondents know well what are the alternatives not stated explicitly. More frequently, however, the entry 'other items' reflects ignorance with regard to the omitted alternatives. The author of the questionnaire may guess vaguely what they are, but he is not in a position to specify them precisely. Endeavours to do so do not serve the purpose in this case, since such a precise specification could only be made at the price of disregarding those alternatives 'which cannot be foreseen'. This suggests the solution that in such situations a question with the entry 'other items' be treated not as a single question, but as a concretion of two questions, one of which is closed, and the other is open. The above question would, accordingly, consist of two questions:

1. 'Would you spend an increase of your salary above all on **a.** food, **b.** clothing, **c.** housing, **d.** furniture, **e.** entertainment and travel, **f.** home appliances?'. 2. 'On what else (i.e., except the items specified under (1)) would you spend an increase of your salary?' The first question is a six-place uniquealternative whether-question,[18] and the second is an open question.

Sociological questionnaires often include questions with the entry *'don't know'*, *'no opinion'*, or the like. Here is an example: 'Who should be charged with parental rights and duties if both parents of a child are deprived by court of their parental authority: **a.** municipal authorities, **b.** relatives, **c.** a person indicated by the parents, **d.** a priest, **e.** school authorities, **f.** other persons or institutions (specify which), **g.** I do not know?. Please underline one item only'. It seems that such questions also are to be treated as abbreviations, each of which stands for two different questions. The present example would, accordingly, be a concretion of the following two questions:

1. 'Have you a well formed opinion on the issue of who should be charged with parental rights and duties if both parents of a child are deprived by court

of their parental authority?' 2. "Who should take over such rights and duties: a. municipal authorities, b. relatives, c. a person indicated by the parents, d. a priest, e. school authorities, f. other persons or institutions (specify which)?' Obviously only those persons would be asked the second question who have answered the first in the affirmative. What is the type of these questions? The first is a two-place unique-alternative whether-question. The second could at the first glance be treated as a six-place unique-alternative whether-question. The situation is complicated by the fact that the second question has an 'other' item, which indicates that that question is in turn a concretion of two separate questions, whose type can be identified by the procedure used previously. Thus we have to do here with a complex question which, when recorded in a non-abbreviated form, would divide into three separate questions.

In questionnaires and interviews we can use closed and open questions. Which are better? This obviously depends on the situation and on the objectives of the sociologist. If his objective is to obtain from his respondents exact information on a precisely defined subject, he should use closed questions, since closed questions strictly define the form of the possible direct answers.[19]

In other situations open questions are more useful. In a psychological interview the questions are intended to evoke a sequence of verbal responses in the course of which the attitudes and dispositions of the respondent may freely reveal themselves. In the opinion of psychologists, open questions, because they are loose and do not strictly determine the form of the possible answers, help the hidden mental characteristics of the respondent to reveal themselves freely. They claim that sometimes it is advisable to ask questions about issues with which the respondent is not well acquainted. When trying to answer such a question he will fill the gaps in his knowledge with elements which are projections of his inner self. It is to be emphasized that the belief in the usefulness of open questions in situations of this kind is based on the acceptance of certain empirical statements on the relations between the manner of asking questions and the respondent's verbal responses.

Open questions are also superior to closed ones when it is not clear what is the important thing to ask about. For instance, consider the question: 'How do you usually spend weekends?'[20] A sociologist who makes an interview can, of course, specify a number of things to be covered by such a question, but he is not in a position to foresee them all. Should he nevertheless formulate a closed question which covers only those things he has taken into account, he might lose an opportunity to obtain important information from the respondent.

NOTES

[1] A similar distinction is made in sociology, but it seems that the concepts are somewhat differently interpreted there.

[2] For brevity to be called hereafter 'completeness claim'.

[3] This is a modification of a question in *Zjawiska prawne w opinii publicznej (Legal Issues as Reflected in Public Opinion)*, by A. Podgórecki, Warszawa 1964, p. 88.

[4] Cf. N. Belnap, *An Analysis of Questions*, 1963, p. 32.

[5] A. Podgórecki, *op. cit.*, p. 92.

[6] S. Dzięcielska, *Sytuacja społeczna dziennikarzy polskich (The Social Status of Polish Journalists)*, Warszawa-Wrocław 1962.

[7] This is a slightly modified version of a question in the Podgórecki's book p. 154.

[8] T. Kubiński, 'Przegląd niektórych zagadnień logiki pytań' (A Review of Selected Issues in the Logic of Questions). *Studia Logica*, XVIII, 1966, p. 126. Cf. also *Wstęp do logicznej teorii pytań (An Introduction to the Logical Theory of Questions)*, Warsaw 1971, by the same author.

[9] J. Giedymin, *Problemy, założenia, rozstrzygnięcia (Problems, Assumptions, Decisions)*, Poznań 1964.

[10] Cf. C. F. Cannel, R. L. Kahn, 'The Collection of Data by Interviewing' in: Festinger, D. Katz (eds.), *Research Methods in the Behavioral Sciences*. New York, 1953.

[11] A. Podgórecki, *op. cit.*, p. 156.

[12] A separate issue arises in connection with the item 'with other persons', included in the question. The issue will be discussed below.

[13] From the questionnaire included in the paper by M. Jarosińska and H. Najduchowska, 'Młodzież robotnicza wobec Związku Młodzieży Polskiej w okresie kryzysu' (Attitudes of Young Workers Toward the Polish Youth Union in Its Crisis), in: *Z badań klasy robotniczej i inteligencji (Studies on the Working Class and the Intelligentsia)*, Łódź 1958, p. 131.

[14] Cf. S. Nowak (ed.), *Metody badań socjologicznych (Methods of Sociological Research)*, Warszawa 1965, p. 128.

[15] From a questionnaire in the above quoted paper by M. Jarosińska and H. Najduchowska, p. 132.

[16] Ibid., p. 133.

[17] From a questionnaire included in *Pozycja społeczna urzędników w Polsce Ludowej (The Social Status of Civil Servants and Clerical Staff in Peoples' Poland)* by K. Lutyńska, Warszawa-Wrocław 1965.

[18] The formulation of this question does not make it possible strictly to identify its completeness claim. Perhaps the author intended it to be not a unique-alternative question, but a complete-list question.

[19] The terms 'Open question' and 'closed question' are used in their respective meanings established in the logical theory of questions.

[20] From a questionnaire in the above quoted book by K. Lutyńska, p. 247.

BIBLIOGRAPHY

Adorno T. W. (*et al.*), *The Authoritarian Personality*, New York 1950.
Ajdukiewicz K., *Język i poznanie (Language and Cognition)*, Warszawa, 1960. Polish.
Albert H., 'Ethik und Meta-Ethik'. In: H. Albert, E. Topitsch (Hrsg.), *Werturteilsstreit*, Darmstadt 1971.
Alsleben K., *Ästhetische Redundanz*, Quickborn 1962.
Aqvist L., *A New Approach to the Logical Theory of Interrogatives*. Uppsala 1965.
Asperen van G. M., 'Über die Wertfreiheit einer metaetischen Theorie'. *Bijdragen* 38, 1977.
Banach A., *O kiczu (On Kitsch)*, Krakow, 1968. Polish.
Bar-Hillel Y., *Language and Information*. Reading, Mass. 1964.
Barthes R., 'Eléments de sémiologie', *Communications* No. 4.
Batóg T., *The Axiomatic Method in Phonology*. London 1967.
Becker J., Vostell W., *Happenings*. Reinbek 1965.
Belnap N., *An Analysis of Questions*. California 1963.
Bense M., *Aesthetica* I, II, III, IV. Stuttgart, Krefeld, Baden-Baden 1954, 1956, 1958, 1960.
Berka K., Kreiser L. (Hrsg.), *Logik-Texte*. Berlin 1971.
Birkhoff G. D., 'A Mathematical Theory of Aesthetics and its Applications to Poetry and Music'. In: *Collected Mathematical Papers*, New York 1958.
Black M., *Models and Metaphors*. Ithaca 1962.
Blegvad M., *Competing and Complementary Patterns of Explanation in Social Science*. Copenhagen 1975.
Bose N. K., *Selections from Gandhi*. Ahmedabad 1948.
Büschges G., Lütke-Bornefeld I., (Hrsg.), *Praktische Organisations-forschung*. Reinbek bei Hamburg 1977.
Carnap R., *The Logical Foundations of Probability*. Chicago 1950.
Carnap R., 'Testability and Meaning'. *Philosophy of Science*, 1936, 1937.
Carnap R., 'The Methodological Character of Theoretical Concepts'. *Minnesota Studies in the Philosophy of Science*, vol. I, 1956.
Carus P., *The Gospel of Buddha*. New Delhi 1961.
Chomsky N., *Aspects of the Theory of Syntax*. Cambridge, Mass. 1965.
Czempiel E. O., 'Friede und Konflikt in der Gesellschaftslehre'. *Aus Politik und Zeit Geschichte*, B 20–74.
Dorfles G., *Kitsch. An Anthology of Bad Taste*. London 1969.
Eco U., *La Struttura di Assente*. Milano 1968.
Eco U., *Einführung in die Semantik*. Müchen 1972.
Elton W., (ed.) *Aesthetics and Language*, Oxford 1959.
Essler W. K., *Wissenschaftstheorie. I*. Freidburg-München 1970.
Farnsworth P. R., *The Social Psychology of Music*. New York 1958.
Frank H., *Informationsästhetik*. Waiblingen 1959.

Frey, F. W., Kessler A. R. Rothchile J. E., *Index Construction and Validation*. Massachussetts 1967.
Fromm E., *Der Moderne Mensch und seine Zukunft*. 1960.
Geismann G., *Ethik und Herrschaftsordnung*. Tübingen 1974.
Giedymin J., *Problems, Assumptions, Decisions*. Poznan 1964. Polish.
Giesz L., *Phänomenologie des Kitsches*. Heidelberg 1960.
Gollwitzer G., *Die Kunst als Zeichen*. München 1963.
Goodman N., *Languages of Art*. London 1969.
Grzyb G., *Theoretische Probleme der linguistischen Semantik*. Bielefeld 1974.
Gunzenhäuser R., *Ästhetisches Maß und ästhetische Information*. Quickborn 1962.
Hallett G., *A. Companion to Wittgenstein's 'Philosophical Investigations'*. Ithaca 1977.
Hempel C. G., *Aspects of Scientific Explanation*. New York 1965.
Henri A., *Environments and Happenings*. London 1974.
Hermeren G., *Representation and Meaning in the Visual Arts*. Lund 1969.
Hiż H., 'Questions and Answers'. *The Journal of Philosophy*, LIX, 1962.
Hoerster N., *Utilitaristische Ethik und Verallgemeinerung*. Freiburg – München 1971.
Hubbeling H. G., *Spinoza's Methodology*. Groningen 1964.
Ingarden R., *Experience, Work, Value*. Krakow 1966. Polish.
Kaprow A., *Assemblage, Environments and Happenings*. New York 1968.
Killy W., *Deutscher Kitsch*. Göttingen 1966.
Kirby M., *Happenings. An Illustrated Anthology*. New York 1965.
Kłoskowska A., *Kultura masowa (Mass Culture)*, Warszawa 1964. Polish.
Kmita J., Ławniczak W., 'Znak – Symbol – Alegoria'. In: J. Pelc (ed.), *Studia Semiotyczne*, 1970. Polish.
Koj L., 'On Defining Meaning Families'. *Studia Logica* XXV, 1969.
Kotarbinska J., 'Pojęcie znaku' (The Concept of Sign). *Studia Logica*, IV, 1957. Polish.
Kotarbinska J., 'On Ostensive Definitions'. *Philosophy of Science*, 27, 1960.
Kotarbinski T., *Gnosiology*. London 1966.
Kotarbinski T., *Praxiology*, Oxford 1965.
Kubinski T., *Wstęp do logicznej teorii pytań (An Introduction to the Logical Theory of Questions)*. Warszawa 1971. Polish.
Kuipers T., *Studies in Inductive Probability and Rational Expectation*. Dordrecht 1978.
Kultermann U., *Leben und Kunst*. Tübingen 1970.
Kutschera F., Breitkopf A., *Einführung in die moderne Logik*. Freiburg 1971.
Lazari-Pawlowska I., *Etyka Gandhiego (The Ethics of Gandhi)*. Warszawa 1965. Polish.
Lazarsfeld P. F., Pasanella A. K., Rosenberg M. (eds.), *Continuities in the Language of Social Research*. New York 1972.
Lenk H., 'Kann die sprachanalytische Moralphilosophie neutral sein?' In: H. Albert, E. Topitsch (Hrsg), *Wissenschaftslehre und Gesellschaft*. Darmstadt 1971.
Levi-Strauss C., *Anthropologie Structurale*. Paris 1958.
Lotman Ju. M., 'Sur la délimitation linguistique et littéraire de la notion de structure'. *Linguistics* 6.
Lucie-Smith E., *Movements in Art Since 1945*. London 1975.
Lutynski J., 'On Valuation and the Manichean Attitude in the Social Sciences'. *Kultura i Społeczeństwo* No. 4, 1958. Polish.
Lützeler H., 'Die außerwissenschaftliche Kunsterfahrung'. *Jahrbuch für Ästhetik und allgemeine Kunstwissenschaft*, Bd. VII, 1962.

Maser S., *Numerische Ästhetik*. Stuttgart 1971.
Mazur M., *Qualitative Theory of Information*. Warszawa 1970. Polish.
McLuhan M., *Understanding Media*. London 1968.
Mooij J. J. A., *A Study of Metaphor*. Amsterdam 1976.
Moles A., *Theorie de l'information et perception esthetique*. Paris 1958.
Morawski S., 'Happening'. *Dialog* No. 9, 10, 1971. Polish.
Nowak L., 'Wartość – Idealizacja – Wartościowanie. In: I. Lazari-Pawlowska (ed.), *Metaetyka*. Warszawa 1975. Polish.
Nowak S., *Studia z metodologii nauk społecznych*. Warszawa 1965. Polish.
Oelmüller W., *Die unbefriedigte Aufklärung*. Frankfurt-M. 1969.
Ossowska M., *Moral Thought in the English Enlightenment*. Warszawa 1966. Polish.
Ossowski S., *Die Besonderheiten der Sozialwissenschaften*. Frankfurt-M. 1973.
Pawlowski T., *Methodologische Probleme in den Geistes- und Sozialwissenschaften*. Braunschweig-Warszawa 1976.
Pawlowski T., *Über Normen der Begriffsbildung*. Paderborn 1977.
Pawlowski T., *Beiträge zum Problem der Interpretation und Wertung des Ästhetischen*. Paderborn 1977.
Pawlowski T., *Begriffsbildung und Definition*. Berlin 1980.
Pelc J., 'Meaning as an Instrument'. In: J. Pelc (ed.), *Studies in Functional Logical Semiotics*. The Hague – Paris 1971.
Phillips W., (ed.), *Art and Psychoanalysis*. Cleveland 1963.
Podgórecki A., *Zjawiska prawne w opinii publicznej*. Warszawa 1964. Polish.
Poser H., 'Das Scheitern des logischen Positivismus an modaltheoretischen Problemen'. *Studium Generale* 24, 1971.
Posner R., 'Diskurs als Mittel der Aufklärung'. In: M. Gerhard (Hrsg.), *Linguistik und Sprachphilosophie*. München 1974.
Przelecki M., *The Logic of Empirical Theories*. London 1969.
Ptaszkowska H., *Happenings in Poland*. Współczesność 1969. Polish.
Rader M. (ed.), *A Modern Book of Esthetics*. New York 1964.
Rapp F., 'Technik und Naturwissenschaften'. In: H. Lenk, S. Moser (Hrsg.), *Techne, Technik, Technologie*. Pullach 1973.
Richter G., *Kitsch-Lexikon von a–z*. Gütersloh 1970.
Savigny E., *Grundkurs im wissenschaftlichen Definieren*. München, 1970.
Schmidt S. J., *Bedeutung und Begriff*. Braunschweig 1969.
Schweitzer T., *Methodenprobleme des interkulturellen Vergleichs*. Köln 1978.
Sohm H. (Hrsg.), *Happening und Fluxus*. Köln 1970.
Stachowiak H., *Allgemeine Modell Theorie*. Wien 1973.
Stegmüller W., *Probleme und Resultate der Wissenschaftstheorie und analytischen Philosophie*. Berlin 1970.
Stevenson C. L., *Facts and Values*. New Haven 1963.
Suppes P., Zinnes J. L., 'Basic Measurement Theory'. In: *Handbook of Mathematical Psychology*. New York 1963.
Szczepanski J., *Socjologiczne zagadnienia wyższego wykształcenia*. Warszawa 1963. Polish.
Tatarkiewicz W., *Dzieje sześciu pojęć*. Warszawa 1975. Polish.
Tielsch E., 'Die Logik des Freiheitsbegriffs'. *Zeitschrift für Philosophische Forschung*, 1974.

Topitsch E., *Sozialphilosophie zwischen Ideologie und Wissenschaft*. Neuwied-Rhein 1966.
Turk H., 'Social Cohesion Through Variant Values'. *American Sociological Review*, 1963.
Wallis M., *Jugendstil*. Warschau-Dresden 1974.
Walther E., 'Ein als Zeichen verwendetes Natur-Objekt'. *Semiosis* 5, 1977.
Wellek R., *Concepts of Criticism*. New Haven 1963.
Wiehl R., 'Reflexionsprozesse und Handlungen'. *Neue Hefte für Philosophie*, Heft 9.
Wittgenstein L., *Philosophical Investigations*. New York 1957.
Wróblewski J., 'Natura a reguły postępowania'. In: I. Lazari-Pawlowska (ed.), *Metaetyka*. Warszawa 1975. Polish.
Zimmermann J., *Sprachanalytische Ästhetik*. Stuttgart 1980.

SUBJECT INDEX

Aesthetic value judgment 162, 170n.
   factors which influence it 163–168
   objective conception of 170–172
   subjective conception of 169–171
Answers 205n.
   complete 212
   direct 211
   indirect 211
   partial 212

Beauty 162n.
   and aesthetic experience 175
   an objective conception of 171n.
   the concept of 173–175
Boolean algebra 201

Chance 119n.
   and its role in contemporary art 119, 125n., 148
   the aesthetic function of 125–126
   the varieties of 120–123
Concepts
   absolute 97
   classificatory 3, 99
   comparative 3, 99
   dispositional 23
   historical 100
   metrical 3n.
   relative 97
   universal 100
Cumulative development of science 52

Definiendum 59
Definiens 59
Definition 46, 57n., 101, 186
   adequate 115, 171
   analytic 66–70, 101, 193
   complete 53, 60
   ostensive 103, 111, 158
   stipulative 69–70, 101
   the formal correctness of 46
   the scientific usefulness of 47–49, 176
Derivative measurement 8

Equivalence definition 25, 53, 115, 186
   and partial criteria 30
Explication 81, 102
Expression 130, 150
   variants of 151

Fundamental measurement 8

Happening 112n.
   and meaning families 136–139
   conceptual elements in 139n.
   examples of 113, 119
   features of 116n.
   semantic functions in 117, 130n., 146
   the definability of 115, 135, 138
   the role of the audience in 127–128
Homogeneous sets 47, 51, 109, 144, 146
Homomorphism 4, 5, 7

Indicator 23, 181n., 198
   and its transference 191n.
   cultural 198
   definitional 185–188, 193
   factual 185–186, 191
   probabilistic 189–190
Indicatum 183–186
Informational aesthetics 77n.
   and aesthetic information 86
   and measurement 79–80, 84
   and semantic information 85
   and statistical (Shannonian) information 78–79, 85, 89
   and the maximal effect 79–82

225

SUBJECT INDEX

(Informational aesthetics)
    the concept of sign in 77–78, 89
Interpretation of art-works 144n.
    in non-fundamental senses 157–159
    in the fundamental sense 145–146, 157
    the emotional constituent in 152–153
    the formal constituent in 146–147
    the semantical constituent in 148
Interval scale 7–8
Isomorphism 4

Kitsch 91n.
    and repetition 106–108
    features of 93, 94, 98, 105
    the definability of 103n.
    the varieties of 92n.

Language 36, 37, 42

Meaning families 23n., 146n.
    examples of 32, 34, 36, 43, 136
    partial definability of 30
    the extension of 23, 35, 37, 47, 50
    the logical structure of 24–26, 30–35
    the scientific usefulness of 31, 47–49, 136
Meaningfulness
    of quantitative statements 4, 8–11, 16–21, 84
    of terms 16, 17
Measurement 3n.
    in the informational aesthetics 85
    in the social sciences 11–13, 187
    representation problem in 5
    uniqueness problem in 5–6
    unit of 4

Observable properties 158, 181, 183
Open concepts 24, 137–138
Ordinal scale 6, 8

Pansemiotism 197
    and the semiotic theory of culture 199n.

Partial definitions 25, 30, 35, 38, 60, 104, 137, 186, 189
    and dispositional terms 23, 104, 186
    negative criteria 30, 38, 137, 189
    positive criteria 30, 35, 137, 189
Persuasive argumentation 65n.
Persuasive definition 55n., 65n., 106
    examples of 59, 62–64, 106
    in the objective sense 66n.
    in the subjective sense 66n.
    variants of 59, 61, 64
Persuasive function of language 44, 55, 57, 72
Pornography 45, 56
Principle of economy 31, 41n.
    and meaning families 31, 42, 43
Properties admitting of degrees 5, 31, 39
Psychoanalysis 102, 144
    and interpretation of art-works 144, 145, 149
    and kitsch 102–103

Questions 204n.
    closed 205, 219
    containing an entry 'don't know' 218
    containing an entry 'other items – specify which' 218
    examples of errors in questions 213n.
    open 205, 219
    the constitutive elements of 207–209
    types of 209n.

Ratio scale 7, 8
Relational systems 6

Scales 5n.
    and additive magnitudes 4
    types of 5–8, 187
Semiotic theory of culture 197n.
    a critical evaluation of 199, 202
    the aims of 197, 199, 202
    the concept of sign in 198–199

Semiotics 149, 197n.
Sign 132, 149, 198–199

Terms
   descriptive 19, 58, 70, 71
   dispositional 23
   emotively active 31, 44–45, 55, 58, 64
   emotively neutral 57, 58, 61
   empirically meaningful 17
   value-laden 45, 57–58, 61, 70–71

AUTHOR INDEX

Adorno, T. W. 22, 195, 221
Ajdukiewicz, K. 208, 221
Albert, H. 73, 161, 221, 222
Alsleben, K. 82, 89, 221
Aquist, L. 221
Asperen, van, G. M. 221

Banach, A. 98, 110, 111, 221
Bar-Hillel, Y. 85, 161, 221
Barthes, R. 197, 203, 221
Batóg, T. 203, 221
Becker, J. 143, 221
Belnap, N. 204, 206, 211, 220, 221
Bense, M. 88, 89, 177, 221
Berka, K. 221
Birkhoff, G. D. 77, 79, 86, 221
Black, M. 161, 177, 221
Blegvad, M. 221
Bose, N. K. 221
Boyle, M. 134, 136
Brecht, G. 133
Breitkopf, A. 222
Büschges, G. 221

Cage, J. 127, 140
Carnap, R. 14ff., 21, 54, 81, 85, 102, 111, 186, 196, 221
Carus, P. 72, 221
Celebonović, A. 102, 111
Chomsky, N. 203, 221
Coutts-Smith, K. 73
Cube, F. 82
Czempiel, E. O. 221

Dali, S. 130
Davidson, D. 14
Dine, J. 131, 132
Dorfles, G. 91, 110, 111, 221

Eco, U. 197, 203, 221
Elton, W. 221

Endell, A. 153, 160
Essler, W. K. 221

Farnsworth, P. R. 177, 221
Filiou, R. 139
Frank, H. 79, 82, 88, 89, 221
Frey, F. W. 195, 222
Fromm, E. 222

Geismann, G. 222
Giedymin, J. 208, 211, 212, 220, 222
Giesz, L. 110, 222
Gollwitzer, G. 54, 222
Gombrowicz, W. 167
Goodman, N. 161, 222
Gregotti, V. 91, 110
Grooms, R. 119
Grzyb, G. 222
Gunzenhäuser, R. 79, 86, 89, 222

Hallett, S. A. 53, 222
Hempel, C. G. 222
Henri, A. 142, 143, 222
Hermeren, G. 160, 222
Hesse, M. B. 161
Higgins, D. 120
Hindemith, P. 150, 151, 160
Hiż, H. 222
Hoerster, N. 222
Hubbeling, H. G. 222
Huxley, A. 57, 72

Ingarden, R. 90, 160, 177, 203, 222

Jones, E. 144, 145, 160
Jung, C. G. 102

Kantor, T. 128, 131
Kaprow, A. 114, 118, 121, 123, 128, 130, 142, 222
Kessler, A. R. 195, 222

Killy, W. 110, 222
Kirby, M. 112, 114, 135ff., 142ff., 222
Kloskowska, A. 203, 222
Koj, L. 26, 27ff., 53, 222
Kotarbińska, J. 111, 160, 161, 203, 222
Kotarbiński, T. 161, 177, 196, 222
Kreiser, L. 221
Kubiński, T. 211, 220, 222
Kuipers, T. 222
Kultermann, U. 142, 222
Kutschera, F. 222

Lazari-Pawlowska, I. 73, 222
Lazarsfeld, P. F. 181, 195, 222
Lebel, J. J. 113, 120, 131, 133, 134
Lenk, H. 73, 222
Levi-Strauss, C. 54, 197, 203, 222
Lotman, Ju. 203, 222
Lucie-Smith, E. 142, 222
Lutoslawski, W. 125, 148
Lutynski, J. 72, 222
Lützeler, H. 161, 223

Maciunas, G. 140
Maser, S. 80, 83ff., 223
McLuhan, M. 223
Moles, A. 82, 89, 223
Mooij, J. J. A. 161, 177, 223
Morawski, S. 136, 143, 223
Morris, C. 203
Munro, T. 177

Nitsch, H. 114, 120, 132, 133, 134
Nowak, L. 223
Nowak, S. 220, 223

Oelmüller, W. 223
Oldenburg, C. 116, 121, 129, 131
Ossowska, M. 73, 161, 177, 223
Ossowski, S. 55, 160, 161, 174, 203, 223

Pasanella, A. K. 195, 222
Pawlowski, T. 54, 72, 89, 111, 196, 203, 223
Peirce, C. S. 203
Pelc, J. 160, 203, 223

Phillips, W. 223
Picasso, P. 155
Podgórecki, A. 215, 220, 223
Pollock, J. 126
Poser, H. 223
Posner, R. 223
Proust, M. 152, 160
Przelecki, M. 161, 177, 223
Ptaszkowska, H. 130, 142, 223

Rader, M. 223
Rapp, F. 223
Richter, G. 111, 223
Rothchile, J. E. 195, 223

Savigny, E. 223
Scheuch, E. K. 196
Schmidt, S. J. 223
Schneeman, C. 115, 120
Schweitzer, T. 223
Seidler, I. 161
Shannon, C. 140
Sohm, H. 142, 143, 223
Stachowiak, H. 223
Stegmüller, W. 196, 223
Stevenson, C. L. 59, 72, 223
Suppes, P. 14, 15, 19, 21, 223
Szczepański, J. 73, 223

Tarski, A. 19
Tatarkiewicz, W. 160, 174, 224
Turk, H. 12, 224

Vautier, B. 141
Vostell, W. 118, 133, 136, 138, 221

Wallis, M. 160, 174, 177, 203, 224
Walther, E. 224
Weitz, M. 54
Wellek, R. 161, 224
Whiteman, R. 114, 134
Wiehl, R. 224
Wittgenstein, L. 23, 24, 25, 32, 53, 54, 224
Wróblewski, J. 224

Zimmermann, J. 224
Zinnes, J. L. 21, 223

SYNTHESE LIBRARY

Studies in Epistemology, Logic, Methodology,
and Philosophy of Science

Managing Editor:
JAAKKO HINTIKKA (Florida State University)

Editors:
DONALD DAVIDSON (University of Chicago)
GABRIEL NUCHELMANS (University of Leyden)
WESLEY C. SALMON (University of Arizona)

1. J. M. Bochénski, *A Precis of Mathematical Logic.* 1959.
2. P. L. Guiraud, *Problèmes et méthodes de la statistique linguistique.* 1960.
3. Hans Freudenthal (ed.), *The Concept and the Role of the Model in Mathematics and Natural and Social Sciences.* 1961.
4. Evert W. Beth, *Formal Methods. An Introduction to Symbolic Logic and the Study of Effective Operations in Arithmetic and Logic.* 1962.
5. B. H. Kazemier and D. Vuysje (eds.), *Logic and Language. Studies Dedicated to Professor Rudolf Carnap on the Occasion of His Seventieth Birthday.* 1962.
6. Marx W. Wartofsky (ed.), *Proceedings of the Boston Colloquium for the Philosophy of Science 1961-1962.* Boston Studies in the Philosophy of Science, Volume I. 1963.
7. A. A. Zinov'ev, *Philosophical Problems of Many-Valued Logic.* 1963.
8. Georges Gurvitch, *The Spectrum of Social Time.* 1964.
9. Paul Lorenzen, *Formal Logic.* 1965.
10. Robert S. Cohen and Marx W. Wartofsky (eds.), *In Honor of Philipp Frank.* Boston Studies in the Philosophy of Science, Volume II. 1965.
11. Evert W. Beth, *Mathematical Thought. An Introduction to the Philosophy of Mathematics.* 1965.
12. Evert W. Beth and Jean Piaget, *Mathematical Epistemology and Psychology.* 1966.
13. Guido Küng, *Ontology and the Logistic Analysis of Language. An Enquiry into the Contemporary Views on Universals.* 1967.
14. Robert S. Cohen and Marx W. Wartofsky (eds.), *Proceedings of the Boston Colloquium for the Philosophy of Science 1964-1966. In Memory of Norwood Russell Hanson.* Boston Studies in the Philosophy of Science, Volume III. 1967.
15. C. D. Broad, *Induction, Probability, and Causation. Selected Papers.* 1968.
16. Günther Patzig, *Aristotle's Theory of the Syllogism. A Logical-Philosophical Study of Book A of the Prior Analytics.* 1968.
17. Nicholas Rescher, *Topics in Philosophical Logic.* 1968.
18. Robert S. Cohen and Marx W. Wartofsky (eds.), *Proceedings of the Boston Colloquium for the Philosophy of Science 1966-1968.* Boston Studies in the Philosophy of Science, Volume IV. 1969.

19. Robert S. Cohen and Marx W. Wartofsky (eds.), *Proceedings of the Boston Colloquium for the Philosophy of Science 1966-1968*. Boston Studies in the Philosophy of Science, Volume V. 1969.
20. J. W. Davis, D. J. Hockney, and W. K. Wilson (eds.), *Philosophical Logic*. 1969.
21. D. Davidson and J. Hintikka (eds.), *Words and Objections. Essays on the Work of W. V. Quine*. 1969.
22. Patrick Suppes, *Studies in the Methodology and Foundations of Science. Selected Papers from 1911 to 1969*. 1969.
23. Jaakko Hintikka, *Models for Modalities. Selected Essays*. 1969.
24. Nicholas Rescher *et al.* (eds.), *Essays in Honor of Carl G. Hempel. A Tribute on the Occasion of His Sixty-Fifth Birthday*. 1969.
25. P. V. Tavanec (ed.), *Problems of the Logic of Scientific Knowledge*. 1969.
26. Marshall Swain (ed.), *Induction, Acceptance, and Rational Belief*. 1970.
27. Robert S. Cohen and Raymond J. Seeger (eds.), *Ernst Mach: Physicist and Philosopher*. Boston Studies in the Philosophy of Science, Volume VI. 1970.
28. Jaakko Hintikka and Patrick Suppes, *Information and Inference*. 1970.
29. Karel Lambert, *Philosophical Problems in Logic. Some Recent Developments*. 1970.
30. Rolf A. Eberle, *Nominalistic Systems*. 1970.
31. Paul Weingartner and Gerhard Zecha (eds.), *Induction, Physics, and Ethics*. 1970.
32. Evert W. Beth, *Aspects of Modern Logic*. 1970.
33. Risto Hilpinen (ed.), *Deontic Logic: Introductory and Systematic Readings*. 1971.
34. Jean-Louis Krivine, *Introduction to Axiomatic Set Theory*. 1971.
35. Joseph D. Sneed, *The Logical Sstructure of Mathematical Physics*. 1971.
36. Carl R. Kordig, *The Justification of Scientific Change*. 1971.
37. Milic Capek, *Bergson and Modern Physics*. Boston Studies in the Philosophy of Science, Volume VII. 1971.
38. Norwood Russell Hanson, *What I Do Not Believe, and Other Essays* (ed. by Stephen Toulmin and Harry Woolf). 1971.
39. Roger C. Buck and Robert S. Cohen (eds.), *PSA 1970. In Memory of Rudolf Carnap*. Boston Studies in the Philosophy of Science, Volume VIII. 1971.
40. Donald Davidson and Gilbert Harman (eds.), *Semantics of Natural Language*. 1972.
41. Yehoshua Bar-Hillel (ed.), *Pragmatics of Natural Languages*. 1971.
42. Sören Stenlund, *Combinators, λ-Terms and Proof Theory*. 1972.
43. Martin Strauss, *Modern Physics and Its Philosophy. Selected Papers in the Logic, History, and Philosophy of Science*. 1972.
44. Mario Bunge, *Method, Model and Matter*. 1973.
45. Mario Bunge, *Philosophy of Physics*. 1973.
46. A. A. Zinov'ev, *Foundations of the Logical Theory of Scientific Knowledge (Complex Logic)*. (Revised and enlarged English edition with an appendix by G. A. Smirnov, E. A. Sidorenka, A. M. Fedina, and L. A. Bobrova.) Boston Studies in the Philosophy of Science, Volume IX. 1973.
47. Ladislav Tondl, *Scientific Procedures*. Boston Studies in the Philosophy of Science, Volume X. 1973.
48. Norwood Russell Hanson, *Constellations and Conjectures* (ed. by Willard C. Humphreys, Jr.). 1973.

49. K. J. J. Hintikka, J. M. E. Moravcsik, and P. Suppes (eds.), *Approaches to Natural Language.* 1973.
50. Mario Bunge (ed.), *Exact Philosophy — Problems, Tools, and Goals.* 1973.
51. Radu J. Bogdan and Ilkka Niiniluoto (eds.), *Logic, Language, and Probability.* 1973.
52. Glenn Pearce and Patrick Maynard (eds.), *Conceptual Change.* 1973.
53. Ilkka Niiniluoto and Raimo Tuomela, *Theoretical Concepts and Hypothetico-Inductive Inference.* 1973.
54. Roland Fraissé, *Course of Mathematical Logic* — Volume 1: *Relation and Logical Formula.* 1973.
55. Adolf Grünbaum, *Philosophical Problems of Space and Time.* (Second, enlarged edition.) Boston Studies in the Philosophy of Science, Volume XII. 1973.
56. Patrick Suppes (ed.), *Space, Time, and Geometry.* 1973.
57. Hans Kelsen, *Essays in Legal and Moral Philosophy* (selected and introduced by Ota Weinberger). 1973.
58. R. J. Seeger and Robert S. Cohen (eds.), *Philosophical Foundations of Science.* Boston Studies in the Philosophy of Science, Volume XI. 1974.
59. Robert S. Cohen and Marx W. Wartofsky (eds.), *Logical and Epistemological Studies in Contemporary Physics.* Boston Studies in the Philosophy of Science, Volume XIII. 1973.
60. Robert S. Cohen and Marx W. Wartofsky (eds.), *Methodological and Historical Essays in the Natural and Social Sciences. Proceedings of the Boston Colloquium for the Philosophy of Science 1969-1972.* Boston Studies in the Philosophy of Science, Volume XIV. 1974.
61. Robert S. Cohen, J. J. Stachel, and Marx W. Wartofsky (eds.), *For Dirk Struik. Scientific, Historical and Political Essays in Honor of Dirk J. Struik.* Boston Studies in the Philosophy of Science, Volume XV. 1974.
62. Kazimierz Ajdukiewicz, *Pragmatic Logic* (transl. from the Polish by Olgierd Wojtasiewicz). 1974.
63. Sören Stenlund (ed.), *Logical Theory and Semantic Analysis. Essays Dedicated to Stig Kanger on His Fiftieth Birthday.* 1974.
64. Kenneth F. Schaffner and Robert S. Cohen (eds.), *Proceedings of the 1972 Biennial Meeting, Philosophy of Science Association.* Boston Studies in the Philosophy of Science, Volume XX. 1974.
65. Henry E. Kyburg, Jr., *The Logical Foundations of Statistical Inference.* 1974.
66. Marjorie Grene, *The Understanding of Nature. Essays in the Philosophy of Biology.* Boston Studies in the Philosophy of Science, Volume XXIII. 1974.
67. Jan M. Broekman, *Structuralism: Moscow, Prague, Paris.* 1974.
68. Norman Geschwind, *Selected Papers on Language and the Brain.* Boston Studies in the Philosophy of Science, Volume XVI. 1974.
69. Roland Fraissé, *Course of Mathematical Logic* — Volume 2: *Model Theory.* 1974.
70. Andrzej Grzegorczyk, *An Outline of Mathematical Logic. Fundamental Results and Notions Explained with All Details.* 1974.
71. Franz von Kutschera, *Philosophy of Language.* 1975.
72. Juha Manninen and Raimo Tuomela (eds.), *Essays on Explanation and Understanding. Studies in the Foundations of Humanities and Social Sciences.* 1976.

73. Jaakko Hintikka (ed.), *Rudolf Carnap, Logical Empiricist. Materials and Perspectives.* 1975.
74. Milic Capek (ed.), *The Concepts of Space and Time. Their Structure and Their Development.* Boston Studies in the Philosophy of Science, Volume XXII. 1976.
75. Jaakko Hintikka and Unto Remes, *The Method of Analysis. Its Geometrical Origin and Its General Significance.* Boston Studies in the Philosophy of Science, Volume XXV. 1974.
76. John Emery Murdoch and Edith Dudley Sylla, *The Cultural Context of Medieval Learning.* Boston Studies in the Philosophy of Science, Volume XXVI. 1975.
77. Stefan Amsterdamski, *Between Experience and Metaphysics. Philosophical Problems of the Evolution of Science.* Boston Studies in the Philosophy of Science, Volume XXXV. 1975.
78. Patrick Suppes (ed.), *Logic and Probability in Quantum Mechanics.* 1976.
79. Hermann von Helmholtz: *Epistemological Writings. The Paul Hertz/Moritz Schlick Centenary Edition of 1921 with Notes and Commentary by the Editors.* (Newly translated by Malcolm F. Lowe. Edited, with an Introduction and Bibliography, by Robert S. Cohen and Yehuda Elkana.) Boston Studies in the Philosophy of Science, Volume XXXVII. 1977.
80. Joseph Agassi, *Science in Flux.* Boston Studies in the Philosophy of Science, Volume XXVIII. 1975.
81. Sandra G. Harding (ed.), *Can Theories Be Refuted? Essays on the Duhem-Quine Thesis.* 1976.
82. Stefan Nowak, *Methodology of Sociological Research. General Problems.* 1977.
83. Jean Piaget, Jean-Blaise Grize, Alina Szeminska, and Vinh Bang, *Epistemology and Psychology of Functions.* 1977.
84. Marjorie Grene and Everett Mendelsohn (eds.), *Topics in the Philosophy of Biology.* Boston Studies in the Philosophy of Science, Volume XXVII. 1976.
85. E. Fischbein, *The Intuitive Sources of Probabilistic Thinking in Children.* 1975.
86. Ernest W. Adams, *The Logic of Conditionals. An Application of Probability to Deductive Logic.* 1975.
87. Marian Przelecki and Ryszard Wójcicki (eds.), *Twenty-Five Years of Logical Methodology in Poland.* 1977.
88. J. Topolski, *The Methodology of History.* 1976.
89. A. Kasher (ed.), *Language in Focus: Foundations, Methods and Systems. Essays Dedicated to Yehoshua Bar-Hillel.* Boston Studies in the Philosophy of Science, Volume XLIII. 1976.
90. Jaakko Hintikka, *The Intentions of Intentionality and Other New Models for Modalities.* 1975.
91. Wolfgang Stegmüller, *Collected Papers on Epistemology, Philosophy of Science and History of Philosophy.* 2 Volumes. 1977.
92. Dov M. Gabbay, *Investigations in Modal and Tense Logics with Applications to Problems in Philosophy and Linguistics.* 1976.
93. Radu J. Bogdan, *Local Induction.* 1976.
94. Stefan Nowak, *Understanding and Prediction. Essays in the Methodology of Social and Behavioral Theories.* 1976.
95. Peter Mittelstaedt, *Philosophical Problems of Modern Physics.* Boston Studies in the Philosophy of Science, Volume XVIII. 1976.

96. Gerald Holton and William Blanpied (eds.), *Science and Its Public: The Changing Relationship.* Boston Studies in the Philosophy of Science, Volume XXXIII. 1976.
97. Myles Brand and Douglas Walton (eds.), *Action Theory.* 1976.
98. Paul Gochet, *Outline of a Nominalist Theory of Proposition. An Essay in the Theory of Meaning.* 1980. (Forthcoming.)
99. R. S. Cohen, P. K. Feyerabend, and M. W. Wartofsky (eds.), *Essays in Memory of Imre Lakatos.* Boston Studies in the Philosophy of Science, Volume XXXIX. 1976.
100. R. S. Cohen and J. J. Stachel (eds.), *Selected Papers of Léon Rosenfeld.* Boston Studies in the Philosophy of Science, Volume XXI. 1978.
101. R. S. Cohen, C. A. Hooker, A. C. Michalos, and J. W. van Evra (eds.), *PSA 1974: Proceedings of the 1974 Biennial Meeting of the Philosophy of Science Association.* Boston Studies in the Philosophy of Science, Volume XXXII. 1976.
102. Yehuda Fried and Joseph Agassi, *Paranoia: A Study in Diagnosis.* Boston Studies in the Philosophy of Science, Volume L. 1976.
103. Marian Przelecki, Klemens Szaniawski, and Ryszard Wójcicki (eds.), *Formal Methods in the Methodology of Empirical Sciences.* 1976.
104. John M. Vickers, *Belief and Probability.* 1976.
105. Kurt H. Wolff, *Surrender and Catch: Experience and Inquiry Today.* Boston Studies in the Philosophy of Science, Volume LI. 1976.
106. Karel Kosík, *Dialectics of the Concrete.* Boston Studies in the Philosophy of Science, Volume LII. 1976.
107. Nelson Goodman, *The Structure of Appearance.* (Third edition.) Boston Studies in the Philosophy of Science, Volume LIII. 1977.
108. Jerzy Giedymin (ed.), *Kazimierz Ajdukiewicz: The Scientific World-Perspective and Other Essays, 1931-1963.* 1978.
109. Robert L. Causey, *Unity of Science.* 1977.
110. Richard E. Grandy, *Advanced Logic for Applications.* 1977.
111. Robert P. McArthur, *Tense Logic.* 1976.
112. Lars Lindahl, *Position and Change. A Study in Law and Logic.* 1977.
113. Raimo Tuomela, *Dispositions.* 1978.
114 Herbert A. Simon, *Models of Discovery and Other Topics in the Methods of Science.* Boston Studies in the Philosophy of Science, Volume LIV. 1977.
115. Roger D. Rosenkrantz, *Inference, Method and Decision.* 1977.
116. Raimo Tuomela, *Human Action and Its Explanation. A Study on the Philosophical Foundations of Psychology.* 1977.
117. Morris Lazerowitz, *The Language of Philosophy. Freud and Wittgenstein.* Boston Studies in the Philosophy of Science, Volume LV. 1977.
118. Stanislaw Leśniewski, *Collected Works* (ed. by S. J. Surma, J. T. J. Srzednicki, and D. I. Barnett, with an annotated bibliography by V. Frederick Rickey). 1980. (Forthcoming.)
119. Jerzy Pelc, *Semiotics in Poland, 1894-1969.* 1978.
120. Ingmar Pörn, *Action Theory and Social Science. Some Formal Models.* 1977.
121. Joseph Margolis, *Persons and Minds. The Prospects of Nonreductive Materialism.* Boston Studies in the Philosophy of Science, Volume LVII. 1977.
122. Jaakko Hintikka, Ilkka Niiniluoto, and Esa Saarinen (eds.), *Essays on Mathematical and Philosophical Logic.* 1978.
123. Theo A. F. Kuipers, *Studies in Inductive Probability and Rational Expectation.* 1978.

124. Esa Saarinen, Risto Hilpinen, Ilkka Niiniluoto, and Merrill Provence Hintikka (eds.), *Essays in Honour of Jaakko Hintikka on the Occasion of His Fiftieth Birthday*. 1978.
125 Gerard Radnitzky and Gunnar Andersson (eds.), *Progress and Rationality in Science*. Boston Studies in the Philosophy of Science, Volume LVIII. 1978.
126. Peter Mittelstaedt, *Quantum Logic*. 1978.
127. Kenneth A. Bowen, *Model Theory for Modal Logic. Kripke Models for Modal Predicate Calculi*. 1978.
128. Howard Alexander Bursen, *Dismantling the Memory Machine. A Philosophical Investigation of Machine Theories of Memory*. 1978.
129. Marx W. Wartofsky, *Models: Representation and the Scientific Understanding*. Boston Studies in the Philosophy of Science, Volume XLVIII. 1979.
130. Don Ihde, *Technics and Praxis. A Philosophy of Technology*. Boston Studies in the Philosophy of Science, Volume XXIV. 1978.
131. Jerzy J. Wiatr (ed.), *Polish Essays in the Methodology of the Social Sciences*. Boston Studies in the Philosophy of Science, Volume XXIX. 1979.
132. Wesley C. Salmon (ed.), *Hans Reichenbach: Logical Empiricist*. 1979.
133. Peter Bieri, Rolf-P. Horstmann, and Lorenz Krüger (eds.), *Transcendental Arguments in Science. Essays in Epistemology*. 1979.
134. Mihailo Marković and Gajo Petrović (eds.), *Praxis. Yugoslav Essays in the Philosophy and Methodology of the Social Sciences*. Boston Studies in the Philosophy of Science, Volume XXXVI. 1979.
135. Ryszard Wójcicki, *Topics in the Formal Methodology of Empirical Sciences*. 1979.
136. Gerard Radnitzky and Gunnar Andersson (eds.), *The Structure and Development of Science*. Boston Studies in the Philosophy of Science, Volume LIX. 1979.
137. Judson Chambers Webb, *Mechanism, Mentalism, and Metamathematics. An Essay on Finitism*. 1980.
138. D. F. Gustafson and B. L. Tapscott (eds.), *Body, Mind, and Method. Essays in Honor of Virgil C. Aldrich*. 1979.
139. Leszek Nowak, *The Structure of Idealization. Towards a Systematic Interpretation of the Marxian Idea of Science*. 1979.
140. Chaim Perelman, *The New Rhetoric and the Humanities. Essays on Rhetoric and Its Applications*. 1979.
141. Wlodzimierz Rabinowicz, *Universalizability. A Study in Morals and Metaphysics*. 1979.
142. Chaim Perelman, *Justice, Law, and Argument. Essays on Moral and Legal Reasoning*. 1980.
143. Stig Kanger and Sven Ohman, *Philosophy and Grammar. Papers on the Occasion of the Quincentennial of Uppsala University*. 1980.
144. Tadeusz Pawlowski, *Concept Formation in the Humanities and the Social Sciences*. 1980.
145. Jaakko Hintikka and David Gruender, *History and Philosophy of Science: Their Interface in 1978. Proceedings of the Second Joint International Conference*. 2 volumes. 1980.
146. Evandro Agazzi, *Modern Logic – a Survey. Historical, Philosophical, and Mathematical Aspects of Modern Logic and its Applications*. 1980.